THE CANADIAN SOLDIER

IN NORTH-WEST EUROPE, 1944-1945

Jean BOUCHERY

Computer graphics and maps by Jean-Marie MONGIN
Translated from the French by Alan McKAY

HISTOIRE & COLLECTIONS - PARIS

FROM THE BEACHES OF NORMANDY TO THE BALTIC
THE CANADIAN SOLDIER

After the very lively interest shown in the first two volumes of the *'British Soldier from D-Day to VE-Day'*, I have here decided to pay tribute to his North American cousin: the Canadian Soldier during the Liberation of Europe.

The 21st Army Group technical trilogy is now complete, *From Normandy to the Baltic'*, being a fitting title.

But let's go back to some essentials.

The purpose *'The Canadian Soldier in North-West Europe'* is to bring together in a pleasing and attractive format (without however claiming to be comprehensive) all the material details concerning the Canadian soldier, the 'Canuck', as he was affectionately called.

The period covered extends from the Normandy Beaches, 6 June 1944 to 2 May 1945, the historic date when the 1st Canadian Parachute Battalion met up with the Soviet Army, at Wismar, a German town on the Baltic.

The ambition of this book is to offer basic documentation for military history enthusiasts who wish to acquire detailed information about the Canadian Army, not to forget the militaria collectors, model-makers and those taking part in historical reenactments; they will all find elements to satisfy their hobbies or interests in this book.

The Canucks, very close to French hearts, crossed the Ocean long before the Americans did and hurled themselves against the concrete of the Atlantic Wall as early as 1942.

I hope this book is worthy of their exploits.

Jean Bouchery

CONTENTS

INTRODUCTION

The owner of our first two volumes in the 'From Normandy to the Baltic' trilogy must not be surprised to find that some of the material in this book is the same as in the other two volumes.

The explanation given below has been taken from 'Victory Campaign' by Colonel C.P. Stacey, in the 1960 edition of this work which is absolutely essential reading for anyone interested in the Canadian Army in 1944 and 1945. It is worth noting that whilst not being an exact copy of the British Army, the organisation of the Canadian Army followed the same basic lines, be it at an organisational level, or weaponry and equipment which was mainly supplied by Canadian industry.

'In July 1943 and in prevision for the attack across the Channel planned for Spring 1944, the 21st Army Group was set up, with the 1st Canadian Army and the 2nd British Army.

'There was now the problem of supplying these two armies. It rapidly became clear that a specifically Canadian organisation would have meant an enormous waste of manpower which was greatly needed elsewhere. Besides, the demands of war could require that during a campaign, Canadian divisions be integrated in a British army corps or vice-versa, that British divisions be included in a Canadian army corps (or for example, a Canadian soldier who had an unserviceable rifle could replace it with a British one).

In such circumstances, managing the flow of such supplies separately would have been far too complex and totally incompatible

Above. **Normandy 19 June 1944, in the village of Villons-les-Buissons, North of Caen, Lt L. L. Smith of the Stormont Dundas and Glengarry Highlanders offers sweets to some children. At this date and at their age, these children did not know what it was to eat a real bar of chocolate, an orange or sweets other than those obtained from chemical production.** *(PA 135960)*

with the efficient operation of an army group in the field.

This is why during the battle for Northwest Europe, there was no specifically Canadian supply system for its Army. Supplying certain Canadian articles, like battledress or supplies which were intended to improve the lot of the ordinary soldiers were shipped from Britain ; but they were stored in British depots and Canadian officers supervised their distribution.

Most of the supplies for the Canadian Army, ammunition, fuel, food, weapons, radios, medical stores, came from British warehouses (except for vehicles used in front-line units: the Canadian command wanted 4 x 4 vehicles whereas a lot of the British vehicles were only 4 x 2).

This organisation was considered to have been entirely satisfactory, a happy solution to the huge administrative problems which had come up during the campaign in Northwest Europe.'

CANADA AT WAR

Canada is a parliamentary monarchy with the title of Dominion within the Commonwealth. The Head of State is the King or Queen of England. Executive power is handled by the Prime minister, designated by the majority of the Members of Parliament, themselves elected by universal suffrage. The National Anthem was 'God save the King', replaced by 'O Canada' in 1980.

The Militia in 1939

On the eve of the declaration of war, the organisation of the Militia (or Canadian Army) was as follows :

The ACTIVE MILITIA, or CANADIAN ARMY A, was made up of 4,261 professionals. In September 1939, the units of the permanent active militia or Permanent Force were the following:

Cavalry: The Royal Canadian Dragoons and Lord Strathcona's Horse (Royal Canadians)

Artillery (*Royal Canadian Artillery*): Three motorised batteries (Horse Artillery) and five ordinary batteries.

Engineers (*Corps of Royal Canadian Engineers*): 1 Field Company and 13 detachments.

Signals (*Royal Canadian Corps of Signals*): 13 detachments and 2 Fortress Establishments.

Infantry: the Royal Canadian Regiment, Princess Patricia's Canadian Light Infantry and

Left. **August 1941: the Canadian Prime Minister W.L. McKenzie-King inspecting the 1st Infantry Division in Great Britain. He is talking with Major-General G.R. Pearkes, at the time commanding officer of the division.** *(PA 132774)*

the Royal 22nd Regiment.

Supply (*Royal Canadian Army Service Corps*): 15 detachments.

Medical (*Royal Canadian Army Medical Corps*): 15 detachments.

Ordnance (*Royal Canadian Ordnance Corps*): 12 detachments.

Veterinary Service (*Royal Canadian Veterinary Corps*): 8 Detachments.

Pay (*Royal Canadian Army Pay Corps*): 12 detachments

Staff (*Corps of Military Staff Clerks*): 12 Detachments

THE NON-PERMANENT ACTIVE MILITIA (NPAM), OR CANADIAN ARMY B, had about 51,500 reservists, training on a part-time basis (on certain evenings during the week, week-ends and during the summer manoeuvres). It was made up of infantry (88 regiments), cavalry (18 regiments), artillery and auxiliary units, all lacking in proper equipment. The Non-Permanent Militia was an important reserve of officers and NCOs who had at least a basic level of training.

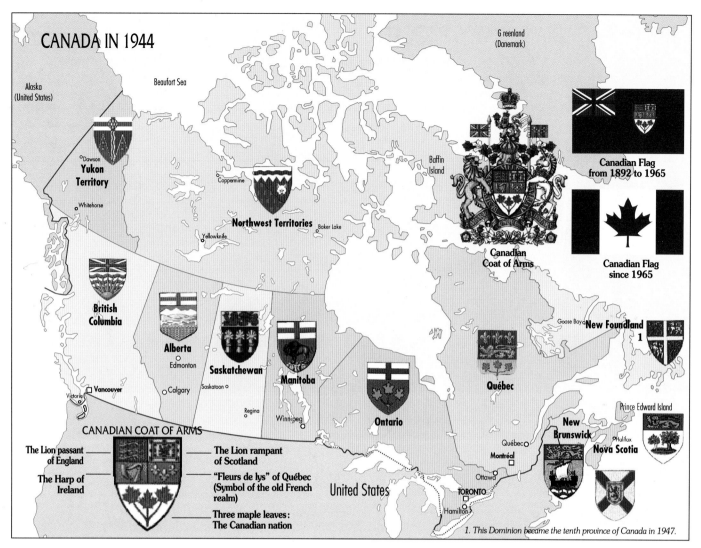

CANADA IN 1944

Alaska (United States)

Beaufort Sea

Greenland (Danemark)

Canadian Flag from 1892 to 1965

Canadian Flag since 1965

°Dawson
Yukon Territory
° Whitehorse

°Coppermine
Northwest Territories
°Yellowknife
Baker Lake

Baffin Island

Canadian Coat of Arms

British Columbia

Alberta
° Edmonton

Saskatchewan
Saskatoon °

Manitoba

Goose Bay ° **New Foundland** 1

Victoria □ Vancouver
° Calgary
Regina °
Winnipeg °

Ontario

Québec

Prince Edward Island

Québec ○
Montréal □

New Brunswick
° Halifax
Nova Scotia

CANADIAN COAT OF ARMS

The Lion passant of England

The Harp of Ireland

The Lion rampant of Scotland

"Fleurs de lys" of Québec (Symbol of the old French realm)

Three maple leaves: The Canadian nation

United States

Ottawa □
TORONTO □
Hamilton ○

1. This Dominion became the tenth province of Canada in 1947.

When war was declared, several Non-Permanent militia units were mobilised. The members of these units were invited to volunteer for active service (and to serve overseas). The others, those who had priority civilian jobs, those who were unfit or too old were assigned to the reserve battalion of the regiment which had just been put on the active list, and remained in Canada.

Mobilisation

On 10 September, after a vote in Parliament, unlike in 1914, Canada itself declared war against Germany, seven days after Great Britain. Here Canada showed London that it was making its own choice.

On 21 June 1940 the Mobilisation Law on national resources was passed. It imposed compulsory military service in the country but did not force any soldier to serve abroad against his will. There were thus two categories of soldiers, the General Service volunteer, ready to serve anywhere, and the conscripted soldier, who would only serve overseas if he volunteered to do so. In the spring of 1941, there were nowhere near enough volunteers, especially in the infantry.

On 27 April 1942, by referendum, the government asked the Canadian people to free them from their commitment to send only volunteers overseas. By a 64 % to 36% majority, the Canadians overwhelmingly agreed. The main opposition came from French-speaking Québec which had not forgotten the 1917 conscription. This referendum divided the country in two, as it had done during WWI.

On 22 November 1944, the Canadian Prime Minister W. L . McKenzie-King decided to send 16 000 conscripts overseas (National Resources Mobilisation Act - NRMA). Some of the men rebelled a few days later.

On January 3, 1945 the first group of 12, 908 conscripts left Halifax for England. On 23 February, 9,677 men were shipped to the Continent and 2,643 were assigned to combat units. In all, these recruits suffered losses of 313 casualties, of which 69 killed.

The Conscripts

In order to be drafted, the Canadian citizen had to be between 19 and 45 years old, five feet tall, five feet six inches for the artillery, the engineers and the armoured units. He had to weigh 121 lbs and have a 31-inch chest (33 inches for the artillery, the engineers and armoured units).

Daily pay for men serving abroad in 1944-45 was Can $ 1.2 for a private, $3 for a Sergeant, $5 for Lieutenants and Captains and $10 for a Lieutenant-Colonel, to which must be added $0.75 for other ranks and $2 for officers as a daily supplement for all volunteers for parachute duty.

The number of annual engagements for National Service was 65,383

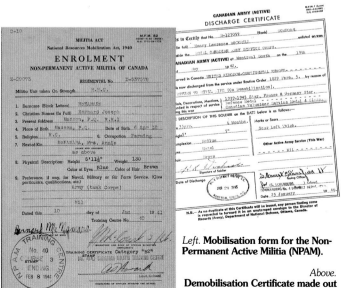

Left. **Mobilisation form for the Non-Permanent Active Militia (NPAM).**

Above.
Demobilisation Certificate made out in January 1946.

1. In 1944, Can $4.47= FF200 of the period ; at the time a French worker earned FF1 700 per month on average.

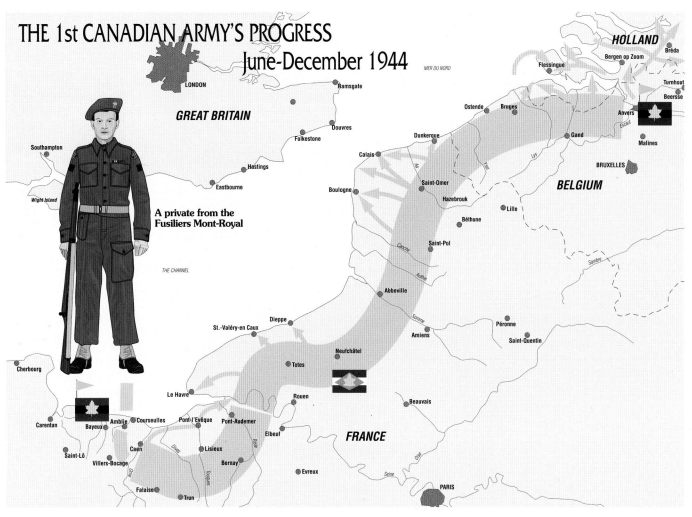

THE 1st CANADIAN ARMY'S PROGRESS
June-December 1944

MER DU NORD

HOLLAND

GREAT BRITAIN

LONDON

Ramsgate

Douvres

Folkestone

Hastings

Southampton

Eastbourne

Wight Island

A private from the
Fusiliers Mont-Royal

THE CHANNEL

Calais

Boulogne

Dunkerque

Saint-Omer

Hazebrouck

Béthune

Lille

Ostende
Bruges

Gand

Anvers

Malines

BRUXELLES

BELGIUM

Bergen op Zoom
Bréda
Flessingue
Turnhout
Beersse

Escaut

Lys

Aa

Yser

Sambre

Saint-Pol

Canche

Authie

Abbeville

Somme

Péronne

Saint-Quentin

St.-Valéry-en Caux
Dieppe

Totes

Neufchâtel

Beauvais

Amiens

Le Havre

Rouen

Elbeuf

Cherbourg

Carentan
Bayeux
Amblie
Courseulles
Pont-l'Evêque
Pont-Audemer

Caen
Lisieux
Bernay
Evreux

Saint-Lô
Villers-Bocage

Orne
Dives
Touques
Risle
Oise
Seine

FRANCE

Falaise
Trun

PARIS

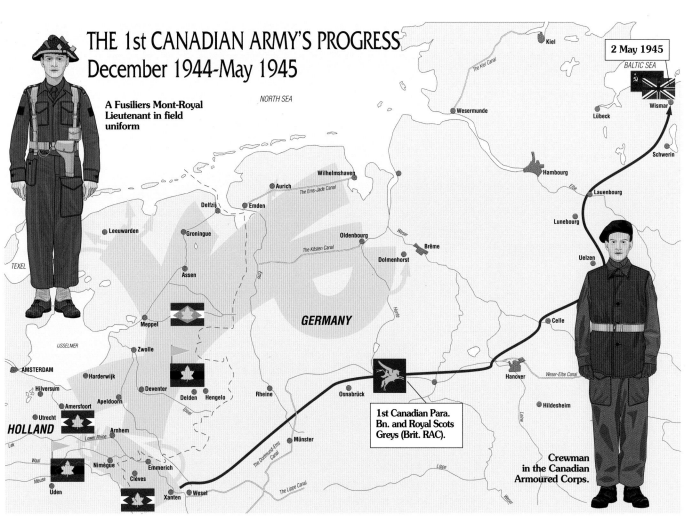

THE 1st CANADIAN ARMY'S PROGRESS
December 1944-May 1945

A Fusiliers Mont-Royal
Lieutenant in field
uniform

NORTH SEA

Kiel

The Kiel Canal

2 May 1945

BALTIC SEA

Wismar

Lübeck

Schwerin

Wesermunde

Hambourg

Lauenbourg

Wilhelmshaven

Aurich

The Ems-Jade Canal

Delfzil
Emden

Leeuwarden

Groningue

TEXEL

Oldenbourg

The Köstèn Canal

Dolmenhorst

Brême

Weser

Lunebourg

Uelzen

Assen

Meppel

IJSSELMER

Zwolle

AMSTERDAM

Hilversum

Harderwijk

Deventer

Delden
Hengelo

Celle

GERMANY

Hunte

Ems

Rheine

Osnabrück

1st Canadian Para.
Bn. and Royal Scots
Greys (Brit. RAC).

Hanover

Weser-Elbe Canal

Leine

Hildesheim

Utrecht
Amersfoort
Apeldoorn

HOLLAND

Arnhem

Lower Rhine

Lek
Waal

Nimègue

Emmerich

Münster

The Dortmund-Ems Canal

Weser

Lippe

Crewman
in the Canadian
Armoured Corps.

Meuse

Uden

Clèves

Xanten
Wesel

The Lippe Canal

5

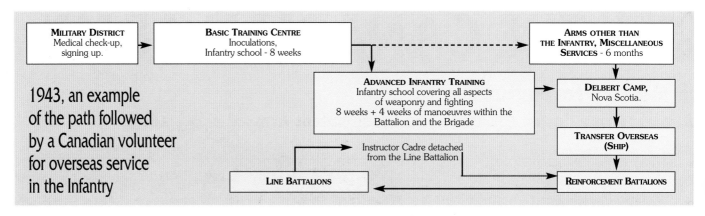

1943, an example of the path followed by a Canadian volunteer for overseas service in the Infantry

| MILITARY DISTRICT — Medical check-up, signing up. | → | BASIC TRAINING CENTRE — Inoculations, Infantry school - 8 weeks | ⟶ | ARMS OTHER THAN THE INFANTRY, MISCELLANEOUS SERVICES - 6 months |

ADVANCED INFANTRY TRAINING — Infantry school covering all aspects of weaponry and fighting 8 weeks + 4 weeks of manoeuvres within the Battalion and the Brigade

DELBERT CAMP, Nova Scotia.

TRANSFER OVERSEAS (SHIP)

Instructor Cadre detached from the Line Battalion

LINE BATTALIONS

REINFORCEMENT BATTALIONS

---

men in 1939, 118,591 in 1940, 100,644 in 1941, 132,659 in 1942, 72,711 in 1943, 59,281 in 1944 and 33,689 in 1945, for a total of 582 888 volunteers. The Canadian population at that time was 11,507,000 .

Two Languages

English was the official language in the Canadian Army. All orders, messages, organisation charts, etc. were in English.

Four regiments in the 1st Canadian Army were French-speaking (the Régiment de la Chaudière, the 22nd Royal Régiment, the Fusiliers Mont-Royal and the Régiment de Maisonneuve). In these regiments the officers had to speak both languages, and at small unit level, all orders and service orders were in French.

French-speaking soldiers having some rudiments of English could be assigned in English-speaking units where they would fulfill non-operational tasks.

Some manuals and issue items (e.g. rations) were drawn up in both languages and had bilingual instructions.

Below.
Holland June 1945, General Crerar talking with officers from the Régiment de la Chaudière. Although this was a French-speaking regiment, these officers who were bilingual do have a very British style and manner. (PA 1922265)

Above.
Bilingual poster for war loans.

Left.
Debert Camp at Truro (Nova Scotia) was a assembly point for troops before going overseas.
(Doc. J. Garnier)

Right.
Poster to encourage voluntary conscription. The presence of a man in dungarees is meant to show that volunteers can be assigned as labour in industry.

Waging the war

H.M. George VI
His Majesty's Governor General, Major-General the earl of Athlone
The Primer Minister W. L. McKenzie-King
Defence Minister Colonel J. L. Ralston (July 1940 to November 1944) then General A.G.L. Mc Naughton (from Nov. 1944)
Chief of the General Staff Lieutenant-General J. C. Murchie

CHAPTER 1 THE CANADIAN ARMY

1. Military Formations
Armies, Army Corps, Divisions and Independent Armoured Brigades

Made up of two or three army corps, the field army was meant to carry out strategic plans for the High Command.

It drew up its own units and support services which could, if needs be, be attached to units on the line.

From 23 July 1944, the 1st Canadian Army was made up of its own units but also of British divisions and other Allied units.

An Army Corps was made up of two or three divisions, the most current format being two infantry and one armoured divisions. In the same way as the Army, the Army Corps was made up of combat and support units, among which an armoured car reconnaissance regiment.

The divisions were the main combat units for the command and were in immediate contact with the enemy. They could be transferred from one corps to another according to the needs of the battle.

The division itself: each division in the line — about 16 000 men — was supported by 25 000 men spread out between the Army, Army Corps and Lines of communication and maintenance area support units. This strength of 41 000 men was supported by 8,000 vehicles and machines of all types, i.e. about one wheeled or tracked vehicle for every five men.

Infantry Division

This powerful formation was organised around three 3-battalion infantry brigades. A very large contingent of support units enabled the division to fight for a long time.

The Armoured Division

As a force which could strike and follow through, the Armoured Division included a three-regiment armoured brigade with a motorised infantry battalion and a three-battalion infantry brigade. The lorries of the *Royal Canadian Army Service Corps* provided the transport. Within the division, the Armoured Reconnaissance regiment was in fact a fourth tank regiment, equipped and organised in the same way as the other armoured regiments. Thus four groups could be made up consisting mainly of an armoured regiment and an infantry battalion. Reconnaissance was carried out by the regimental reconnaissance troops.

The Independent Armoured Brigade

Although they had been trained so that they could be committed en bloc, these brigades were general reserve

---

THE ORDER OF PRECEDENCE

CAVALRY
- Royal Canadian Dragoons
- Lord Strathcona's Horse (Royal Canadians)
- 8th Princess Louise's (New Brunswick) Hussars
- The Governor General's Horse Guards
- 4th Princess Louise's Dragoon Guards
- The Elgin Regiment
- Ontario Regiment
- The Sherbrooke Fusiliers Regiment *
- The Three Rivers Regiment
- First Hussars
- The Prince Edward Island Light Horse
- 17th Duke of York's Royal Canadian Hussars
- The British Columbia Regiment (Duke of Connaught's Own Rifles)
- 12th Manitoba Dragoons
- The South Alberta Regiment
- 14th Canadian Hussars (VIII Recce Regiment)
- The Calgary Regiment *
- The British Columbia Dragoons
- The Fort Garry Horse.

ARMS AND SERVICES

Arms
- Canadian Armoured Corps
- The Royal Canadian Artillery
- Corps of Royal Canadian Engineers
- Royal Canadian Corps of Signals
- Canadian Infantry Corps

Services
- Royal Canadian Army Service Corps
- Royal Canadian Army Medical Corps
- Canadian Dental Corps

- Royal Canadian Ordnance Corps
- Royal Canadian Electrical and Mechanical Engineers
- Royal Canadian Army Pay Corps
- Corps of Military Staff Clerks
- Canadian Postal Corps
- Canadian Chaplain Service
- Canadian Provost Corps
- Canadian Women's Army Corps
- Canadian Intelligence Corps
- Canadian Forestry Corps

General list. INFANTRY

Regular Force
- The Royal Canadian Regiment
- Princess Patricia's Canadian Light Infantry
- Royal 22ᵉ Régiment

Foot Guards
- Governors General's Foot Guards *
- Canadian Grenadier Guards *

Militia
- The Queen's Own Rifles of Canada
- The Black Watch of Canada (Royal Highland Regiment)
- The Royal Regiment of Canada
- The Royal Hamilton Light Infantry
- The Hastings and Prince Edward Regiment
- The Lincoln and Welland Regiment
- The Perth Regiment
- The Highland Light Infantry of Canada
- The Lorne Scots (Peel, Dufferin and Halton Reg.)
- The Lanark and Renfrew Regiment (RCA)

- The Stormont, Dundas and Glengarry Highlanders (Glengarrians)
- Le Régiment de la Chaudière
- Les Fusiliers Mont Royal
- The Princess Louise Fusiliers
- The Carleton and York Regiment
- The New Brunswick Rangers
- The North Shore (New Brunswick) Regiment
- West Nova Scotia Regiment
- The North Nova Scotia Highlanders
- The Cape Breton Highlanders
- Le Régiment de Maisonneuve
- The Cameron Highlanders of Ottawa
- The Royal Winnipeg Rifles
- The Essex Scottish
- 48th Highlanders of Canada
- The Algonquin Regiment
- The Argyll and Sutherland Highlanders of Canada (Princess Louise's)
- The Lake Superior Regiment
- The Regina Rifle Regiment
- The Queen's Own Cameron Highlanders of Canada
- The Calgary Highlanders
- The Westminster Regiment
- Seaforth, Canada
- The Saskatoon Light Infantry (MG),
- The Canadian Scottish Regiment
- The Royal Montréal Regiment
- 49th The Loyal Edmonton Regiment
- The Toronto Scottish
- The Irish Regiment
- South Saskatchewan Regiment

---
* Became Armoured Regiments.

units whose job was to support the infantry division. They were made up of three tank regiments with several light support elements.

Town and province names for regiments

The principal sources were :

- The name of the town or the province where recruitment took place (see map page 4).

- In honour of one of the members of the British Royal family or one of the Kingdom's noble families.

- The names of Scottish regiments indicating, for most of them, a link with a British regiment. They were made up of soldiers whose families emigrated at the end of the 19th century.

For example :

- *The Lorne Scots:* the Marquis of Lorne, Governor-General of Canada in 1878, the husband of Princess Louise.

- *Princess Patricia's Canadian Light Infantry:* Princess Patricia was Queen Victoria's grand-daughter, born in 1886.

- *The Elgin Regiment:* Lord Elgin, Governor of Canada from 1840 -1854.

- *8th Princess Louise's* (North Brunswick) *Hussars, 4th Princess Louise's Dragoon Guards, Princess Louise's Fusiliers:* Princess Louise was one of Victoria's daughters, born in 1848.

- *The Mont-Royal Fusiliers:* Mont-Royal is the hill dominating the city of Quebec.

- *The Hastings and Prince Edward, Prince*

Percentage of personnel in the various units of the 21st Army Group*

FIGHTING UNITS

Artillery	18 % **
Infantry	14 %
Engineers	13 %
Armour	6 %
Signals	5 %
Total	**56 %**

SERVICES

Army Service corps	15 %
Pioneers	10 %
Electrical and Mechanical Engineers	5 %
Medical	4 %
Chaplains, Stores, equipment, Pay, Intelligence, Provost	10 %
Total (for all services)	**44 %**

* Percentages were calculated on the basis of 660,000 men in August 1944.
** The relative size of the artillery was due to doctrines in fashion after the lessons learnt in WWI.

British Corps without equivalent In the Canadian Army

British Army	**Tasks carried out by (Canadian Army)**
— Reconnaissance Corps	Canadian Arm. Corps
— Pioneer Corps	Royal Can. Engineers
— Royal Army Veterinary Corps	Disbanded in 1940
— Royal Army Educational Corps	Can. Intelligence Corps
— Army Catering Corps	RCASC
— Army Physical Training Corps	Canadian Infantry Corps

THE ARMY IN N-W EUROPE, commands, strengths, means

Group, Unit	Average Strength	Symbol	Under the command of a
Army Group	600 000		Field Marshall
Army	150 000		General
Corps *	60 000		Lieutenant-General
Division	15 000 18 000		Major-General
Brigade	3 500		Brigadier
Battalion Regiment (CAC, RCA)	850		Lieutenant-Colonel
Company, Squadron	130		Major
Platoon	37		Lieutenant or 2nd Lieutenant
Section	10	Bren Group	Corporal

(see map page 4).

REGIMENTS KEPT IN CANADA
or disbanded in Great-Britain without having taken part in operations during the period 1944-1945

● **15th Alberta Light Horse:** disbanded in January 1945 in Great Britain.

● **Brockville Rifles:** disbanded in June 1943 in Canada, personnel transferred to the Stormont, Dundas and Glengarry Highlanders and to the Rocky Mountain Rangers.

● **Canadian Fusiliers (City of London Regiment):** converted into an infantry training battalion in November 1944 in Great Britain

● **Dufferin and Haldimand Rifles of Canada:** training regiment kept in Canada.

● **6th Duke of Connaught's Royal Canadian Hussars:** disbanded in January 1943, personnel transferred to Headquarters, 5th Armoured Division

● **Essex Regiment (Tank):** disbanded in March 1944 in Great Britain.

● **St. Laurent Fusiliers:** disbanded in January 1945 in Great Britain.

● **Grey and Simcoe Foresters:** disbanded in November 1943 in Great Britain.

● **Halifax Rifles:** disbanded in November 1943 in Great Britain.

● **7th/11th Hussars:** disbanded in January 1943 in Great Britain, personnel transferred to HQ, 5th Armoured Division.

● **Irish Fusiliers of Canada:** disbanded in January 1945 in Great Britain.

● **Kent Regiment:** kept in Canada as a training regiment.

● **King's Own Rifles of Canada:** kept in Canada as a training regiment.

● **Midland Regiment:** transferred to Great Britain in January 1945, personnel transferred to other regiments.

● **Oxford Rifles:** transferred to Great Britain in January 1945, personnel transferred to other regiments.

● **Princess of Wales' Own Regiment:** disbanded in October 1943, personnel transferred to the Stormont, Dundas and Glengarry Highlanders.

● **Chateauguay Regiment:** disbanded in Great Britain in January 1945, personnel transferred to other regiments.

● **Hull Regiment:** converted into an infantry training battalion in Great Britain in November 1944.

● **Joliette Regiment:** disbanded in Great Britain in January 1945, personnel transferred to other regiments.

● **Levis Regiment:** disbanded in October 1943 in Canada.

● **Montmagny Regiment:** disbanded in September 1944 in Great Britain.

● **Royal Rifles of Canada:** annihilated at Hong Kong in December 1941. Re-formed and transferred to Great Britain in January 1945 where it remained.

● **Saint-John Fusiliers:** disbanded in Great Britain in January 1945, personnel transferred to other regiments.

● **16/22nd Saskatchewan Horse:** disbanded in Great Britain in November 1943.

● **Victoria Rifles of Canada:** disbanded in Great Britain in November 1944 personnel transferred to other regiments.

● **The Quebec Voltigeurs:** disbanded in November 1943 in Great Britain.

● **Winnipeg Grenadiers:** annihilated at Hong Kong in December 1941. Re-formed in January 1942 and kept in Great Britain as an infantry training battalion.

● **Winnipeg Light Infantry:** disbanded in Great Britain in January 1945, personnel transferred to other regiments.

CANADIAN REGIMENTS IN THE ORDER OF BATTLE, 1944-45

alphabetical order	1st Army	I Corps	II Corps	1st Armoured Brigade	2nd Armoured Brigade	1st Infantry Division	2nd Infantry Division	3rd Infantry Division	4th Armoured Division	5th Armoured Division	Assignment
The Algonquin Regiment									●		Infantry Battalion
The Argyll and Sutherland Highlanders of Canada									●		Infantry Battalion
The Black Watch of Canada (Royal Highland Reg.)							●				Infantry Battalion
The British Columbia Dragoons										●	9th Armoured Regiment
The British Columbia Regiment									●		28th Armoured regiment
The Calgary Highlanders							●				Infantry Battalion
The Calgary Regiment				●							14th Armoured Regiment
Cameron Highlanders of Ottawa								●			Machine Gun Battalion
Canadian Grenadier Guards									●		22nd Armoured Regiment
Canadian Scottish Regiment								●			Infantry Battalion
Cape Breton Highlanders										●	Infantry Battalion
Carleton and York Highlanders						●					Infantry Battalion
14th Canadian Hussars							●				8th Reconnaissance Regiment
Elgin Regiment	●										Armoured Delivery Regiment
Essex Scottish							●				Infantry Battalion
First Hussars					●						6th Armoured Regiment
Fort Garry Horse					●						10th Armoured Battalion
Fusiliers Mont Royal							●				Infantry Battalion
Governor General's Foot Guards									●		21st Armoured Regiment
Governor General's Horse Guards										●	3rd Armoured Reconnaissance Regiment
Hastings and Prince Edward Regiment						●					Infantry Battalion
48th Highlanders of Canada						●					Infantry Battalion
Highland Light Infantry of Canada								●			Infantry Battalion
Irish Regiment of Canada										●	Infantry Battalion
Lake Superior Regiment									●		Infantry Battalion (motor.)
Lanark and Renfrew Scottish Regiment		●									1st Light Anti-Aircraft Regiment
Lincoln and Welland Regiment									●		Infantry Battalion
Lord Strathcona's Horse (Royal Canadians)										●	2nd Armoured Regiment
Lorne Scots	●					●	●	●	●	●	Headquarters Defence Company
12th Manitoba Dragoons			●								18th Armoured Car Regiment
Loyal Edmonton Regiment						●					Infantry Battalion
New Brunswick Rangers									●		10th Independent Machine Gun Company
North Shore Regiment								●			Infantry Battalion
North Nova Scotia Highlanders								●			Infantry Battalion
Ontario Regiment				●							11th Armoured Regiment
Perth Regiment										●	Infantry Battalion
Prince Edward Island Light Horse			●								Headquarters Defence Company
8th Princess Louise's (New Brunswick) Hussars										●	5th Armoured Regiment
Princess Louise's Fusiliers										●	11th Independent Machine Gun Company
4th Princess Louise's Dragoon Guards						●					4th Reconnaissance Regiment
Princess Patricia's Canadian Light Infantry						●					Infantry Battalion
Queen's Own Cameron Highlanders of Canada								●			Infantry Battalion
Queen's Own Cameron Rifles of Canada								●			Infantry Battalion
Régiment de la Chaudière								●			Infantry Battalion
Régiment de Maisonneuve							●				Infantry Battalion
Regina Rifle Regiment								●			Infantry Battalion
Royal Canadian Dragoons		●									1st Armoured Car Regiment
Royal Canadian Regiment						●					Infantry Battalion
Royal Hamilton Light Infantry							●				Infantry Battalion
Royal Montreal Regiment	●										Headquarters Defence Battalion
Royal Regiment of Canada							●				Infantry Battalion
Royal 22e Régiment						●					Infantry Battalion
Royal Winnipeg Rifles								●			Infantry Battalion
Saskatoon Light Infantry						●					Machine Gun Battalion
Seaforth Highlanders of Canada						●					Infantry Battalion
17th Duke of York's Royal Canadian Hussars								●			7th Reconnaissance Regiment
Sherbrooke Fusiliers					●						27th Armoured Regiment
South Alberta Regiment									●		29th Armoured Reconnaissance Regiment
South Saskatchewan Regiment							●				Infantry Battalion
Stormont, Dundas and Glengarry Highlanders								●			Infantry Battalion
Three Rivers Regiment				●							Armoured Regiment
Toronto Scottish Regiment							●				Machine Gun Battalion
Westminster Regiment										●	Infantry Battalion (Motor.)
West Nova Scotia Regiment						●					Infantry Battalion

Edward's Island Light Horse: Prince Edward was the son of Queen Victoria, the future King Edward VII.

- *The Lanark and Renfrew Scottish Regiment:* towns of the Lowlands of Scotland.

- *The Maisonneuve Regiment:* Monsieur Chomedey de Maisonneuve, a French gentleman who was the founder of the town of Montreal in 1642.

- *Lord Strathcona's Horse* (Royal Canadians): Lord Strathcona was a Scottish engineer and financier who promoted the building of the railway linking the Atlantic to the Pacific in 1885 (the crossed tools at the centre of the cap badge symbolised this huge enterprise.

Lord Strathcona was the regiment's patron when it was formed up in 1900.

- *The Toronto Scottish Regiment:* a regiment affiliated to the Lon-

don Scottish.

- *The Black Watch* (Royal Highland) *of Canada*: a regiment affiliated to the Black Watch.

The order of precedence

The order of precedence of regiments (page 4) was determined by the date on which the regiment was formed. Organisational charts, tables and all official documents systematically presented the regiments in this order, whether written across the page or in columns.

Formed in December 1883, the Royal Canadian is the oldest of infantry regiments and therefore takes precedence at the top of the list. Formed in May 1920, the Toronto Scottish Regiment brings up the rear.

THE 1st CANADIAN ARMY

1. Organisation

The following tables present the general organisation of the Canadian forces (units, arms and services) in Western Europe for the period 1944-45.

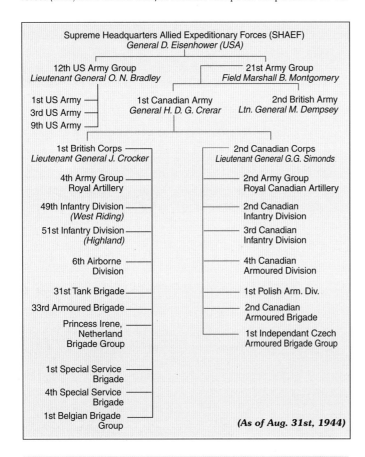

Supreme Headquarters Allied Expeditionary Forces (SHAEF)
General D. Eisenhower (USA)

12th US Army Group — *Lieutenant General O. N. Bradley*
21st Army Group — *Field Marshall B. Montgomery*

1st US Army / 3rd US Army / 9th US Army
1st Canadian Army — *General H. D. G. Crerar*
2nd British Army — *Ltn. General M. Dempsey*

1st British Corps — *Lieutenant General J. Crocker*
2nd Canadian Corps — *Lieutenant General G.G. Simonds*

4th Army Group Royal Artillery
49th Infantry Division (West Riding)
51st Infantry Division (Highland)
6th Airborne Division
31st Tank Brigade
33rd Armoured Brigade
Princess Irene, Netherland Brigade Group
1st Special Service Brigade
4th Special Service Brigade
1st Belgian Brigade Group

2nd Army Group Royal Canadian Artillery
2nd Canadian Infantry Division
3rd Canadian Infantry Division
4th Canadian Armoured Division
1st Polish Arm. Div.
2nd Canadian Armoured Brigade
1st Independant Czech Armoured Brigade Group

(As of Aug. 31st, 1944)

1st CANADIAN ARMY 1944-1945

General Officer Commanding: General H.D.G. Crerar, C.H., CB, DSO, from 20 March 1944.

Date of formation: Headquarters Staff on 6 April 1942 in Great Britain. Operational from 23 July in Normandy when I British Corps joined II Canadian Corps.

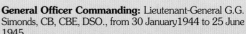

465	**25th Armoured Delivery Regiment (The Elgin Regiment): a replacement unit for armoured vehicles and their crews.**
157	**1st Armoured Carrier Regiment (see pages 152-153)**
459	**1st Canadian Army Headquarters Defence Battalion (Royal Montreal Regiment)**

UNITS ASSIGNED TO 1ST CANADIAN ARMY HQ

1st CANADIAN CORPS

General Officer Commanding: Lieutenant-General C. Foulkes, CB, CBE, DSO., from 10 November 1944 to 17 July 1945.

Activation: December 1940 in Great Britain.

Campaigns and Battles: Sicily, Italy 1943-1945. Northwest Europe from March 1945 in Holland.

Composition:
1st Armoured brigade,
1st Infantry Division,
5th Armoured Division.
Main units assigned to Army Corps HQ:

● **CAC**

- *1st Armoured car Regiment (The Royal Canadian Dragoons) Army Corps Reconnaissance.*

● **RCA**
- *7th Anti-Tank Regiment*
- *1st Survey Regiment*
- *1st Light Anti-Aircraft Regiment (Lanark and Renfrew Scottish Regiment)*

● **RCE**
- *9th Field park Company*
- *12th, 13th, 14th Field companies*

● **RCCS - CIC**
17
- *1st Corps Signals*
- *1st Corps Defence Company (Lorne Scots)*
● **RCASC**
- *1st Headquarters Corps Company*
- *1st Corps Transport Company*
- *No 31 Corps Troops Company*
- *No 32 Corps troops Company*
● **RCOC**
- *No 1 Corps and Army Troops Sub-Park*
● **RCEME**
- *1st Corps Troops Workshop*

2nd CANADIAN CORPS

General Officer Commanding: Lieutenant-General G.G. Simonds, CB, CBE, DSO., from 30 January 1944 to 25 June 1945.

Activation: January 1943 in Great Britain. Operational from 7 July 1944 in Normandy

Composition:
2nd Armoured Brigade,
2nd Infantry Division,
3rd Infantry Division,
1st Polish Armoured Division
(1st August 1944),
4th Armoured Division
(8th August 1944).
Main units assigned to Army Corps HQ:

● **CAC**

18th Armoured car Regiment (12th Manitoba Dragoons): Army Corps Reconnaissance.
● **RCA**
- *6th Anti-Tank Regiment*
- *2nd Survey Regiment*
- *6th Light Anti-Aircraft Regiment*

● **RCE**
- *8th Field park Company*
- *29th, 30th, 31st Field companies*
● **RCCS CIC**
17
- *2nd Corps Signals*
- *2nd Corps Defence Company (The Prince Edward Island Light Horse)*
● **RCASC**
- *No 2 Headquarters Corps Car Company*
- *2nd Corps Transport Company*
- *No 33 Corps Troops Company*
- *No 34 Corps troops Company*
● **RCOC**
- *No 2 Corps and Army Troops Sub-Park*
● **RCEME**
- *2nd Corps Troops Workshop*

Campaigns and Battles: North-west Europe. The first elements landed on 6 June 1944 with I British Corps.

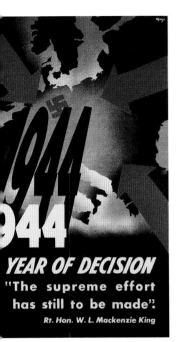

1st CANADIAN ARMY TROOPS, GREAT HEADQUARTERS & LINES OF COMMUNICATION TROOPS, 5th MAY 1945

1st Army Group, Royal Canadian Artillery

- *11th Army Field Regiment*
- *1st Medium Regiment*
- *2nd Medium Regiment*
- *5th Medium Regiment*

2nd Army Group, Royal Canadian Artillery

- *19th Army Field Regiment*
- *3rd Medium Regiment*
- *4th Medium Regiment*
- *7th Medium Regiment*
- *2nd Heavy Anti-Aircraft Regiment (Mobile)*
- *1st Rocket Battery*
- *1st Radar Battery*

(See pp. 18-19)

Royal Canadian Engineers, 1st Canadian Army Troops

- *10th Field Park Company*
- *5th Field Company*
- *20th Field Company*
- *23rd Field Company*

2nd Canadian Army Troops

- *11th Field Park Company*
- *32nd Field Company*
- *33rd Field Company*
- *34th Field Company*
- *No 1 Workshop and Park Coy.*
- *1st Field (Air) Survey Company*
- *2nd Field Survey Company*
- *3rd Field (Reproduction) Survey Company*
- *1st Radar Battery*

GHQ and L of C troops

- *1st Mechanical Equipment Coy.*
- *1st Mechanical Equipment Park Coy.*
- *2nd Battalion, R.C.E.*
- *3rd Battalion, R.C.E.*
- *1st Road Construction Coy*
- *2nd Road Construction Coy*
- *1st Drilling Company*
- *2nd Drilling Company*
- *No 1 Railway Operating Coy*
- *No 2 Railway Operating Coy*
- *No 1 Railway Workshop Coy.*

Royal Canadian Corps of Signals 1st Army Signals L of C Signals

- *1st Air Support Signals Unit*
- *No 1 Special Wireless Section*
- *No 2 Special Wireless Section*
- *No 3 Special Wireless Section*

Royal Canadian Army Service Corps 1st Canadian Army Troops

- *No 1 Army HQ Car Coy*
- *No 35 Army Troops Composite Coy*
- *No 36 Army Troops Composite Coy*
- *No 81 Artillery Company*
- *No 82 Artillery Company*
- *No 41 Army Transport Company*
- *No 45 Army Transport Company*
- *No 47 Army Transport Company*
- *No 63 Army Transport Company*
- *No 64 Army Transport Company*
- *No 1 Motor Ambulance Convoy*
- *No 2 Motor Ambulance Convoy*

GHQ and L of C troops and Base Troops

- *No 66 General Transport Coy*
- *No 69 General Transport Company*
- *No 1 Base Transport Company*
- *No 65 Tank Transporter Company*
- *No 85 Brigade Company*
- *No 86 Brigade Company*

Royal Canadian Ordnance Corps

- *No 201 Infantry Ordnance Sub-Park*
- *No 202 Infantry Ord. Sub-Park*
- *No 203 Infantry Ord. Sub-Park*
- *No 204 Armoured Ord. Sub-Park*
- *No 205 Armoured Ordnance Sub-Park*
- *No 1 Corps and Army Troops Sub-Park*
- *No 2 Corps and Army Troops Sub-Park*

Royal Canadian Electrical and Mechanical Engineers

- *First Army Troops Workshop*
- *1st General Troops Workshop*
- *No 1 Infantry Troops Workshop*
- *No 2 Infantry Troops Workshop*
- *No 3 Infantry Troops Workshop*
- *No 4 Armoured Troops Wksp*
- *No 5 Armoured Troops Wksp*
- *No 1 Tank Troops Workshop*
- *No 2 Tank Troops Workshop*
- *No 1 Recovery Company*
- *No 2 Recovery Company*
- *No 3 Recovery Company*
- *No 1 Advanced Base Workshop*
- *No 2 Advanced Base Workshop*

Canadian Postal Corps

- *No 1 Army Base Post Office*

Royal Canadian Army Medical Corps, 1st Can. Army Troops

- *First Canadian Army Troops:*
- *No 2 Casualty Clearing Station*
- *No 3 Casualty Clearing Station*
- *No 4 Casualty Clearing Station*
- *No 5 Casualty Clearing Station*
- *No 6 Casualty Clearing Station*

GHQ and L of C troops

- *No 1 General Hospital*
- *No 2 General Hospital*
- *No 3 General Hospital*
- *No 5 General Hospital·*
- *No 6 General Hospital*
- *No 7 General Hospital*
- *No 8 General Hospital*
- *No 10 General Hospital*
- *No 12 General Hospital*
- *No 16 General Hospital*
- *No 20 General Hospital*
- *No 21 General Hospital*
- *No 2 Convalescent Depot*
- *No 3 Convalescent Depot*

Canadian Dental Corps

- *No 1 Dental Company*
- *No 2 Dental Company*
- *No 3 Dental Company*
- *No 4 Dental Company*
- *No 5 Dental Company*
- *No 6 Dental Company*
- *No 8 Dental Company*
- *No 9 Dental Company*
- *No 11 Base Dental Company*
- *No 12 Base Dental Company*

Canadian Provost Corps

- *No 7 Provost Company*
- *No 8 Provost Company*
- *No 11 Provost Company*
- *No 13 Provost Company*
- *No 15 Provost Company*
- *No 16 Provost Company*
- *No 1 L. of C. Provost Company*
- *No 2 L. of C. Provost Company*

Canadian Forestry Corps

No 1 Forestry Group:
- *No 1 Company*
- *No 5 Company*
- *No 9 Company*
- *No 14 Company*
- *No 15 Company*
- *No 16 Company*
- *No 25 Company*
- *No 27 Company*
- *No 28 Company*
- *No 30 Company*

OTHER ATTACHED ALLIED UNITS
temporarily to the Canadian Army during the Campaign

— **18th October 1944:**
- **52nd British Infantry Division** *(Lowland)*
- **104th US Infantry Division.**

— **5th May 1945:**
BRITISH UNITS
- **3rd Infantry Division**
- **49th Infantry Division** *(West Riding)*
- **4th Army Group, Royal Artillery**
- **31st Anti-Aircraft Brigade**
- **74th Anti-Aircraft Brigade**

- **107th Anti-Aircraft Brigade**
These last three artillery units had been converted into infantry units.
- **4th Commando Brigade**
- **308th Infantry Brigade**
BELGIAN UNITS
- **1st Belgian Infantry Brigade**
DUTCH UNITS
- **'Prinses Irene' Brigade Group**
POLISH UNITS
- **1st Polish Armoured Division**

Miscellaneous

- *Canadian Section, HQ 1st Echelon, 21 Army Group*
- *Canadian Section, HQ 2nd Echelon, 21 Army Group*
- *No 2 Base Reinforcement Group*
- *No 3 Base Reinforcement Group*
- *Headquarters 1st Canadian Army Terminals*
- *Headquarters Army Troop Area 1st Canadian Army*
- *No 3 Non-Effective Transit Depot*
- *No 3 Public Relations Group*

2. The Infantry Divisions

THE INFANTRY DIVISION

Organisation of a Canadian Infantry Division
Tactical Grouping or *Brigade Group*

During the principal operations, an independent armoured brigade was attached to the infantry division.

Each of its armoured regiments was thus attached to one of the three infantry brigades, one squadron of tanks per infantry battalion.

JUNIOR INFANTRY BRIGADE

SECOND INFANTRY BRIGADE

SENIOR INFANTRY BRIGADE

ARMOURED REGIMENT Canadian Armoured Corps
— Squadron ------- Infantry Battalion (No 3)
— Squadron ------- Infantry Battalion (No 2)
— Squadron ------- Infantry Battalion (No 1)

Medium Machine Gun Company

Field Regiment Royal Canadian Artillery

Anti-Tank Battery Royal Canadian Artillery

Field Company Royal Canadian Engineers

Transport Company Royal Canadian Army Service Corps

Field Ambulance Royal Can. Army Medical Corps

Infantry Brigade Workshop RCEME

13 July 1944 in Normandy, a company of the 3rd Canadian Infantry Division marching towards the front.
(IWM B-5549)

THE STRENGTH OF THE INFANTRY DIVISION

	Officers	OR		Officers	OR
			Supply and Transport		
			HQ RCASC	10	35
			— 3 Infantry Brigade Companies	9	**308** (x 3)
			(2 Transport Platoons each)		
			— 1 Divisional Troops Company	9	291
(Headquarters)	**40**	**123**	(2 Transport Platoons)		
Armoured Corps			**Medical**		
— *Reconnaissance Regiment*	**43**	**777**	— 3 Field Ambulances	12	**230** (x 3)
Artillery			— 2 Field Dressing Stations	6	**89** (x 3)
— *Headquarters, RCA*	**10**	**31**	— 1 Field Hygiene section	2	27
— *3 Field Regiments*	**38**	**632** (x 3)			
(HQ, three 25-pdr batteries)			**Ordnance**		
— *1 Anti-Tank Regiment*			— *Ordnance Field Park*	**2**	**78**
● *Headquarters*	**8**	**56**	**Electrical and Mechanical Engineers**		
● *3 anti-tank batteries*	**7**	**142** (x 3)	— HQ RCEME	6	18
— *1 Light anti-aircraft Regiment*			— 3 Infantry Brigade workshops	6	**184** (x 3)
● *Headquarters*	**7**	**41**	— 1 LAA Workshop (A)	1	28
● *3 Light anti-aircraft batteries*	**9**	**170** (x 3)	— 4 Light Aid Detachments (A)	1	**15** (x 4)
— *1 CMO staff (A)*	**5**	**43**	— 6 Light Aid Detachments (B)	1	**13** (x 6)
Engineers			— 1 Light Aid Detachment (D)	1	46
— *Headquarters RCE*	**7**	**27**	**Provost**		
— *1 Field Park Company*	**4**	**112**	— *Provost Company*	**3**	**112**
— *1 Bridge Platoon*	**1**	**40**	**Intelligence**		
— *3 Field Companies*	**7**	**249** (x 3)	— *Field Security Section*	**1**	**13**
Signals			**TOTAL**	**917**	**17 158**
— *Divisional Signals*	**29**	**714**			
Infantry			**ATTACHED UNITS FROM ARMY CORPS**		
— *Machine Gun Battalion*	**37**	**701**			
— *Defence & Employment Platoon*	**1**	**60**	**Ordnance**		
— *3 Infantry Brigades*			— *Infantry Ordnance Sub Park*	**4**	**130**
● *Headquarters*	**18**	**52** (x 3)	— *Mobile Laundry and Bath Unit*	**3**	**63**
● *Ground Defence platoon*	—	**27** (x 3)	**Pay corps**		
● *3 Infantry Battalions*	**38**	**812** (x 3)	— *Field Cash Office*	**2**	**5**

1st Infantry Division

Date of activation: 1 September 1939 in Canada, transferred to Great Britain in December 1939.

General Officer Commanding: Major-General H.W. Foster, CBE, DSO, from 1 December 1944 to 15 August 1945

Brigadiers in 1945 :
1st Infantry Brigade: Brigadier J.D.B. Smith
2nd Infantry Brigade: Brigadier M. P. Bogert
3rd Infantry Brigade: Brigadier J.P.E Bernatchez
Divisional Artillery:
Brigadier W.S. Ziegler

Campaigns and Battles: *Operation Husky*, landing in Sicily on 10 July 1943. Italian campaign from September 1943 to March 1945. North-west Europe Campaign from March to May 1945 in Holland (Appeldorn).
The Division was disbanded on 15 September 1945 in Holland.

NB: On 12 June 1940, an infantry section from the 1st Infantry Brigade landed at Brest and was stationed in the Laval/Sablé-sur-Sarthe area before re-embarking on the 17th without having taken part in operations.

The units of the Royal Canadian Corps of Signals adopted the number of the unit to which they were attached, painted red.
Example:
Vehicle code sign for a unit attached to the Headquarters of the 1st Infantry Brigade.

81

2nd Infantry Division

Date of activation: February 1940 in Canada, transferred to Great Britain in December 1940.

General Officer Commanding: Major-General C. Foulkes, CBE, from 11 January to November 1944.
Major-General A.B. Matthews, CBE, DSO, ED, from 10 November 1944 to 8th October 1945

Brigadiers in 1945:
4th Infantry Brigade: Brigadier S. Lett from 27 February 1944 to 18 July 1944, wounded and evacuated ; Brigadier J.E. Garroney from 3 to 30 August 1944 ; Brigadier F.N. Cabeldu from 31 August to 22 September 1945.
5th Infantry Brigade: Brigadier W.J Megill from 27 February 1944 to 4 June 1945.
6th Infantry Brigade: Brigadier H.A. Young from 27 July 1944 to 25 August 1944 ; Brigadier F.A. Clift from 26 to 29 August 1944, wounded and evacuated ; Brigadier J.G. Gauvreau from 30 August to 26 October 1944, wounded and evacuated ; Brigadier R.H. Keefler from 10 November 1944 to 23 March 1945. Brigadier J.V. Allard from 25 March to 27 September 1945.

Divisional: Brigadier R.H. Keefler from 8 November 1943 to 9 November 1944 ; Brigadier F. D. Lace from 10 November 1944 to 4 October 1945.

Campaigns and Battles: Dieppe, 19 August 1942 * ; landed in Normandy on 7 July 1944, committed at Caen on the 18th then on the right bank of the Orne, Bourguébus Ridge, Falaise, the Forêt de la Londe, Scheldt, Hochwald, Xanten, Groningen and Oldenburg.
The Division was disbanded in September 1945 in Canada.

* *see Appendix 1*

1st Canadian Infantry Division (March 1945)

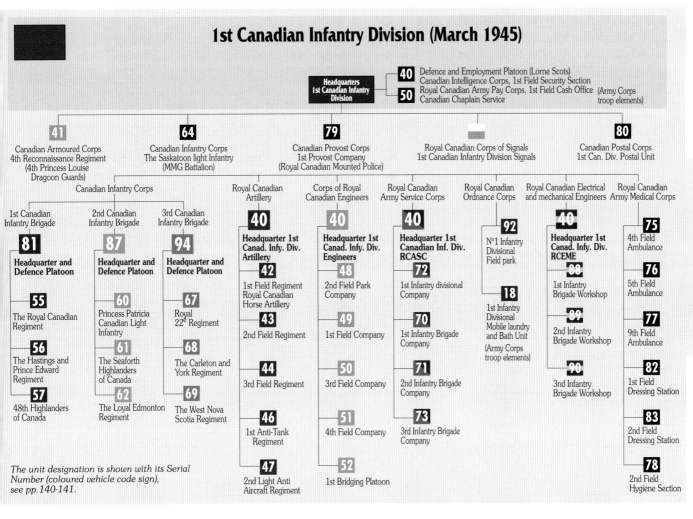

Headquarters 1st Canadian Infantry Division

- **40** Defence and Employment Platoon (Lorne Scots)
  Canadian Intelligence Corps, 1st Field Security Section
- **50** Royal Canadian Army Pay Corps, 1st Field Cash Office
  Canadian Chaplain Service *(Army Corps troop elements)*

41 Canadian Armoured Corps
4th Reconnaissance Regiment
(4th Princess Louise Dragoon Guards)

64 Canadian Infantry Corps
The Saskatoon light Infantry
(MMG Battalion)

79 Canadian Provost Corps
1st Provost Company
(Royal Canadian Mounted Police)

Royal Canadian Corps of Signals
1st Canadian Infantry Division Signals

80 Canadian Postal Corps
1st Can. Div. Postal Unit

Canadian Infantry Corps

1st Canadian Infantry Brigade
- **81** Headquarter and Defence Platoon
- **55** The Royal Canadian Regiment
- **56** The Hastings and Prince Edward Regiment
- **57** 48th Highlanders of Canada

2nd Canadian Infantry Brigade
- **87** Headquarter and Defence Platoon
- **60** Princess Patricia Canadian Light Infantry
- **61** The Seaforth Highlanders of Canada
- **62** The Loyal Edmonton Regiment

3rd Canadian Infantry Brigade
- **94** Headquarter and Defence Platoon
- **67** Royal 22ᵉ Regiment
- **68** The Carleton and York Regiment
- **69** The West Nova Scotia Regiment

Royal Canadian Artillery
- **40** Headquarter 1st Canad. Infy. Div. Artillery
- **42** 1st Field Regiment Royal Canadian Horse Artillery
- **43** 2nd Field Regiment
- **44** 3rd Field Regiment
- **46** 1st Anti-Tank Regiment
- **47** 2nd Light Anti Aircraft Regiment

Corps of Royal Canadian Engineers
- **40** Headquarter 1st Canad. Infy. Div. Engineers
- **48** 2nd Field Park Company
- **49** 1st Field Company
- **50** 3rd Field Company
- **51** 4th Field Company
- **52** 1st Bridging Platoon

Royal Canadian Army Service Corps
- **40** Headquarter 1st Canadian Inf. Div. RCASC
- **72** 1st Infantry divisional Company
- **70** 1st Infantry Brigade Company
- **71** 2nd Infantry Brigade Company
- **73** 3rd Infantry Brigade Company

Royal Canadian Ordnance Corps
- **92** N°1 Infantry Divisional Field park
- **18** 1st Infantry Divisional Mobile laundry and Bath Unit *(Army Corps troop elements)*

Royal Canadian Electrical and mechanical Engineers
- **40** Headquarter 1st Canad. Infy. Div. RCEME
- **88** 1st Infantry Brigade Workshop
- **89** 2nd Infantry Brigade Workshop
- **90** 3nd Infantry Brigade Workshop

Royal Canadian Army Medical Corps
- **75** 4th Field Ambulance
- **76** 5th Field Ambulance
- **77** 9th Field Ambulance
- **82** 1st Field Dressing Station
- **83** 2nd Field Dressing Station
- **78** 2nd Field Hygiene Section

The unit designation is shown with its Serial Number (coloured vehicle code sign), see pp.140-141.

2nd Canadian Infantry Division

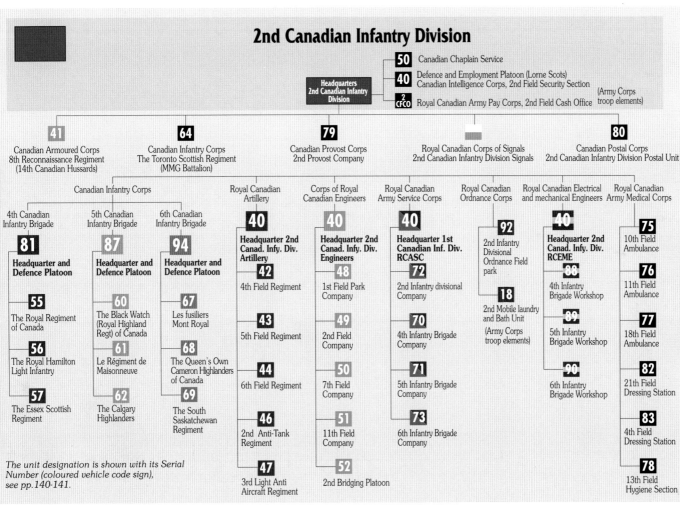

Headquarters 2nd Canadian Infantry Division

- **50** Canadian Chaplain Service
- **40** Defence and Employment Platoon (Lorne Scots)
  Canadian Intelligence Corps, 2nd Field Security Section
- **2 CFCO** Royal Canadian Army Pay Corps, 2nd Field Cash Office *(Army Corps troop elements)*

41 Canadian Armoured Corps
8th Reconnaissance Regiment
(14th Canadian Hussards)

64 Canadian Infantry Corps
The Toronto Scottish Regiment
(MMG Battalion)

79 Canadian Provost Corps
2nd Provost Company

Royal Canadian Corps of Signals
2nd Canadian Infantry Division Signals

80 Canadian Postal Corps
2nd Canadian Infantry Division Postal Unit

Canadian Infantry Corps

4th Canadian Infantry Brigade
- **81** Headquarter and Defence Platoon
- **55** The Royal Regiment of Canada
- **56** The Royal Hamilton Light Infantry
- **57** The Essex Scottish Regiment

5th Canadian Infantry Brigade
- **87** Headquarter and Defence Platoon
- **60** The Black Watch (Royal Highland Regt) of Canada
- **61** Le Régiment de Maisonneuve
- **62** The Calgary Highlanders

6th Canadian Infantry Brigade
- **94** Headquarter and Defence Platoon
- **67** Les fusiliers Mont Royal
- **68** The Queen's Own Cameron Highlanders of Canada
- **69** The South Saskatchewan Regiment

Royal Canadian Artillery
- **40** Headquarter 2nd Canad. Infy. Div. Artillery
- **42** 4th Field Regiment
- **43** 5th Field Regiment
- **44** 6th Field Regiment
- **46** 2nd Anti-Tank Regiment
- **47** 3rd Light Anti Aircraft Regiment

Corps of Royal Canadian Engineers
- **40** Headquarter 2nd Canad. Infy. Div. Engineers
- **48** 1st Field Park Company
- **49** 2nd Field Company
- **50** 7th Field Company
- **51** 11th Field Company
- **52** 2nd Bridging Platoon

Royal Canadian Army Service Corps
- **40** Headquarter 1st Canadian Inf. Div. RCASC
- **72** 2nd Infantry divisional Company
- **70** 4th Infantry Brigade Company
- **71** 5th Infantry Brigade Company
- **73** 6th Infantry Brigade Company

Royal Canadian Ordnance Corps
- **92** 2nd Infantry Divisional Ordnance Field park
- **18** 2nd Mobile laundry and Bath Unit *(Army Corps troop elements)*

Royal Canadian Electrical and mechanical Engineers
- **40** Headquarter 2nd Canad. Infy. Div. RCEME
- **88** 4th Infantry Brigade Workshop
- **89** 5th Infantry Brigade Workshop
- **90** 6th Infantry Brigade Workshop

Royal Canadian Army Medical Corps
- **75** 10th Field Ambulance
- **76** 11th Field Ambulance
- **77** 18th Field Ambulance
- **82** 21th Field Dressing Station
- **83** 4th Field Dressing Station
- **78** 13th Field Hygiene Section

The unit designation is shown with its Serial Number (coloured vehicle code sign), see pp.140-141.

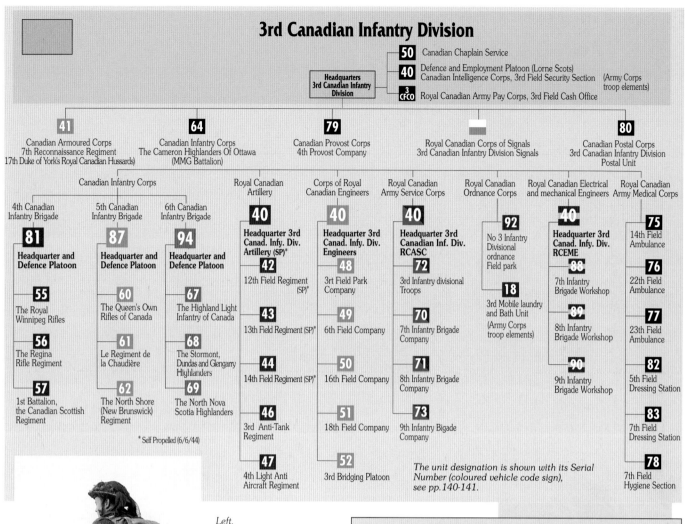

3rd Canadian Infantry Division

Headquarters 3rd Canadian Infantry Division

- **50** Canadian Chaplain Service
- **40** Defence and Employment Platoon (Lorne Scots)
  Canadian Intelligence Corps, 3rd Field Security Section (Army Corps troop elements)
- **3 CFCO** Royal Canadian Army Pay Corps, 3rd Field Cash Office

41 Canadian Armoured Corps
7th Reconnaissance Regiment
17th Duke of York's Royal Canadian Hussards)

64 Canadian Infantry Corps
The Cameron Highlanders Of Ottawa
(MMG Battalion)

79 Canadian Provost Corps
4th Provost Company

Royal Canadian Corps of Signals
3rd Canadian Infantry Division Signals

80 Canadian Postal Corps
3rd Canadian Infantry Division
Postal Unit

Canadian Infantry Corps

4th Canadian Infantry Brigade

81 Headquarter and Defence Platoon

55 The Royal Winnipeg Rifles

56 The Regina Rifle Regiment

57 1st Battalion, the Canadian Scottish Regiment

5th Canadian Infantry Brigade

87 Headquarter and Defence Platoon

60 The Queen's Own Rifles of Canada

61 Le Regiment de la Chaudière

62 The North Shore (New Brunswick) Regiment

6th Canadian Infantry Brigade

94 Headquarter and Defence Platoon

67 The Highland Light Infantry of Canada

68 The Stormont, Dundas and Glengarry Highlanders

69 The North Nova Scotia Highlanders

* Self Propelled (6/6/44)

Royal Canadian Artillery

40 Headquarter 3rd Canad. Infy. Div. Artillery (SP)*

42 12th Field Regiment (SP)*

43 13th Field Regiment (SP)*

44 14th Field Regiment (SP)*

46 3rd Anti-Tank Regiment

47 4th Light Anti Aircraft Regiment

Corps of Royal Canadian Engineers

40 Headquarter 3rd Canad. Infy. Div. Engineers

48 3rt Field Park Company

49 6th Field Company

50 16th Field Company

51 18th Field Company

52 3rd Bridging Platoon

Royal Canadian Army Service Corps

40 Headquarter 3rd Canadian Inf. Div. RCASC

72 3rd Infantry divisional Troops

70 7th Infantry Brigade Company

71 8th Infantry Brigade Company

73 9th Infantry Bigade Company

Royal Canadian Ordnance Corps

92 No 3 Infantry Divisional ordnance Field park

18 3rd Mobile laundry and Bath Unit (Army Corps troop elements)

Royal Canadian Electrical and mechanical Engineers

40 Headquarter 3rd Canad. Infy. Div. RCEME

88 7th Infantry Brigade Workshop

89 8th Infantry Brigade Workshop

90 9th Infantry Brigade Workshop

Royal Canadian Army Medical Corps

75 14th Field Ambulance

76 22th Field Ambulance

77 23th Field Ambulance

82 5th Field Dressing Station

83 7th Field Dressing Station

78 7th Field Hygiene Section

The unit designation is shown with its Serial Number (coloured vehicle code sign), see pp. 140-141.

Left.
Caen July 1944. A Lance-Corporal of the 3rd Infantry Division in combat gear. The entrenching tool has been replaced by a bigger General Service shovel. In its place is a mess tin in a waterbottle holder. It contains a cold meal.
(*PAC 463403*)

Below.
Holland April 1944. An infantry section from the Perth Regiment, 11th Infantry Brigade, 5th Canadian Armoured Division.
(*PAC 145884*)

3rd Infantry Division

Date of activation: from 5 September 1940 in Canada, transferred to Great Britain in July 1941.

General Officer Commanding: Major-General R.F.L. Keller, CBE, from 8 September 1942 to 8 August 1944, wounded following an 8th Air Force air raid, evacuated ; Major-General D.C. Spry, DSO, from 18 August 1944 to 22 March 1945 ; Major-General R.H. Keefler, CBE, DSO, ED from 25 March to 19 November 1945.

Brigadiers in 1945:
7th Infantry Brigade: Brigadier H.W. Foster from 28 January 1944 to 28 August 1944 ; Brigadier J.G. Spragge from 26 August 1944 to 20 February 1945 ; Brigadier T.G. Gibson from 24 April 19454 to 3 June 1945.
8th Infantry Brigade: Brigadier K.G. Blackadder from 20 January 1942 to 28 September 1944 ; Brigadier J.A. Roberts from 30 October 1944 to 14 August 1945.
9th Infantry Brigade: Brigadier D.G. Cunningham from 25 November 1943 to 7 August 1944 ; Brigadier J.M. Rockingham from 8 August 1944 to 4 June 1945.
Divisional Artillery: Brigadier P.A.S. Todd from 27 December 1943 to 9 November 1944. Brigadier E.R. Suttie from 10 November 1944 to 3 April 1945. Brigadier L.G. Clarke from 4 April to 20 November 1945.

Campaigns and Battles: 6 June 1944, Normandy, then Caen, Carpiquet, Bourguébus Ridge, Falaise, le Laison, Boulogne-sur-Mer, Scheldt, Rhineland, Hochwald, the Rhine, Occupation of Germany (Canadian Army Occupation Force -CAOF) up to 15 May 1946.
The Division was disbanded on 20 June 1946 in Germany.

ARMAMENT AND TRANSPORT

ARMAMENT			
- Pistols, revolvers	1011	- 6-Pounder antitank gun	78
- Rifles	11254	- 17-Pounder antitank gun	32
- Sten Machine Carbine	6525	**VEHICLES and MACHINES**	
- Bren LMG	1262	- Motor-bikes	983
- Vickers Heavy Machine Guns	40	- Miscellaneous light vehicles	495
- 2-in. Mortars	283	- Armoured cars	31
- 3-in. Mortars	60	- Scout cars	32
- 4.2-in. Mortars	16	- Bren carriers Half-Tracks,	595
- PIATs	436	Truck, 15-cwt, Arm. carrier 4x4	
- 20-mm AA gun	71	- Ambulances	52
- 40-mm AA gun	36	- 15-cwt trucks	881
- 40-mm self-propelled AA gun	18	- 3-ton trucks	1056
- 25-Pounder gun howitzer	72	- various tractors	205
		- Trailers	226

14

3. The Armoured Division

ARMAMENT and TRANSPORT

ARMAMENT

- Pistols, revolvers	2 324
- Rifles	6 689
- Sten Machine carbine	6 204
- Bren LMG	1 376
- Vickers MG	22
- 2 in. Mortars	132
- 3 in. Mortars	24
- 4.2 in. Mortars	4
- PIATs	302
- 20-mm AA gun	87
- 40-mm AA gun *(towed)*	36
- 40-mm AA gun *(self-propelled)*	18
- 25-Pounder Gun howitzer *(towed)*	24
- 25-Pounder Gun howitzer *(self-propelled)*	24
- 6-Pounder antitank gun *(towed)*	30
- 17-Pounder antitank gun *(towed)*	24
- 17-Pounder antitank gun *(self-propelled)* **US M-10**	24

VEHICLES and MACHINES

- Motor-bikes	853
- Miscellaneous light cars, Jeeps	390
- Scout-Cars	87
- Bren carriers, Half-Tracks	261
- Ambulances	36
- 15-cwt trucks	789
- 3-Ton. trucks	1 309
- Various tractors	130
- Various trailers	219
- Armoured Command vehicles	19
- Recovery vehicles	14
- Ambulances	36

TANKS

- Medium tanks [1]	246
- Anti-Aircraft tanks	27
- Stuart Light tanks	63
- Forward observation tanks	27
- Bridging tanks	3

1. Sherman tanks only .

4th Armoured Division

Date of Constitution: March 1942 in Canada by converting the 4th Infantry Division, transferred to Great Britain in October 1942.

General Officer Commanding: Major-General G. Kitching, DSO, relieved on 21 August 1944; Major-General H.W. Foster from 22 August 1944 to 30 November 1944 ; Major-General C. Vokes, CBE, DSO from 1st December 1944 to 5 June 1945.

Brigadiers in 1945:
4th Armoured Brigade: Brigadier E.L. Booth, 23 August 1944, killed 14 August 1944 ; Brigadier R.W. Moncel from 19 August 1944 to 9 July 1945.
10th Armoured Brigade: Brigadier J.C. Jefferson from 27 April to 5 May 1945.
Divisional Artillery: Brigadier J.N. Lane from 1 April 1944 to 9 November 1944 Brigadier C.M. Drury from 10 November 1944 to 26 June 1945.

Campaigns and Battles: landed in Normandy on 31 July 1944 and committed for the first time on 8 August during Operation Totalize to the north of Falaise, Chambois, the Seine, the Somme, the Scheldt, Rhineland, Hochwald, the North Sea. The Division was disbanded in December 1945 in Canada.

THE ARMOURED DIVISION STRENGTH

	Officers	ORs
Headquarters		
— *Armoured Division HQ* Administrative unit	52	251
Armoured Corps		
— *Armoured Reconnaissance Regiment*	38	647
— *Headquarters Armoured Brigade*	23	99
— *3 Armoured Regiments*	38	647 *(x 3)*
Artillery		
— *Headquarters, RCA*	13	38
— *Field Regiment*	38	632
— *Field Regiment (Self-propelled)*	39	610
— *1 Anti-Tank Regiment*		
● *Headquarters*	7	54
● *2 anti-tank batteries*	7	169 *(x 2)*
● *2 anti-tank batteries*	7	173 *(x 2)*
— *1 Light anti-aircraft Regiment*		
● *Headquarters*	7	41
● *3 Light anti-aircraft batteries*	9	170 *(x 3)*
— *1 CMO staff (B)*	4	31
Engineers		
— *1 Field Park Squadron*	4	112
— *1 Bridge Troop*	1	40
— *2 Field Squadrons*	7	249 *(x 2)*
Signals		
— *Armoured Divisional Signals*	26	697
Infantry		
— *Headquarters Infantry Brigade*	18	52
— *Independent Defence Platoon*		27
— *3 Infantry Battalions*	38	816 *(x 3)*
— *1 Motor Battalion (lorried infantry)*	36	815
Supply and Transport		
HQ RCASC	10	35
— *1 Armoured Brigade Company (5 Transport Platoons)*	11	369
— *1 Infantry Brigade Company (3 Transport Platoons)*	13	450
— *1 Armd Divisional Troops Coy (3 Transport Platoons)*	10	359
Medical		
— *1 Light Field Ambulance*	9	180
— *1 Field Ambulance*	12	230
— *1 Field Dressing Station*	6	89
— *Field Hygiene section*	2	27
Ordnance *Armd Div. Ordnance Field Park*	2	66
Electrical and Mechanical Engineers		
— *HQ RCEME*	5	17
— *1 Armoured Brigade workshops*	8	277
— *1 Infantry Brigade workshops*	6	184
— *1 LAA Workshop (A)*	1	28
— *1 Light Aid Detachment (A)*	1	15
— *5 Light Aid Detachments (B)*	1	13 *(x 5)*
— *4 Light Aid Detachments (C)*	1	24 *(x 4)*
— *1 Light Aid Detachment (D)*	1	37
— *1 Light Aid Detachment (D)*	1	42
Postal *Divisional Postal Unit*	1	21
Provost *Provost Company*	3	112
Intelligence *Field Security Section*	1	13
Miscellaneous *Employment Platoon*		34
TOTAL	*742*	*13837*
ARMY CORPS ELEMENTS		
Ordnance		
— *Infantry Ordnance Sub Park*	4	123
— *Mobile Laundry and Bath Unit*	3	63
Canadian Pay Corps *Field Cash Office*	2	5

4th Canadian Armoured Division

Headquarters 4th Canadian Armoured Division

- **50** Canadian Chaplain Service
- **40** Defence and Employment Platoon (Lorne Scots)
  Canadian Intelligence Corps, 4th Field Security Section
  (Army Corps troop elements)
- **4 CFCO** Royal Canadian Army Pay Corps, 4th Field Cash Office

The unit designation is shown with its Serial Number (coloured vehicle code sign), see pp.140-141.

- **465** D. Squadron Elgin Regiment (25th Armoured Delivery Regt) Canadian Armoured Corps
- **45** Canadian Armoured Corps 29th Armoured Reconnaissance Reg. (The South Alberta Regiment)
- **64** Canadian Infantry Corps 10th Independant Machine Gun Company (The New Brunswick Rangers)
- **43** Canadian Provost Corps 8th Provost Company
- Royal Canadian Corps of Signals 4th Armd. Div. Signals
- **44** Canadian Postal Corps 4th Canad. Ard. Div. Postal Section

Canadian Armoured Corps 4th Canadian Armoured Brigade
- **50** Headquarter
- **51** 21st Armoured Regiment (The Governor General's Foot Guards)
- **52** 22nd Armoured Regiment (The Canadian Grenadier Guards)
- **53** 28th Armoured Regiment (The British Columbia Regiment)
- **54** The Lake Superior Regiment (Motor, Infantry Corps)

Canadian Infantry Corps 10th Canadian Infantry Brigade
- **60** Headquarter and Defence Platoon
- **61** The Lincoln and Welland Regiment
- **62** The Algonquin Regiment
- **63** The Argyll and Sutherland Highlanders of Canada

Royal Canadian Artillery
- **40** Headquarter 4th Canadian Ard. Div. Artillery
- **74** 15th Field Regiment
- **76** 23rd Field Regiment (Self Propelled)
- **77** 5th Anti-Tank Regiment
- **73** 8th Light-Anti Aircraft Regiment

Corps of Royal Canadian Engineers
- **42** 6th Field Park Squadron
- **41** 8th Field Squadron
- **46** 9th Field Squadron
- **52** 4th Ard Div. Bridging Troop

Royal Canadian Army Service Corps
- **80** Headquarter 4th Ard. Div. RCASC
- **84** 4th Ard. Div. Troop Company
- **82** 4th Ard. Div. Transport Company
- **81** 4th Ard. Brigade Company
- **83** 10th Infantry Brigade Company

Royal Canadian Ordnance Corps
- **97** 4th Ard. Div. Ordnance Field park Squadron
- **72** 4th Mobile Laundry and Bath Unit
  (Army Corps troop elements)

Royal Canadian Electrical and Mechanical Engineers
- **40** Headquarter 4th Ard. Div. RCEME
- **99** 4th Ard. Brigade Workshop
- **100** 10th Infy. Brigade Workshop

1. Sherman tanks equipped all Armoured Regiments in armoured divisions and Independent Armoured Brigades. The main types were the Sherman III (M4A2) and Sherman V (M4A4). One Sherman Firefly with the 17-pdr gun was allocated per Troop, depending on availability

Royal Canadian Army Medical Corps
- **89** 12th Field Ambulance
- **90** 15th Field Ambulance
- **92** 12th Field Hygiene Section
- **93** 12th Field Dressing Station

5th Canadian Armoured Division (March 1945)

The unit designation is shown with its Serial Number (coloured vehicle code sign), see pp.140-141.

Headquarters 5th Canadian Armoured Division

- **50** Canadian Chaplain Service
- **40** 7th Defence and Employment Platoon (Lorne Scots) Canadian Intelligence Corps, 7th Field Security Section (Army Corps troop elements)
- **61** Royal Canadian Army Pay Corps, 5th Field Cash Office

45 Canadian Armoured Corps 3rd Armoured Reconnaissance Reg. (Governor General's Horse Guards)

64 Canadian Infantry Corps 11th Independent Machine Gun Company (Princess Louise's Fusiliers)

43 Canadian Provost Corps 5th Provost Company

Royal Canadian Corps of Signals 5th Armd. Div. Signals

44 Canadian Postal Corps 5th Canad. Armoured. Div. Postal Section

Canadian Armoured Corps 5th Canadian Armoured Brigade
- **50** Headquarter
- **51** 2nd Armoured Regiment (Lord Strathcona's Horse, Royal Canadians)
- **52** 5th Armoured Regiment (8th Princess Louise's New Brunswick Hussars)
- **53** 9th Armoured Regiment (The British Columbia Dragoons)
- **54** The Westminster Regiment (Motor, Infantry Corps)

Canadian Infantry Corps 11th Canadian Infantry Brigade
- **60** Headquarter and Defence Platoon
- **61** The Perth Regiment
- **62** The Cape Breton Highlanders
- **63** The Irish Regiment of Canada

Royal Canadian Artillery
- **40** Headquarter 5th Ard. Div. Artillery
- **74** 17th Field Regiment
- **76** 8th Field Regiment (Self Propelled)
- **77** 4th Anti-Tank Regiment
- **73** 5th Light-Anti Aircraft Regiment

Corps of Royal Canadian Engineers
- **42** 4th Field Park Squadron
- **41** 1st Field Squadron
- **46** 10th Field Squadron
- **52** 5th Ard Div. Bridging Troop

Royal Canadian Army Service Corps
- **80** Headquarter 5th Ard. Div. RCASC
- **84** 5th Ard. Div. Troop Company
- **82** 5th Ard. Div. Transport Company
- **81** 5th Ard. Brigade Company
- **83** 11th Infantry Brigade Company

Royal Canadian Ordnance Corps
- **97** No 5 Armoured Divisional ordnance Field Park Squadron
- **19** 5th Mobile and Bath Unit (Army Corps troop elements)

Royal Canadian Electrical and Mechanical Engineers
- **40** Headquarter 5th Ard. Div. RCEME
- **99** No 5 Armoured Brigade Workshop
- **100** No 11 Infantry Brigade Workshop

Royal Canadian Army Medical Corps
- **89** 7th Field Ambulance
- **90** 24th Field Ambulance
- **92** 11th Field Hygiene Section
- **93** 13th Field Dressing Station

Left.
A Canadian Sherman Vc Firefly (Hybrid). This machine with a well-protected glacis was photographed during the winter of 1944-45 on the Dutch-German border.
(PAC)

Date of activation: February 1941 in Canada, transferred to Great Britain between October and November 1941.

General Officer Commanding: Major-General B.M. Hoffmeister, CBE, DSO, ED
Brigadiers in 1945:
5th Armoured Brigade: Brigadier H.I. Cumberland from 7 June 1944 to 11 November 1945
11th Infantry Brigade: Brigadier I.S. Johnston from 24 June 1944 to 6 June 1945
Divisional Artillery: Brigadier J.S. Ross from 19 December 1944 to 19 November 1945.

Campaigns and Battles: Italy from November 1943 until the beginning of 1945, Liri Valley, Gothic Line, North-west Europe from March to May 1945: Appeldorn (Holland).

---

4. Independent Armoured Brigades

Originally called Army Tank Brigades they were renamed Armoured Brigades in June 1943.

AFVs AND MOTOR TRANSPORT IN THE INDEPENDENT ARMOURED BRIGADE

MOTOR TRANSPORT		ARMOUR	
- Motorcycles, solo	17	- Stuart Light tank	33
- Misc. light cars, Jeeps	16	- Sherman tanks	186
- Carriers, Universal	4	- AA tanks	8
- Scout-cars	16	- Bridge-laying tanks	3
- Half-Tracks	7		
- 15-cwt lorries	52		
- 3-Ton trucks	55		

2nd Armoured Brigade (Independent)

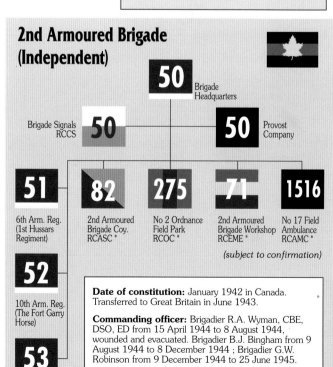

50 Brigade Headquarters

50 Brigade Signals RCCS

50 Provost Company

- **51** 6th Arm. Reg. (1st Hussars Regiment)
- **52** 10th Arm. Reg. (The Fort Garry Horse)
- **53** 27th Arm. Reg. (The Sherbrooke Fusiliers Reg.)
- **82** 2nd Armoured Brigade Coy. RCASC *
- **275** No 2 Ordnance Field Park RCOC *
- **71** 2nd Armoured Brigade Workshop RCEME *
- **1516** No 17 Field Ambulance RCAMC *

(subject to confirmation)

Date of constitution: January 1942 in Canada. Transferred to Great Britain in June 1943.

Commanding officer: Brigadier R.A. Wyman, CBE, DSO, ED from 15 April 1944 to 8 August 1944, wounded and evacuated. Brigadier B.J. Bingham from 9 August 1944 to 8 December 1944 ; Brigadier G.W. Robinson from 9 December 1944 to 25 June 1945.

Campaigns and Battles: landed in Normandy on 6 June 1944, then Caen, Vaucelles, Falaise, Chambois, Calais, Rhineland, Hochwald, Appeldorn (Holland)

1st Armoured Brigade (Independent), 1945

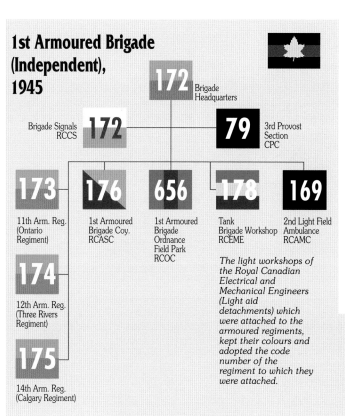

172 Brigade Headquarters

Brigade Signals RCCS **172**

79 3rd Provost Section CPC

173 11th Arm. Reg. (Ontario Regiment)

174 12th Arm. Reg. (Three Rivers Regiment)

175 14th Arm. Reg. (Calgary Regiment)

176 1st Armoured Brigade Coy. RCASC

656 1st Armoured Brigade Ordnance Field Park RCOC

178 Tank Brigade Workshop RCEME

169 2nd Light Field Ambulance RCAMC

The light workshops of the Royal Canadian Electrical and Mechanical Engineers (Light aid detachments) which were attached to the armoured regiments, kept their colours and adopted the code number of the regiment to which they were attached.

STRENGTH OF THE INDEPENDENT ARMOURED BRIGADE

	Officers	OR
Headquarters		
— Armoured Brigade HQ	28	215
Armoured Corps		
— 3 Armoured Regiments	38	647 (x3)
Signals		
— Armoured Brigade Signals	3	148
Supply and Transport		
— Armoured Brigade Company	12	434
(4 Transport Platoons)		
Medical		
— Light Field Ambulance	9	180
Ordnance		
Armoured Brigade Ordnance Field Park	3	90
Electrical and Mechanical Engineers		
— Armoured Brigade Workshop	8	277
— 3 Light Aid Detachments (C)	1	24 (x3)
Provost		
— Provost Company	1	16
TOTAL	**180**	**3 376**

Date of Constitution: February 1941 in Canada, transferred to Great Britain in July 1941.
Commanding Officer: Brigadier W.C. Murphy, DSO, ED, from 27 February 1944 to 25 June 1945.
Campaigns and Battles: Dieppe, 19 August 1942 (Calgary Regiment). Sicily from 13 July to 17 August 1943. Italy from 9 September 1943 to March 1945: Cassino II , Gustav Line, Liri Valley, Hitler Line. North-west Europe from March to May 1945: Apeldoorn (Holland).

The ARMS and SERVICES

1. Canadian Armoured Corps

It became the Royal Canadian Armoured Corps in August 1945.

CANADIAN ARMOURED CORPS REGIMENTS
Numbering adopted in 1943

CAC Regiment	Units
1st Armoured Car Regt	Royal Canadian Dragoons
2nd Armoured Regiment	Lord Strathcona's Horse (RC)
3rd Armoured Recce Regiment	Governor General's Horse Guards
4th Recce Regiment	IV Princess Louise's Dragoon Guards
5th Armoured Regiment	8th Princess Louise's (N.B.) Hussars
6th Armoured Regiment	1st Hussars
7th Recce Regiment	17th D. of Y. Royal Canadian Hussars
8th Recce Regiment	14th Canadian Hussars
9th Armoured Regiment	British Columbia Dragoons
10th Armoured Regiment	Fort Garry Horse
11th Armoured Regiment	Ontario Regiment (Tank)
12th Armoured Regiment	Three Rivers Regiment (Tank)
14th Armoured Regiment	Calgary Regiment (Tank)
15th Armoured Regiment	6th D. of C. Royal Canadian Hussars
16th Armoured Regiment	7/11th Hussars *
17th Armoured Regiment	Prince Edward Island Light Horse
18th Armoured Car Regiment	12th Manitoba Dragoons
19th Armoured Regiment	New Brunswick Regiment (Tank) *
20th Army Tank Bn	16/22nd Saskatchewan Horse *
21st Armoured Regiment	Governor General's Foot Guards
22nd Armoured Regiment	Canadian Grenadier Guards
23rd Army Tank Bn	Halifax Rifles *
24th Recce Regiment	Voltigeurs de Québec *
25th Armoured Delivery Regiment	Elgin Regiment
26th Army Tank Regiment	Grey and Simcoe Foresters *
27th Armoured Regiment	Sherbrooke Fusiliers Regiment
28th Armoured Regiment	British Columbia Regiment
29th Armoured Recce Regiment	South Alberta Regiment
30th Recce Regiment	Essex Regiment (Tank) *
31st Recce Regiment	15th Alberta Light Horse *
32nd Recce Regiment	Royal Montreal Regiment

*See page 7, the list of regiments disbanded in Great Britain and not committed in NW-Europe.

RECONNAISSANCE REGIMENT

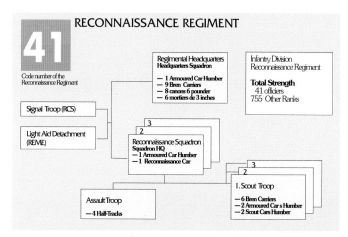

41 Code number of the Reconnaissance Regiment

Signal Troop (RCS)

Light Aid Detachment (REME)

Regimental Headquarters Headquarters Squadron
— 1 Armoured Car Humber
— 9 Bren Carriers
— 8 canons 6 pounder
— 6 mortiers de 3 inches

Infantry Division Reconnaissance Regiment
Total Strength
41 officers
755 Other Ranks

Reconnaissance Squadron Squadron HQ
— 1 Armoured Car Humber
— 1 Reconnaissance Car

1. Scout Troop
— 6 Bren Carriers
— 2 Armoured Car s Humber
— 2 Scout Cars Humber

Assault Troop
— 4 Half-Tracks

The reconnaissance regiments of Infantry Divisions and Army Corps were all armoured cavalry, and thus came under the Canadian Armoured Corps.

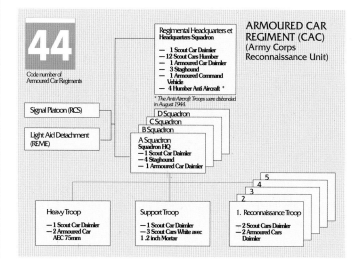

44 Code number of Armoured Car Regiments

Signal Platoon (RCS)

Light Aid Detachment (REME)

Regimental Headquarters et Headquarters Squadron
— 1 Scout Car Daimler
— 12 Scout Cars Humber
— 1 Armoured Car Daimler
— 3 Staghound
— 1 Armoured Command Vehicle
— 4 Humber Anti Aircraft *
* The Anti-Aircraft Troops were disbanded in August 1944.

ARMOURED CAR REGIMENT (CAC)
(Army Corps Reconnaissance Unit)

D Squadron
C Squadron
B Squadron
A Squadron Squadron HQ
— 1 Scout Car Daimler
— 4 Staghound
— 1 Armoured Car Daimler

Heavy Troop
— 1 Scout Car Daimler
— 2 Armoured Car ABC 75mm

Support Troop
— 1 Scout Car Daimler
— 3 Scout Cars White avec 1 .2 inch Mortar

1. Reconnaissance Troop
— 2 Scout Cars Daimler
— 2 Armoured Cars Daimler

THE ARMOURED REGIMENT, 1944-1945
Example of The 22nd Armoured Regiment (Canadian Grenadier Guards), The second regiment in the 4th Armoured Brigade, 4th Armoured Division

Formation sign
of the 4th Canadian
Armoured Division

Table realised thanks to the kind help of Messrs Christopher Johnson and Donald Graves, the authors of 'The South Albertas: a Canadian Regiment at War'.

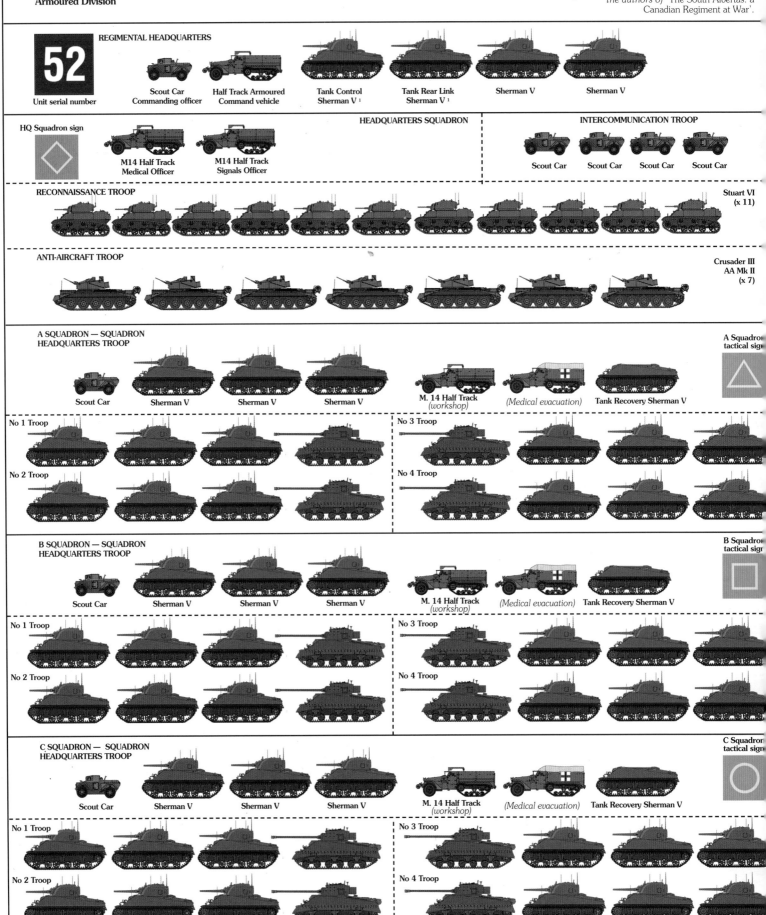

REGIMENTAL HEADQUARTERS

52 Unit serial number

Scout Car Commanding officer — Half Track Armoured Command vehicle — Tank Control Sherman V [1] — Tank Rear Link Sherman V [1] — Sherman V — Sherman V

HQ Squadron sign

HEADQUARTERS SQUADRON

M14 Half Track Medical Officer — M14 Half Track Signals Officer

INTERCOMMUNICATION TROOP

Scout Car — Scout Car — Scout Car — Scout Car

RECONNAISSANCE TROOP

Stuart VI (x 11)

ANTI-AIRCRAFT TROOP

Crusader III AA Mk II (x 7)

A SQUADRON — SQUADRON HEADQUARTERS TROOP

Scout Car — Sherman V — Sherman V — Sherman V — M. 14 Half Track *(workshop)* — *(Medical evacuation)* — Tank Recovery Sherman V

A Squadron tactical sign

No 1 Troop
No 2 Troop
No 3 Troop
No 4 Troop

B SQUADRON — SQUADRON HEADQUARTERS TROOP

Scout Car — Sherman V — Sherman V — Sherman V — M. 14 Half Track *(workshop)* — *(Medical evacuation)* — Tank Recovery Sherman V

B Squadron tactical sign

No 1 Troop
No 2 Troop
No 3 Troop
No 4 Troop

C SQUADRON — SQUADRON HEADQUARTERS TROOP

Scout Car — Sherman V — Sherman V — Sherman V — M. 14 Half Track *(workshop)* — *(Medical evacuation)* — Tank Recovery Sherman V

C Squadron tactical sign

No 1 Troop
No 2 Troop
No 3 Troop
No 4 Troop

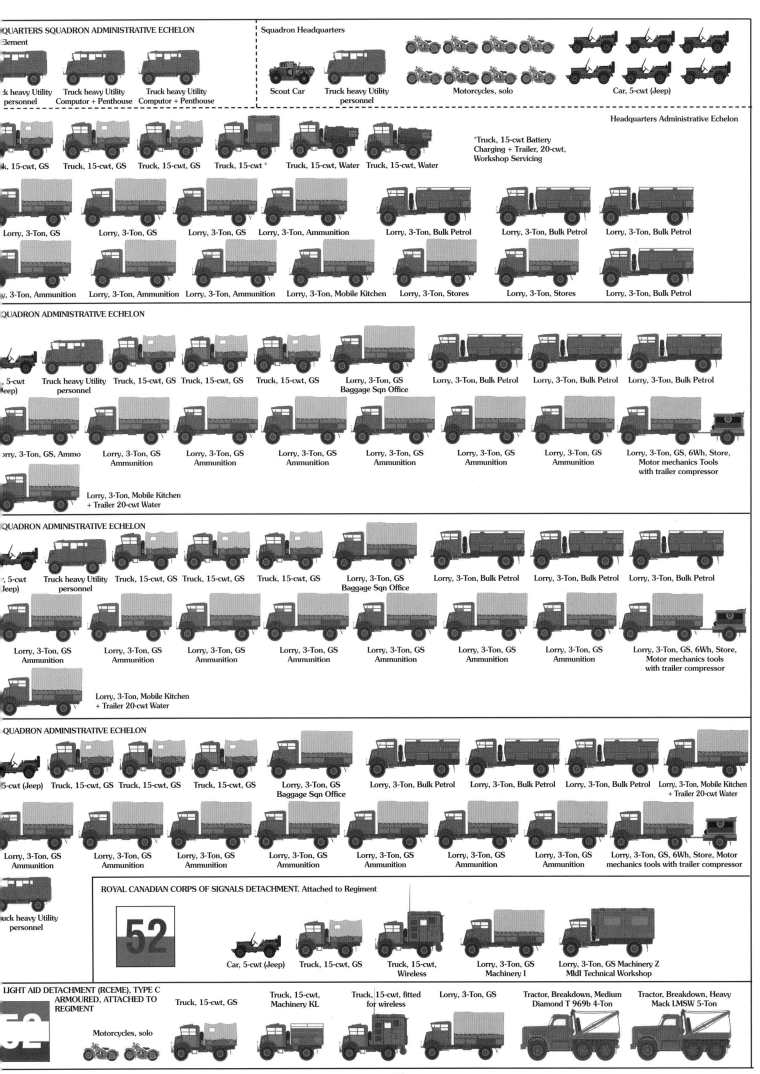

QUARTERS SQUADRON ADMINISTRATIVE ECHELON
Element

Squadron Headquarters

| k heavy Utility | Truck heavy Utility | Truck heavy Utility |
| personnel | Computor + Penthouse | Computor + Penthouse |

Scout Car | Truck heavy Utility personnel | Motorcycles, solo | Car, 5-cwt (Jeep)

Headquarters Administrative Echelon

k, 15-cwt, GS | Truck, 15-cwt, GS | Truck, 15-cwt, GS | Truck, 15-cwt * | Truck, 15-cwt, Water | Truck, 15-cwt, Water

*Truck, 15-cwt Battery Charging + Trailer, 20-cwt, Workshop Servicing

Lorry, 3-Ton, GS | Lorry, 3-Ton, GS | Lorry, 3-Ton, GS | Lorry, 3-Ton, Ammunition | Lorry, 3-Ton, Bulk Petrol | Lorry, 3-Ton, Bulk Petrol | Lorry, 3-Ton, Bulk Petrol

, 3-Ton, Ammunition | Lorry, 3-Ton, Ammunition | Lorry, 3-Ton, Ammunition | Lorry, 3-Ton, Mobile Kitchen | Lorry, 3-Ton, Stores | Lorry, 3-Ton, Stores | Lorry, 3-Ton, Bulk Petrol

QUADRON ADMINISTRATIVE ECHELON

, 5-cwt (eep) | Truck heavy Utility personnel | Truck, 15-cwt, GS | Truck, 15-cwt, GS | Truck, 15-cwt, GS | Lorry, 3-Ton, GS Baggage Sqn Office | Lorry, 3-Ton, Bulk Petrol | Lorry, 3-Ton, Bulk Petrol | Lorry, 3-Ton, Bulk Petrol

rry, 3-Ton, GS, Ammo | Lorry, 3-Ton, GS Ammunition | Lorry, 3-Ton, GS Ammunition | Lorry, 3-Ton, GS Ammunition | Lorry, 3-Ton, GS Ammunition | Lorry, 3-Ton, GS Ammunition | Lorry, 3-Ton, GS Ammunition | Lorry, 3-Ton, GS, 6Wh, Store, Motor mechanics Tools with trailer compressor

Lorry, 3-Ton, Mobile Kitchen + Trailer 20-cwt Water

QUADRON ADMINISTRATIVE ECHELON

, 5-cwt (eep) | Truck heavy Utility personnel | Truck, 15-cwt, GS | Truck, 15-cwt, GS | Truck, 15-cwt, GS | Lorry, 3-Ton, GS Baggage Sqn Office | Lorry, 3-Ton, Bulk Petrol | Lorry, 3-Ton, Bulk Petrol | Lorry, 3-Ton, Bulk Petrol

Lorry, 3-Ton, GS Ammunition | Lorry, 3-Ton, GS Ammunition | Lorry, 3-Ton, GS Ammunition | Lorry, 3-Ton, GS Ammunition | Lorry, 3-Ton, GS Ammunition | Lorry, 3-Ton, GS Ammunition | Lorry, 3-Ton, GS Ammunition | Lorry, 3-Ton, GS, 6Wh, Store, Motor mechanics tools with trailer compressor

Lorry, 3-Ton, Mobile Kitchen + Trailer 20-cwt Water

QUADRON ADMINISTRATIVE ECHELON

5-cwt (Jeep) | Truck, 15-cwt, GS | Truck, 15-cwt, GS | Truck, 15-cwt, GS | Lorry, 3-Ton, GS Baggage Sqn Office | Lorry, 3-Ton, Bulk Petrol | Lorry, 3-Ton, Bulk Petrol | Lorry, 3-Ton, Bulk Petrol | Lorry, 3-Ton, Mobile Kitchen + Trailer 20-cwt Water

Lorry, 3-Ton, GS Ammunition | Lorry, 3-Ton, GS Ammunition | Lorry, 3-Ton, GS Ammunition | Lorry, 3-Ton, GS Ammunition | Lorry, 3-Ton, GS Ammunition | Lorry, 3-Ton, GS Ammunition | Lorry, 3-Ton, GS, 6Wh, Store, Motor mechanics tools with trailer compressor

uck heavy Utility personnel

ROYAL CANADIAN CORPS OF SIGNALS DETACHMENT. Attached to Regiment

52

Car, 5-cwt (Jeep) | Truck, 15-cwt, GS | Truck, 15-cwt, Wireless | Lorry, 3-Ton, GS Machinery I | Lorry, 3-Ton, GS Machinery Z MkII Technical Workshop

LIGHT AID DETACHMENT (RCEME), TYPE C ARMOURED, ATTACHED TO REGIMENT

Truck, 15-cwt, GS | Truck, 15-cwt, Machinery KL | Truck, 15-cwt, fitted for wireless | Lorry, 3-Ton, GS | Tractor, Breakdown, Medium Diamond T 969b 4-Ton | Tractor, Breakdown, Heavy Mack LMSW 5-Ton

Motorcycles, solo

19

▣ Royal Canadian Artillery

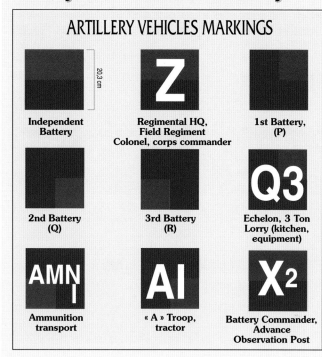

ARTILLERY VEHICLES MARKINGS

Independent Battery	**Z** **Regimental HQ, Field Regiment** **Colonel, corps commander**	**1st Battery, (P)**
2nd Battery (Q)	**3rd Battery (R)**	**Q3** **Echelon, 3 Ton Lorry (kitchen, equipment)**
AMN I **Ammunition transport**	**AI** **« A » Troop, tractor**	**X²** **Battery Commander, Advance Observation Post**

(marking: 20,3 cm height)

▤ Royal Canadian Engineers

The Engineers provided assault troops and carried out various tasks on the battlefield and the rear.

At divisional level the Field Companies (Squadrons in the Armoured Divisions) operated with a strength of 7 officers and 250 NCOs and other ranks (Combat engineers companies).

The Field Park Company included a workshop, store, various earthmoving vehicles including bulldozers and specialised equipment.

The Bridging Platoon had equipment for building Bailey bridges with a span of 25 metres and weight loading of 40 tonnes at their disposal. The larger bridging operations were carried out by the engineer companies at army corps or army level.

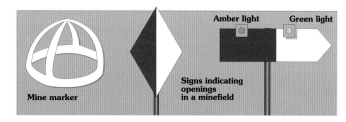

Mine marker — Signs indicating openings in a minefield — Amber light — Green light

22 June 1944 in Normandy. Sapper C.W. Stevens of the 18th Field Company Royal Canadian Engineers in the process of defusing a Teller mine. Using a mirror was vital for seeing whether the mine itself was not booby-trapped. *(PAC)*

ROYAL CANADIAN ARTILLERY - Regiments in divisions

RCHA — shoulder slip-on

HQ RCA 1st Canadian Infantry Division
1st Field Regiment R.C.H.A.
— « A » Battery R.C.H.A.
— « B » Battery R.C.H.A.   24 x 25-pdr. (towed)
— « C » Battery R.C.H.A.

2 RCA

2nd Field Regiment
— 7th Field Battery
— 8th Field Battery   24 x 25-pdr. (towed)
— 10th Field Battery

3 RCA

3rd Field Regiment
— 19th Field Battery
— 77th Field Battery   24 x 25-pdr. (towed)
— 92nd Field Battery

1 A/TRCA

1st Anti-Tank Regiment
— 27th Anti-Tank Battery   18 x 17-pdr (SP)
— 51st Anti-Tank Battery   18 x 17-pdr (towed)
— 57th Anti-Tank Battery
— 90th Anti-Tank Battery

2 L AARCA

2nd Light Anti-Aircraft (L.A.A.) Regiment
— 2nd L.A.A. Battery   12 x 40 mm Bofors (SP)
— 5th L.A.A. Battery   12 x 40 mm Bofors (towed)
— 54th L.A.A. Battery   12 x 20 mm Polsten (AA quad)

SP = Self-propelled. AA = Anti-Aircraft. R.C.H.A.: Royal Canadian Horse Artillery.

HQ RCA 2nd Canadian Infantry Division
4th Field Regiment R.C.H.A.
— 2nd Field Battery
— 14th Field Battery   24 x 25-pdr. (towed)
— 26th Field Battery   **4 RCA**

5th Field Regiment
— 5th Field Battery
— 28th Field Battery   24 x 25-pdr. (towed)
— 73rd Field Battery   **5 RCA**

6th Field Regiment
— 13th Field Battery
— 21st Field Battery   24 x 25-pdr. (towed)
— 91st Field Battery   **6 RCA**

2nd Anti-Tank Regiment
— 18th Anti-Tank Battery   18 x 17-pdr (SP)
— 20th Anti-Tank Battery   18 x 17-pdr (towed)
— 23rd Anti-Tank Battery
— 108th Anti-Tank Battery   **2 A/TRCA**

3rd Light Anti-Aircraft Regiment
— 16th L.A.A. Battery   12 x 40 mm Bofors (SP)
— 17th L.A.A. Battery   12 x 40 mm Bofors (towed)
— 38th L.A.A. Battery   12 x 20 mm Polsten (AA quad)   **3 LAARCA**

12 RCA

HQ RCA 3rd Canadian Infantry Division
12th Field Regiment
— 11th Field Battery
— 16th Field Battery   24 x 25-pdr. (towed)*
— 43rd Field Battery

13 RCA

13th Field Regiment
— 22nd Field Battery
— 44th Field Battery   24 x 25-pdr. (towed)*
— 78th Field Battery

14 RCA

14th Field Regiment
— 34th Field Battery
— 66th Field Battery   24 x 25-pdr. (towed)*
— 81st Field Battery

3 A/TRCA

3rd Anti-Tank Regiment
— 4th Anti-Tank Battery   18 x 17-pdr. (SP)
— 52nd Anti-Tank Battery   18 x 17-pdr. (towed)
— 94th Anti-Tank Battery
— 105th Anti-Tank Battery

4 LAARCA

4th Light Anti-Aircraft Regiment
— 32nd L.A.A. Battery   12 x 40 mm Bofors (SP)
— 69th L.A.A. Battery   12 x 40 mm Bofors (towed)
— 100th L.A.A. Battery   12 x 20 mm Polsten (AA quad)

* On 6 June 1944, these units were equipped American M-7 Self-Propelled 105-mm Howitzers, which were later replaced by Sextons.

ROYAL CANADIAN ARTILLERY, Divisional units

HQ RCA 4th Canadian Armoured Division

 `15 RCA`
15th Field Regiment
— 17th Field Battery — 24 x 25-pdr. (towed)
— 195th Field Battery — 10 x 75 mm AFV (OP)
— 110th Field Battery

`23 RCA`
23rd Field Regiment (SP)
— 31st Field Battery
— 36th Field Battery — 24 x 25-pdr. (towed)
— 83rd Field Battery — 6 x 75 mm AFV (OP)

`5 A/TRCA`
5th Anti-Tank Regiment
— 3rd Anti-Tank Battery — 24 x 17-pdr (SP)
— 14th Anti-Tank Battery — 24 x 17-pdr (towed)
— 65th Anti-Tank Battery
— 96th Anti-Tank Battery

`18 LAARCA`
8th Light Anti-Aircraft Regiment
— 70th L.A.A. Battery
— 101st L.A.A. Battery — 24 x 40 mm Bofors (SP)
— 102nd L.A.A. Battery — 12 x 20 mm Polsten (AA quad)

HQ RCA 5th Canadian Armoured Division

`8 RCA`
8th Field Regiment (SP)
— 61st Field Battery — 24 x 25-pdr. (towed)
— 71st Field Battery — 6 x 75 mm AFV (OP)
— 107th Field Battery

`17 RCA`
17th Field Regiment (SP)
— 37th Field Battery
— 60th Field Battery — 24 x 25-pdr. (towed)
— 76th Field Battery — 10 x 75 mm AFV (OP)

`4 A/TRCA`
4th Anti-Tank Regiment
— 16th Anti-Tank Battery — 24 x 17-pdr (SP)
— 49th Anti-Tank Battery — 24 x 17-pdr (towed)
— 82nd Anti-Tank Battery
— 98th Anti-Tank Battery

`5 LAARCA`
5th Light Anti-Aircraft Regiment
— 41st L.A.A. Battery
— 47th L.A.A. Battery — 24 x 40 mm Bofors (SP)
— 88th L.A.A. Battery — 12 x 20 mm Polsten (AA quad)

ROYAL CANADIAN ARTILLERY, FIRST CANADIAN ARMY. Order of Battle, 8th May 1945

Non-divisional units

Unit serial numbers — Vehicles and Machines
1st Can. Army Artillery, shoulder insignia.
1st Can. Army Formation sign — *Vehicles and Machines*

173 — HQ 1st Canadian Army Group RA

`1 MED.RCA` **174**
1st Medium Regiment
2nd Medium Battery
3rd Medium Battery — 16 x 5.5-in. guns

`2 MED.RCA` **175**
2nd Medium Regiment
18th Medium Battery
25th Medium Battery — 16 x 4.5-in. guns

`5 MED.RCA` **176**
5th Medium Regiment
7th Medium Battery
23th Medium Battery — 16 x 4.5-in. guns

`11 RCA` **173**
11th Army Field Regiment
9th Field Battery
29th Field Battery
40th Field Battery — 24 x 105 mm (SP)

25
665 Air OP Squadron
666 Air OP Squadron
(Royal Canadian Air Force) — Auster AOP light aircraft x 2

181 — HQ 2nd Canadian Army Group RA

`3 MED.RCA` **182**
3rd Medium Regiment — 16 x 4.5-in. guns
5th Medium Battery
87th Medium Battery

`4 MED.RCA` **183**
4th Medium Regiment — 16 x 5.5-in. guns
50th Medium Battery
58th Medium Battery

`7 MED.RCA` **184**
7th Medium Regiment — 16 x 5.5-in. guns
12th Medium Battery
45th Medium Battery

`19 RCA` **45**
19th Army Field Regt. — 24 x 105 mm (SP) [1]
55th Field Battery
63rd Field Battery
99th Field Battery

`2 HAARCA` **260**
2nd H.A.A. Regiment [2] — 24 x 3.7-in A.A.
1st H.A.A. Battery
8th H.A.A. Battery
11th H.A.A. Battery

14
1st Can. Rocket Battery. — 36 Land Masters rocket launchers (see p. 138)
Created on 26.10.44 originally from assets of 112th Battery of the 6th L.A.A Regt.

? — 1st Radar Battery

1. Took part in the landings on 6 June 1944 in support of 3rd Infantry Division.
2. Heavy anti-aircraft guns.

1st Canadian Corps Artillery shoulder insignia
1st Can. Corps Formation sign — *Vehicles and Machines*

HQ RCA 1st Canadian Corps

 `1 SVYRCA` **10**
1st Survey Regiment
1st Survey Battery
2nd Survey Battery

 `7A/TRCA` **2**
7th Anti-tank Regiment — 24 x 17-pdr (SP)
15th A.T. Battery — 24 x 17-pdr (Towed)
104th A.T. Battery
111th A.T. Battery
113th A.T. Battery

 `1 LAARCA` **14**
1st Can. L.A.A. Regt. [1]
35th L.A.A. Battery — 12 x 40 mm Bofors (SP)
89th L.A.A. Battery — 12 x 40 mm Bofors (Towed)
109th L.A.A. Battery — 12 x 20 mm Polsten (on AA Quad)

1. Lanark and Renfrew Scottish Regiment.

2nd Can. Corps Formation sign — *Vehicles and Machines*

HQ RCA 2nd Canadian Corps

 `2 SVYRCA` **10**
2nd Survey Regiment
5th Survey Battery
6th Survey Battery

 `6A/TRCA` **2**
6th Anti-tank Regiment — 24 x 17-pdr (SP)
33rd A.T. Battery — 24 x 17-pdr (Towed)
56th A.T. Battery
74th A.T. Battery
103th A.T. Battery

 `6 LAARCA` **14**
6th Can. L.A.A. Reg.
1st L.A.A. Battery — 12 x 40 mm Bofors (SP)
30th L.A.A. Battery — 12 x 40 mm Bofors (towed)
112th L.A.A. Battery — 12 x 20 mm Polsten (AA quad)

Converted to 1st Canadian Rocket Battery.

4-Ton Diamond T 6x6, Lorry,

Bridge Classification: *12*
A lorry equipped for transporting RCE folding boats. The vehicle was operated and

driven by personnel from the Royal Canadian Army Service Corps.
(PAC Photograph)

Below. **Armoured D7 Caterpillar bulldozer fitted with a Hyster D7 N winch. This equipment was operated by the Royal Canadian Engineers' Field Companies.** *(PAC)*

Bottom, left. **The railways were put back into operation by the Royal Canadian Engineers' Railway Operating Companies. The locomotives were driven by RCASC personnel. This train is full of soldiers about to go on leave in Britain.** *(PAC)*

Above, right.
Normandy 28 August 1944. A Sherman Firefly starting off across a boat bridge built by the Royal Canadian Engineers across the Seine. *(PAC)*

Right.
Normandy, Caen, 29 July 1944. 'Reynolds Bridge' was a Bailey bridge put across the Orne by the 23rd Field Company, RCE.
(PAC 116511)

Mk III "Polish" Mine Detector

How it worked
Held about 4 inches from the ground, the ring created a magnetic field which, when it met a metal object, set off an impulse through the amplifier. This was translated into a sound signal in the operator's headphones. The safety range was about 18 inches for a Teller mine, about 10 inches for an 'S' Mine, about 4 inches for a ZZ - 42

detonator. It equipped RCE Field Companies and the Pioneer Platoon in Infantry Battalions

Below.
Normandy, 18 July 1944, south of Caen. Mine-lifting with the 'Polish' Mk III metal detector.
(PA 131385)

Engineering Equipment

Ostend, Belgium, October 1944. Building a pipeline to supply front line units with petrol. *(PA 130263)*

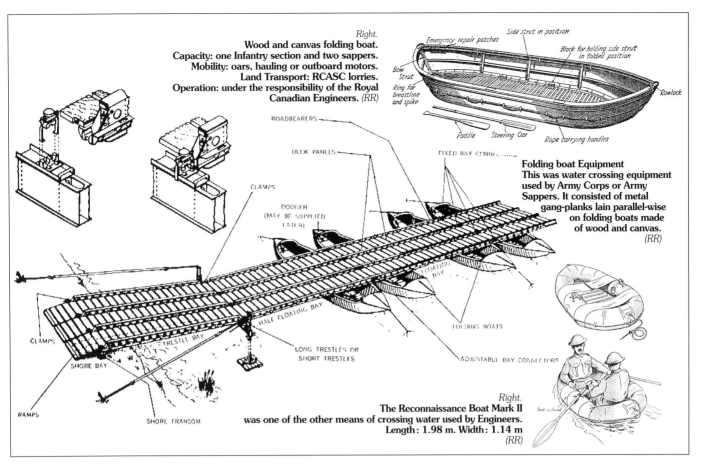

Right.
Wood and canvas folding boat.
Capacity: one Infantry section and two sappers.
Mobility: oars, hauling or outboard motors.
Land Transport: RCASC lorries.
Operation: under the responsibility of the Royal Canadian Engineers. *(RR)*

Emergency repair patches — *Side strut in position*
Block for holding side strut in folded position
Bow Strut
Ring for breastline and spike
Rowlock
Paddle *Steering Oar* *Rope carrying handles*

ROADBEARERS

DECK PANELS

CLAMPS

DODGER (MAY BE SUPPLIED LATER)

FIXED BAY CONNECTORS

Folding boat Equipment
This was water crossing equipment used by Army Corps or Army Sappers. It consisted of metal gang-planks lain parallel-wise on folding boats made of wood and canvas.
(RR)

HALF FLOATING BAY

TRESTLE BAY

LONG TRESTLES OR SHORT TRESTLES

FLOATING BAY

FOLDING BOATS

CLAMPS

SHORE BAY

ADJUSTABLE BAY CONNECTORS

RAMPS

SHORE TRANSOM

Right.
The Reconnaissance Boat Mark II
was one of the other means of crossing water used by Engineers.
Length: 1.98 m. Width: 1.14 m
(RR)

4. Royal Canadian Corps of Signals

Signals units were present at every command level. They used all means of communication: radio, telephone, teletype and runners.

RCCS Vehicles

The vehicles used mainly by the RCCS were the 'Truck, Heavy Utility, Wireless, 15-cwt Chevrolet'; the 'Truck, 15-cwt., Wireless Chevrolet'; the 'Lorry, 3-ton, Cipher Office Chevrolet' and the 'Lorry 3-ton, Command High Power, Chevrolet'

3 ton Chevrolet 4x4, Command high power Lorry

Bridge classification: 8
Length: 16 ft 6 ins.
Width: 7 ft.
Height: 9 ft 8 ins.
Engine: 6 cylinder, 85 hp General Motors petrol.

Transmission: 4 forward gears, one reverse.
Use: High powered radio transmission for liaison between Army Corps and Armies.

Documentation J. Garnier

DIVISIONAL SIGNALS, INFANTRY DIVISION

REGIMENTAL HEADQUARTERS

40

Commanding officer: Lieutenant-colonel.
Second in command: Major.
Adjutant: Captain.
Paymaster, Quartermaster, clerks.
Security section. Light Aid detachment (RCEME)

Strength: 29 officers
714 Other Ranks
—Section A: Inter-divisional and army corps radio liaison.
— Section B: Telephone operators.
— Section C: Liaison. Reconnaissance Regiment.
— Section D: Liaison motorcyclists
— Sections E/F/G: Artillery Regiment
— Section H: Anti-Tank Rgt.
— Section J: Senior Infantry Brigade
— Section K: Second Infantry Brigade
— Section L: Junior Infantry Brigade

1st Company

A
B
C
D

2nd Company

H
G
F
E

3rd Company

L
K
J

M

Section M Headquarters Engineers

See pages 114-115 for a description of signals equipment

5. Infantry
The Battalions

Commanded by a Lieutenant-Colonel, infantry battalions were self-contained units, providing the basic combat element.

5bis. Canadian Infantry Corps

The Corps was officially created on 2 September 1942 in order to supply instructors (Officers and Other Ranks) for the elementary training schools. The Corps controlled all the active and reserve units in Canada and overseas in co-operation with cadre originating from regiments which had already been formed up and, later from units already committed to the fighting. Volunteers enlisting in the infantry after the corps was created wore its cap badge until they were assigned to a regiment.

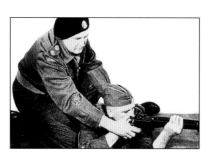

Two musketry instructors demonstrating how to use the No 4 Rifle in a basic training centre.
(RR)

The MEDIUM MACHINE GUN BATTALION (MMG) of the INFANTRY DIVISION

Battalion with support Weapons, mortars and machine guns. Strength: 36 officers, 711 OR.

- Battalion Headquarters
- Light Aid Detachment REME
- Headquarters Company
- Signal Platoon RCS
- Mortar Company — Platoon, Platoon
- Medium Machine Gun Company — Platoon, Platoon
- Medium Machine Gun Company — Platoon
- Medium Machine Gun Company — Platoon, Platoon

4 X 4,2 in. Mortars   4 X .303 Vickers MG

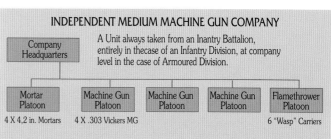

INDEPENDENT MEDIUM MACHINE GUN COMPANY

A Unit always taken from an Inantry Battalion, entirely in thecase of an Infantry Division, at company level in the case of Armoured Division.

- Company Headquarters
- Mortar Platoon — 4 X 4,2 in. Mortars
- Machine Gun Platoon — 4 X .303 Vickers MG
- Machine Gun Platoon
- Machine Gun Platoon
- Flamethrower Platoon — 6 "Wasp" Carriers

Universal Carriers from an Independent Medium Machine Gun Battalion. These machines were fitted with the Vickers .303 machine gun. This unit is the Saskatoon Light Infantry (1st Infantry Division) in Holland in 1945. The Tactical Sign is clearly visible on the front mud guard of the right-hand vehicle.

INFANTRY COMPANY HEADQUARTERS

Officers			
Major (P)	1	.38 Revolver	2
Captain, Second in Command (P)	1	Sten Machine Carbine	1
		No 4 Rifle	13
Warrant Officers/Other ranks		Bren LMG	1
Company Sergeant-Major (CSM) (MC)	1	PIAT	3
Coy. Quartermaster-Sergeant (CQMS) (R)	1	2-inch. Mortar	1
Secretary (R)	1	(signal bombs)	
Corporal (driver, car mechanic) (R)	1		
Corporal (Mess) (R)	1	Bicycles	3
Privates (Supply) (R)	1	Jeep	1
Liaison staff (R)	3	15-cwt Truck GS	3
Cook, Butcher (R)	1	Universal Carrier	1
Orderlies, batmen (R)	4	Radio Sets No 18	
Total	**16**	and No 38	

P = Pistol; MC = Sten Machine Carbine; R = Rifle

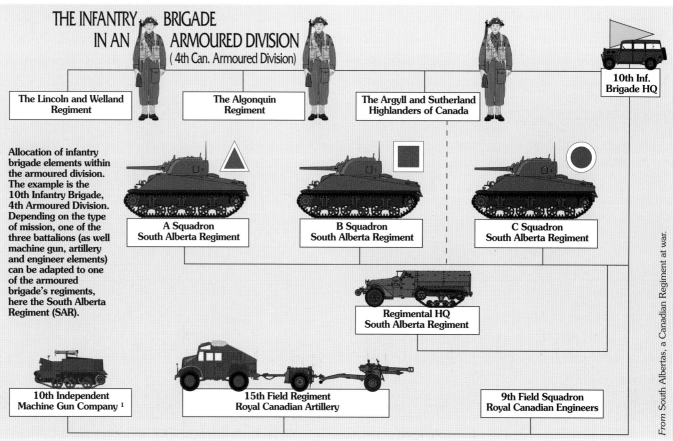

THE INFANTRY BRIGADE IN AN ARMOURED DIVISION
(4th Can. Armoured Division)

10th Inf. Brigade HQ

- The Lincoln and Welland Regiment
- The Algonquin Regiment
- The Argyll and Sutherland Highlanders of Canada

Allocation of infantry brigade elements within the armoured division. The example is the 10th Infantry Brigade, 4th Armoured Division. Depending on the type of mission, one of the three battalions (as well machine gun, artillery and engineer elements) can be adapted to one of the armoured brigade's regiments, here the South Alberta Regiment (SAR).

- A Squadron South Alberta Regiment
- B Squadron South Alberta Regiment
- C Squadron South Alberta Regiment

Regimental HQ South Alberta Regiment

- 10th Independent Machine Gun Company [1]
- 15th Field Regiment Royal Canadian Artillery
- 9th Field Squadron Royal Canadian Engineers

1. The New Brunswick Rangers

From South Albertas, a Canadian Regiment at war.

INFANTRY BATTALION
War strength

Base and reinforcement personnel: 1 Captain, 6 subalterns, 175 Warrant Officers and men. Scottish- and Irish-recruited Battalions: 5 Pipers including 1 Sergeant.

Notes
1. *Lieutenants or Second Lieutenants*
2. *Including 20 stretcher-bearers*
3. *Including 2 sharpshooters.*

	Battalion Headquarters	Headquarters Company — Headquarters	Headquarters Company — Signal Platoon	Headquarters Company — Administrative Platoon	Support Company — Headquarters	Support Company — 3-inch Mortar Platoon	Support Company — Carrier Platoon	Support Company — Anti-Tank Platoon	Support Company — Pioneer Platoon	4 Rifle Companies (A, B, C, D) each — Headquarters	4 Rifle Companies (A, B, C, D) each — Platoon x 3	TOTAL INFANTRY BATTALION
Battalion Commander (Lieutenant-Colonel)	1											1
Second in Command (Major)	1											1
Major or Captain		1			1					1		3
Adjutants (Captain)	1											1
Captains								1	1	1		3
Subalterns [1]	1		1	1		1	1	1	1		1	8
Quartermaster				1								1
TOTAL OFFICERS	4	1	1	2	1	1	2	2	2	2	1	
Warrant Officers and Other Ranks	45[2]	5	35	51	8	41	60	51	21	14[3]	36	
TOTAL	49	6	36	53	9	42	62	53	23	16	37	
Personnel attached. 1 Chaplain (Canadian Chaplain Service)												
Medical Officer (RCAMC)	1											1
Armourers and Mechanics (RCEME)			3			1	1	2				7
Cobbler (RCAOC)				1								1
Cooks (RCASC)				15								15

INFANTRY BATTALION – Armament

Excluding tools supplied with vehicles and machines.

Mine bars	13
Saws	15
Chainsaws	4
Axes	37
Sledgehammers	12
Pickaxes	160
Bill-hooks	8
Spades	198
Shovels	2
Machetes	56
Folding wire-cutters	57
Sand bags	800

Field Engineering (Army Council Instruction War Office, February 5, 1944)

	Battalion Headquarters	Headquarters Company — Headquarters	Headquarters Company — Signal Platoon	Headquarters Company — Administrative Platoon	Support Company — Headquarters	Support Company — 3-inch Mortar Platoon	Support Company — Carrier Platoon	Support Company — Anti-Tank Platoon	Support Company — Pioneer Platoon	4 Rifle Companies (A, B, C, D) each — Headquarters	4 Rifle Companies (A, B, C, D) each — Platoon x 3	TOTAL INFANTRY BATTALION
.38 Revolver	4	1	1	1	1	1	2	2	1	2	1	34
Sten machine carbine	1	1		1	1					1	4	32
No 4 Rifle	44	4	35	32	7	41	60	51	21	13	29	695
Bren LMG	1			3		2	9	6	2	1	3	63
2-inch Mortar	1									1	1	26
3-inch Mortar						6						6
PIAT				3			4	4		3		23
6. Pounder Anti-tank gun								6				6

INFANTRY BATTALION
Motor Transport

	Battalion Headquarters	Headquarters Company — Headquarters	Headquarters Company — Signal Platoon	Headquarters Company — Administrative Platoon	Support Company — Headquarters	Support Company — 3-inch Mortar Platoon	Support Company — Carrier Platoon	Support Company — Anti-Tank Platoon	Support Company — Pioneer Platoon	4 Rifle Companies (A, B, C, D) each — Headquarters	4 Rifle Companies (A, B, C, D) each — Platoon x 3	TOTAL INFANTRY BATTALION
Bicycles	6	3								3	1	33
Motorcycles	5	4	2			3	7		5			26
Jeep	2		1	1	1					3	1	12+1*
15-cwt trucks 4 x 4 **General Service**	2	1	2	1		3	2	2	2	3		28
15-cwt trucks 4 x 4 **Office**	1											1
15-cwt trucks 4 x 4 **900-litre water bowser**					1							1
15-cwt trucks 4 x 4 **Personnel**	1	1										2
3-ton trucks, 4 x 4 **General Service (GS)**				13					1			14
Carriers **Ford Windsor**								12				12
Carriers **Ford T 16**	1						13		1	1		19
Carriers **Universal 3-inch mortar Ford**						7						7
Trailers **10-cwt, General Service**				1					2			3
Trailers **15-cwt. 800-litre water bowser**				1								1

*Chaplain

INFANTRY RIFLE COMPANY

P: Pistol; MC: Sten Machine Carbine; R: Rifle No 4

Platoon Command post	No 4 Rifle	Cartridges	Sten	Mag.	Rds.	Bren LMG	Mag.	Rds.	2-inch Mortar	HE bombs	Smoke bombs	Grenades	Misc.
Platoon Commander Lieut. or 2nd Lieut.													.38 Revolver
Platoon Sergeant	1	50										4	
Lance Corporal (Mortar)	1	50								3	9		
Mortar, No 1			1	5	160				1	3	3		
Mortar, No 2	1	50								6	6		
Liaison (Runner)	1	50										2	
Orderly	1	50											Radio Set No 18 or Set No 38
Three rifle sections each:													
Corporal section commander			1	5	160							2	6 grenades with the command post and 10 grenades per section, of the No 36, 69 and 77 types and types 74 and 75 according to the circumstances.
No 1 Rifle	1	50					2	56 + 50				1	
No 2 Rifle	1	50					2	56 + 50				1	
No 3 Rifle	1	50					2	56 + 50				1	
No 4 Rifle	1	50					2	56 + 50				1	
No 5 Rifle	1	50					2	56 + 50				1	
No 6 Rifle	1	50					2	56 + 50				1	
Bren Group													
Lance-Corporal	1	50					4	112					
Gunner (No 1)						1	4	112					
Amm. bearer (No 2)	1	50					5	140				2	

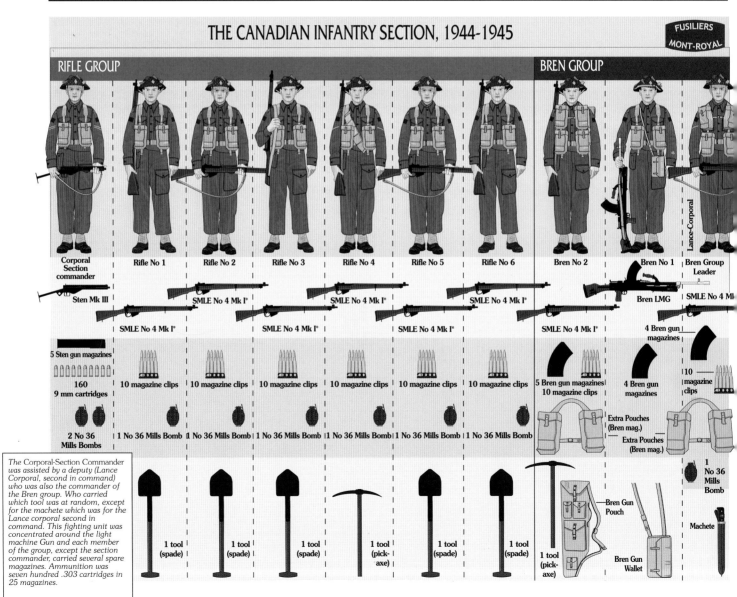

THE CANADIAN INFANTRY SECTION, 1944-1945

FUSILIERS MONT-ROYAL

RIFLE GROUP — BREN GROUP

Corporal Section commander — Sten Mk III — 5 Sten gun magazines — 160 9 mm cartridges — 2 No 36 Mills Bombs — 1 tool (spade)

Rifle No 1 — SMLE No 4 Mk I° — SMLE No 4 Mk I° — 10 magazine clips — 1 No 36 Mills Bomb — 1 tool (spade)

Rifle No 2 — SMLE No 4 Mk I° — 10 magazine clips — 1 No 36 Mills Bomb — 1 tool (spade)

Rifle No 3 — SMLE No 4 Mk I° — SMLE No 4 Mk I° — 10 magazine clips — 1 No 36 Mills Bomb — 1 tool (pick-axe)

Rifle No 4 — SMLE No 4 Mk I° — 10 magazine clips — 1 No 36 Mills Bomb — 1 tool (spade)

Rifle No 5 — SMLE No 4 Mk I° — SMLE No 4 Mk I° — 10 magazine clips — 1 No 36 Mills Bomb — 1 tool (spade)

Rifle No 6 — 10 magazine clips — 1 No 36 Mills Bomb — 1 tool (spade)

Bren No 2 — SMLE No 4 Mk I° — 5 Bren gun magazines 10 magazine clips — Extra Pouches (Bren mag.) — 1 tool (pick-axe)

Bren No 1 — Bren LMG — 4 Bren gun magazines — Extra Pouches (Bren mag.) — Bren Gun Pouch — Bren Gun Wallet

Bren Group Leader — SMLE No 4 Mk I° — 4 Bren gun magazines — 10 magazine clips — 1 No 36 Mills Bomb — Machete

The Corporal-Section Commander was assisted by a deputy (Lance Corporal, second in command) who was also the commander of the Bren group. Who carried which tool was at random, except for the machete which was for the Lance corporal second in command. This fighting unit was concentrated around the light machine Gun and each member of the group, except the section commander, carried several spare magazines. Ammunition was seven hundred .303 cartridges in 25 magazines.

6. Royal Canadian Army Service Corps

This was the transport and logistics service, organised in numbered companies.

The RSASC was present at all levels of the Canadian Army. With its considerable manpower and equipment, it was by far the largest service in the Canadian Army.

The RSASC Units

- Transport sections attached to armoured or infantry brigades. They were made up of five columns of six 3-ton trucks plus three reserve trucks. They also operated columns of petrol bowsers.
- General service units providing personnel, equipment and supplies in field kitchens down to battalion level. They ensured the different food rations were distributed with the help of teams from rear area depots
- Transport companies for the Lines of communication and the rear maintenance areas: road, rail and water transport
- Ambulance companies and their drivers, seconded to the Army Medical Corps.
- Aerial despatching Companies.

Food rations

Two types of rations made up the basic nutrition for troops on campaign: the Field Service Ration and the Compo ration.

Above.
7 August 1944 in Normandy. A Compo Ration Depot set up by the RCASC. Every day front line units would come and draw their rations, according to the ration list.
During the campaign in North-west Europe, the main food for the Canadian Army was based on Compo Rations or meals prepared by field kitchens. During the winter of 1944-45, some units received American 'C' rations which were liked better than British tins.
(PAC 132 903, photo D. I. Grant)

Inset.
One item from a Compo-Ration.

When needed there were the '24-hour' and Emergency ration (issued exceptionally for special operations), and the Haversack Ration handed out when units were being moved by road or rail.

The Field Service Ration

This was the normal ration served to troops as soon as circumstances permitted and was made up of hot meals of fresh, frozen or dehydrated ingredients, prepared in mobile field kitchens by RCASC personnel. It was accompanied by fresh bread made in the field bakeries. The meals were eaten on the spot or brought to the troops in insulated containers.

Composite (14-men) Ration Pack

The Compo Ration was designed to feed 14 men for one day. It had to be supplied immediately after the 24-hour ration had been eaten.

In order to give a bit of variety, there were seven basic menus, in crates marked A, B, C, D, E, F and G, one for each day of the week. These various prepared meals could be heated on the unit's petrol gas fired stoves or on the individual portable cooker that each soldier carried.

As the main part of the Compo Ration was made up of tinned food, its use had to be limited in time and the Field service ration had to be made up

(continued on page 30)

May 1944 in Great Britain. RCASC cooks with the Régiment de Maisonneuve are preparing a meal in a field kitchen.
The food is cooking gently on huge petrol stoves. Two large food containers of 'nosh' are ready to be taken to the soldiers.
(Collection J. Garnier)

Canadian Mess Tin Ration

A box made of paraffin waxed water- and gas-proof cardboard.
Length: 6 ins. Width: 3 ins. Height: 4 ins.
Weight: about 2 lbs. Designed to feed one man for a day.
Contents :
(In English only on the packets)

1. Powdered milk.
2. Biscuits.
3. Cheese.
4. Chocolate, powder or bars.
5. Vitamin C tablets.
6. Salt.
7. Sardines.
8. Spoon and tin-opener.
9. Packet of ten cigarettes.
Not in the picture: the tin of jam and the tin of peanut butter.

Below.
Holland June 1945. A column of RCASC Chevrolet 3-ton 4 x 4 trucks taking part in a victory parade. The front and rear differentials have been painted white for easier night convoy driving during the black-out.
(PAC)

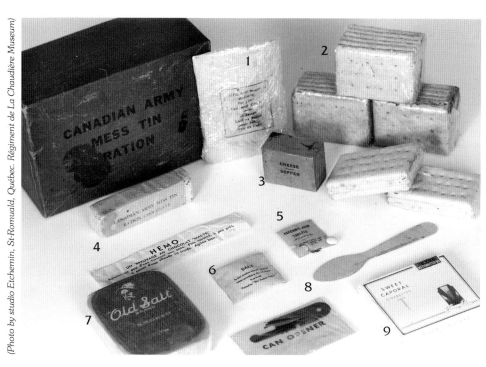

(Photo by studio Etchemin, St-Romuald, Québec. Régiment de La Chaudière Museum)

In the Vaucelles sector, near Caen, 19 July 1944. A regimental field kitchen. The personnel is seconded from the RCASC.
(PA 132728)

24 - Hour Ration Pack

Contents	Quantity
1 - Biscuits	10
2 - Porridge	2 packets
3 - Tea, sugar, milk	2 lumps of mixed ingredients, for preparation of two hot drinks
4 - Dehydrated meat	1 packet
5 - Chocolate with raisins	2 bars
6 - Vitamin-enriched chocolate	1 bar
7 - Sweets	
8 - Chewing-gum	2 packets
9 - Meat broth	2 cubes to be mixed with cold water
10 - Salt	1 bag
11 - Sugar	4 lumps
12 - Toilet paper	4 sheets
13 - Instruction for use	1 leaflet

- **Total weight:** *1,100 kg*
- **Energetic value:** *4,000 calories.*
The ration was kept inside a water- and gas-proof waxed cardboard box.
(L = 15 cm, l = 12 cm, H = 6 cm).
The collapsible cooker and solid fuel were issued separately.

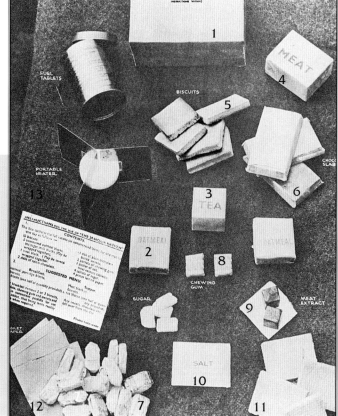

Right.
1. Section-sized petrol stove carried in unit transport or on armoured vehicles.

2. Another Canadian petrol stove. It was also possible to make an expedient stove from a large tin half filled with sand soaked in petrol.

3. Metal boxes containing rations for two or five men (vehicle crews or drivers)

4. Thermos bottle (see details below)

5. Canadian two-part mess tin with cutlery, found in Normandy.

6. Powdered milk
(Private Collection)

Below.
A crate for a British G-menu Compo Ration with some of its contents. Total energy value for one man: 3,600 calories.
Wood and fibre crate: length: 20 ins. Width: 13.5 ins. Height: 11 ins. Total weight: 66 lbs.
On the top of the crate, starting at the back: cutlery and a metal plate, a tin of boiled sweets, a tin of margarine, a tin of meat and vegetables, two Canadian folding cookers and a regulation Canadian pocket knife. The bottles of beer were issued separately or bought from the NAAFI.

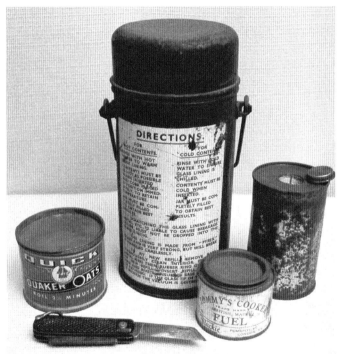

Above.
Thermos bottles holding about two pints; a tin of porridge, a 'Tommy cooker', self-heating tin of soup (see detail below) and a British issue jack-knife.

Right.
A self-heating tin of soup. A lighted candle in the central 'chimney' enabled the tin to be heated whatever the weather conditions. Heinz, the tinned-food company, made the following soups: Tomato, Turtle, Oxtail, and Celery. The Canadian Army was also provided with tins similar to these containing a powdered milk chocolate drink.

8 July 1944 in Normandy, near Carpiquet (Caen). The crew of a Sherman Firefly of the 2nd Canadian Armoured Brigade preparing their meal on two British petrol stoves. A crate of Compo Rations has been attached to the rear left of the tank. The man sitting on the right is wearing the British Denim tank suit.
(PAC 133 978. Photo M.M. Dean)

Haversack Ration

These were travel rations in the form of sandwiches or pies carried inside the mess tin or in the little food sack. Apart from the cold drink (lemonade) in the waterbottle, hot tea was served during the trip or brewed up during a break by the soldier himself.

Emergency Rations

This was a preparation of about 6 ounces of high-vitamin content chocolate contained in a sealed waterproof tin and only distributed to troops on very special missions. It was only to be eaten in the case of no other source of food being available and upon the officer's orders. From 1944 onwards the appearance of the 24-hour Ration meant that the Emergency Ration was used even more exceptionally.

Above.
Compo Pack Type E contents list.

and distributed as quickly as possible.

Apart from the A-G series of Compo Rations, there was a second type of crate, identical in size, numbered 1 to 3 which contained no biscuits. It had to be accompanied with fresh bread when issued.

The crews of armoured vehicles could draw a reserve ration whose contents varied with the number of men per vehicle (*Armoured Fighting Vehicle Ration Pack*). Here are some examples of the main dishes contained in the different crates:

- mutton stew ; pork and vegetables; oxtail and beans ; Steak and kidney in gravy ; steak and vegetables ; salmon.

24-hour Ration Pack (Landing or Assault)

This was a ration pack with a very high energy content taking up only a little space and weighing very little thanks to the use of cardboard and paper packaging. Several ingredients could be eaten hot thanks to the individual cooker. The 24-hour Ration Pack enabled soldiers fighting under extreme conditions to get by whilst waiting for the delivery of the Compo Rations.

During the Normandy Landings, the assault troops were issued with two packs per man, carried in the haversack, one in the upper part of the mess tin, the other in place of the water bottle.

EXAMPLE OF A 'C-MENU' COMPO-RATION

BREAKFAST	Tea	3 cans with sugar and powdered milk
	Sausages	2 cans
	Biscuit	1 can
	Margarine	1 can
DINNER	Irish stew[1]	14 cans
	Pudding	3 cans
TEA	Tea	3 cans with sugar and powdered milk
	Biscuit	1 can
	Margarine	1 can
	Cheese	2 cans
SUPPER	Soup (beef tea)	2 cans
	Biscuits	1 can
EXTRA	Cigarettes	2 tins (1 circular box and 1 flat box, 7 cigarettes per men)
	Sweets	1 tin
	Salt	1 tin
	Matches	1 tin
	Chocolate	1 bar per men
	Toilet Paper	

1. Mutton stew with vegetables and barley.
(From Régiment de La Chaudière Museum, contents list, 1944)

Canadian Emergency Ration.
Metal Box. Height: 3 1/2 ins.
Length: 4 ins. Width: 2 ins.
Weight: 10 1/2 oz..
It contains six bars of very high-calorie content chocolate made by Cadbury's Ltd in Montreal. The text on the tin is in both languages.

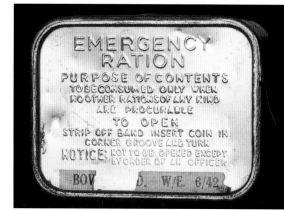

Right.
The British Emergency Ration.
(Photo Studio Etchemin, St Romuald, Quebec. Régiment de la Chaudière Museum)

7. Royal Canadian Army Medical Corps

The medical corps was responsible for the health of the soldiers in the line: i.e. carrying out all the necessary hygiene measures and preventing disease ; care of the sick ; evacuation and care of the wounded ; implementing cleaning-up measures of the battlefields ; billeting ; documentation, statistics and information for the families.

Agreements reached among the Allies' medical authorities engaged in the campaign stipulated that wounded Canadians picked up on the battlefield by American or British medical teams had to be returned to Canadian medical centres as soon as circumstances permitted.

Above.
This tag was tied to the bodies of those killed in action or those who had lost consciousness. It was filled in by an officer or orderly and gave the time and the date of discovery of the body, apparent lesions and if necessary the fact that a tourniquet had been tied on or an injection of morphine given.

Right.
Normandy, June 1944. Inside a requisitioned house, a medical officer and an orderly are giving first aid to a seriously wounded soldier. This type of operation took place at division level in the Advanced Dressing Station. *(PAC)*

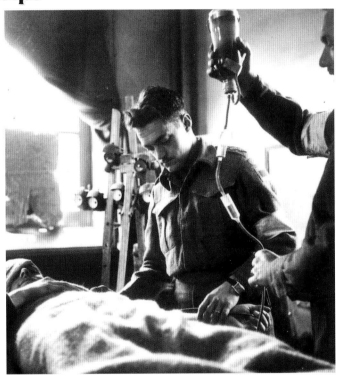

Below, right. **First-aid kit for stretcher-bearers. 1. Dressings Bag. 2. Large waterbottle. 3. Dressing for burns. 4. Bandages and dressings. 5. Individual field dressing. 6. Albuplast, cotton wool. 7. Evacuation tag (filled in by the**

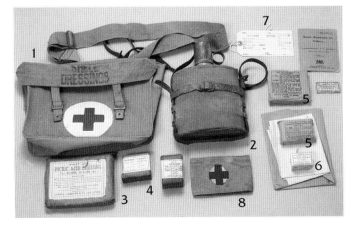

3-Ton Ford 4x4 Ambulance Truck

Bridge Classification: 9
Engine: Ford V-8 petrol.
Capacity: 4 stretcher and 12 sitting casualties.

The vehicle was fitted with a heater for the winter period and a tank for drinking water. *(PAC)*

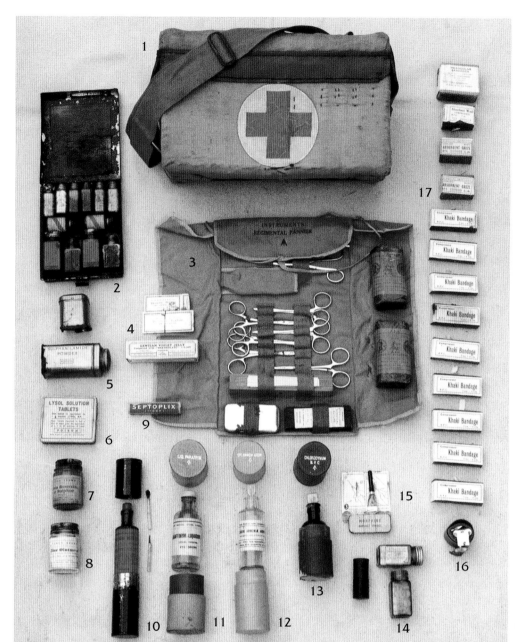

Regimental Pannier

Medical and surgical instruments kit for emergencies and first aid available in each Infantry Battalion.
1. Container. A wicker basket covered in canvas.
2. Metal box containing: Anti-tetanus serum, anti-cathar (salts for regaining consciousness), Mercury chloride (purgative), sodium bi-carbonate, disinfectants (to be drunk in water), cough drops.
3. Minor surgery bag.
4. Antiseptic (gentian violet).
5. Sulfamides.
6. Tablets for sterilising instruments.
7. Antiseptic cream.
8. Zinc oxide scarring cream.
9. Septoflix. Sulfamide antiseptic powder.
10. Iodine.
11. Collyre (for eye burns).
12. Ammoniac liquor
13. Powerful analgesic.
14. Aspirin.
15. Disposable syringe of morphine.
16. Tourniquet.
17. Bandages and dressings.

Below.
First aid outfit for Armoured Fighting Vehicles (British issue)
(RR)

The Infantry Brigade Field Ambulance

This had a strength of 242 officers and other ranks.

Unit transport :
- 8 bicycles
- 17 motorbikes
- 3 Jeeps
- 6 15-cwt General Service trucks
- 12 3-ton GS lorries
- 16 3-ton 4 x 4 ambulances.

The officers were armed with a hand gun ; other personnel had no weapons.

Personnel (drivers, etc.) detached from the RCASC were armed with rifles and Sten guns.

Above.
When a soldier was killed or died of his wounds in hospital, his personal effects were put into his kit bag and sent on to his family.
(RR)

Inset.
The tag tied to the kit bag.

Right.
First aid anaesthetics.
1. Vial of Chloroform in a cotton bag. Breaking the vial enabled the casualty to breathe in the anaesthetic. 2. Morphine shot issued to the officers in combat units. Evacuation teams had to be informed that the wounded man had been given a shot of morphine, so a tag was tied on to the man's uniform or some item of individual equipment.

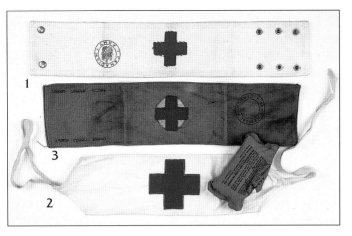

Armbands worn on their left arm by personnel of the Royal Canadian Army Medical Corps, Canadian Dental Corps, stretcher-bearers and chaplains.
1 and 2. Armbands according to the International Geneva Convention.
3. Armband for stretcher-bearer.
4. Canadian issue first field dressing, in a waterproof canvas sealed pouch.
(Private collection)

8. Canadian Dental Corps

This corps was attached to the Royal Canadian Army Medical Corps. It provided dental care as close as possible to the units thanks to specially fitted-out vehicles. Elements of the CDC were also present at all levels, in the various army and army corps hospitals.

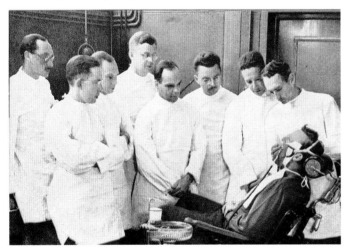

Trainees in a Dental Service school. *(RR)*

9. Royal Canadian Army Ordnance Corps

Above.
Each division had on its roll a Mobile Laundry and Bath Unit operated by the RCAOC, which laundered and exchanged clothes, and normally provided a bath or shower service for each soldier twice a week.
'RR)

The Ordnance corps' task was to stock and issue armament and ammunition, motor transport and armoured vehicles, signals equipment, clothing, some engineer material and medical supplies. Each division or independent brigade had its own Ordnance element, for assembling supplies which to be issued on a regular basis, replenishment being obtained from the depots along the lines of communication and in the rear maintenance areas. The RCAOC was also responsible for the Army Pictorial Service. Whether requisitioned from a states arsenal or a civilian company, all Army issue equipment was checked when it came off the production line ; taken delivery of and signed for by a committee of civil servants from the War Office and officers from the Royal Canadian Army Ordnance Corps.

Mobile Laundry and Bath Units

The RCAOC also maintained laundry and bath/shower units. Each division had one of these units which took charge of laundering and exchanging clothes, and normally allowed each man two baths or showers per week.

10. Royal Canadian Electrical and Mechanical Engineers

This corps was created in February 1944 so that Canadian formations would conform with the British type. These technical personnel came from the Royal Canadian Army Ordnance Corps, which until then had been responsible for repairs and maintenance of equipment in each division.
In each division there was thus a central repair workshop. Light Aid detachments were spread out throughout the various line units.

Repair echelons
First echelon: Tuning, replacing single parts.
Second echelon: Replacing complete units (engine blocks, gearboxes, etc.).
Third echelon: Extensive repairs and servicing, impossible to achieve in the field.
Fourth echelon: Repairs needing heavy equipment.
The first and second echelons took place at division or brigade level, the third and the fourth in heavy workshops of the rear maintenance areas

Mack 6 X 4 Heavy Breakdown Tractor

Bridge Classification: 12
Engine: 160 hp, 6-cylinder Mack petrol engine.
Use: this was a heavy breakdown vehicle to be found in the light workshops of the RCEME seconded to the Armoured Regiments with the Tractor,

Medium Diamond T 969 b. It was equipped with all the tooling necessary for urgent preliminary repairs, with a hoist capable of lifting 8 tonnes and a towing capability of 16 tonnes.
(PAC)

11. Royal Canadian Army Pay Corps

This service was responsible for managing the army's finances and for paying the soldiers. This was carried out by Royal Army Pay Corps officers seconded to the corps *(Field Cash Office)*.

12. Corps of Military Staff Clerks

Administrative personnel assigned to headquarters, under two sections:

- **Section A.** Officers and NCOs employed in administrative functions in district headquarters in Canada, the Army overseas headquarters in London and in the divisions and brigades committed on the continent.

- **Section B.** NCOs and other ranks assigned to the Ottawa Headquarters. The corps also was responsible for the printing and the distribution of operational orders (Field Orders) drawn up by headquarters. Its personnel was made up of soldiers who were unfit for active duty.

A letter sent from Normandy to Canada on 6 August 1944 by Captain Marchand of the Régiment de Maisonneuve. The postmark T.C.2 is that of the 2nd Canadian Infantry Division. The envelope was supplied by a charity and has been passed by the unit censor.

Opposite, right. **An example of the report drawn up by the chaplain (here, G. Marchand, chaplain of the Régiment de Maisonneuve) or by an officer, in the case of the death in action of an officer or a soldier. The place of death and of the temporary grave were indicated according to an army map. The report was then sent to the Military Graves Service (cf. page 36).**

Below .
1. Prayer book for Catholic soldiers.
2. Prayer book for Anglican soldiers.
3. Chaplain's identity card belonging to the chaplain, the Honourable Captain Gérard Marchand* of the Régiment de Maisonneuve,
4. Plastic crucifixes handed out by Christian chaplains.
(* Author of 'Le Régiment de la Maisonneuve vers la Victoire', a highly recommended read.)

13. Canadian Postal Corps

This was the service which ensured the forwarding of mail and packages.

This was of prime importance in order to ensure good morale for the troops fighting overseas.

Left.
**Antwerp, Belgium, December 1944.
A unit of the Canadian Postal Corps attached to the rear maintenance zone sorting parcels sent to the troops.**
(PA 192026)

Postmarks stamped on letters sent to Canada or to Great Britain have a code designating the sender's unit.

AC	Canadian Army
HC	Army Corps
DCA	Armoured Division
TC	Services or divisions
SC	Garrison Services

TC3	3rd Infantry Division
DC4	4th Armoured Division
DC5	5th Armoured Division

The Canadian post offices operating in Continental Europe were :

AC1	1st Canadian Army
HC1	1st Canadian Army Corps
THC1	1st Corps Services
HC2	2nd Canadian Army Corps
THC2	2nd Corps Services
TC2	2nd Infantry Division

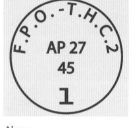

Above.
F.P.O. *Field Post Office*
T.H.C.2 *2nd Corps Services*
AP.27.45 *Date of sending, here 27 April 1945*

	RECTO	Ref. No.1	Army Form W.3314				VERSO			
Serial No.	UNIT	RANK and ARMY NUMBER	NAME and INITIALS				MEANS OF IDENTIFICATION OF BODY	RELIGION	DATE OF DEATH
1	R. de Mais.	L/CPL D140 278	BEAUPRÉ, JAC.		1		disque Livret de paye	R.C	13-8-44
2	R. de MAIS	LIEUT.	DAOUST. G		2		disque Livret de paye	R.C.	13-8-44
3	R. de MAIS.	SOLDAT D109840	CADORETTE R		3		disque + son frère (au régiment)	R.C.	13-8-44
4	R. de MAIS.	SOLDAT D132 815	BOURQUE. MAUR		4		disque d'identité + lettres	R.C.	13-8-44
5	R H C	PTE F 9279	GAMESTER. A.H		5		disque + pay-book	Prot.	13-8-44
6					6				

COUNTRY FRANCE CEMETERY Clair Tizon MAP REF. or LOCATION DETAILS 47/FB (Torigne Bus)

SIGNATURE AND DESIGNATION OF CHAPLAIN OR BURIAL OFFICER
H/Capt. (Signature) Gérard Marchand padre
Date 14-8-1944

Following page, left, from top to bottom
Normandy 1944, a Catholic padre from The 3rd Infantry Division getting ready to say Mass on an improvised altar.
(PAC)

Religious service on a Landing Craft Tank on the eve of D-Day.
(PA 132899)

**Normandy 24 June 1944.
Men from the Régiment de la Chaudière receiving the Holy Sacrament from Padre H.W. Huard.**
(Musée du Régiment de la Chaudière)

**18 March 1945, in Germany.
Jewish religious service. The Star of David has been painted on the vehicle door, on the right. The code number 50 in white on a black background over a white rectangle show that the chaplain is attached to 1st Canadian Army headquarters.**
(PAC)

14. Canadian Chaplain Service

Corps of military Chaplains, all of whom had officer rank. There were Christian (Catholic, Protestant and various other denominations) chaplains as well as Jewish. They were present in all major formations and miscellaneous units.

They held religious services, helped the medical officers at regimental level and gave the comfort of religion to those soldiers who sought it.

15. Canadian Provost Corps

The Canadian Provost Corps was responsible for Court Martials in the theater of operations. Its personnel also provided prison guards and staff at internment camps. The CPC also fielded Military Police units, companies or platoons, within all the big units in the front line and in the rear maintenance areas.

Their main jobs in war zones were the directing of convoys, indicating the itineraries (putting up signposts), guarding prisoners of war, controlling civilians residing or moving about in the military area, checking the behaviour of soldiers on leave, and whether they had the right to be on leave. CPC personnel had at least the rank of Lance-Corporal, and their authority to question soldiers extended up to the rank of Brigadier.

The Royal Canadian Mounted Police supplied a company with the 1st Infantry Division. This unit had its own functions (see pages 28-29)*

1. The red service cap which was particular to the British Military Police was not worn by the Canadian Military Police. It was replaced by the khaki beret introduced for the whole army in 1943.

Above.
Two Lance-Corporals from the Canadian Provost Corps on motorbikes wearing white webbing, special riding breeches and boots. The motorbikes are 16H 500cc Nortons.
(PAC)

Above.
This Canadian Mk II helmet (made by GSW) bears the markings of the Military Police. *(Coll. Jean Bouchery)*

Note. This chapter has been written with the very kind help of Mrs Carmen Harry, curator of the RCMP Museum, and of Jocelyn Garnier

THE PROVOST COMPANY

**3 Officers
2 WOs
113 ORs**

79

A The Company Headquarters consisted of :
- 1 Captain
- 2 Lieutenants
- 1 Regimental Sergeant-Major (RSM)
- 1 Company Quartermaster-Sergeant (CQMS)
- 1 Sergeant
- 4 Drivers
- 1 Corporal (cook - RCASC)
- 1 Private (cook - RCASC)
- 1 motorbike/car mechanic from the RCEME

B

C The company was divided into 6 platoons each consisting of :
- 1 Sergeant
- 2 Corporals
- 12 Lance-Corporals
- 2 Privates (Drivers)

D For its headquarters, the company had at its disposal :
- 4 Jeeps
- 3 motorbikes
- 2 3-ton Lorries

E The transport platoon was equipped with :
- 3 Jeeps
- 2 15-cwt trucks
- 6 motorbikes

F The men in the company were issued with hand guns (revolvers or automatics) except for the cooks, drivers and the mechanic who were given a No 4 Rifle.

Opposite .
Canadian Provost Corps armband, worn on the right sleeve.

Below .
1. Sergeant in the 1st Provost Company, Royal Canadian Mounted Police, in 1943.
2. Corporal of the 1st Provost Company in 1944.
(after the 'Uniforms of the Canadian mounted Police' by James J. Boulton, Turner Warwick Publications inc. 1990)

1   2

---

16. Canadian Women's Army Corps

Canadian Women's Army Corps uniform button.

This women's auxiliary corps was set upon 13 August 1941 in order to free men from certain tasks and send them to combat units.

On 13 March 1942, the CWAC was officially incorporated into the Army [*]. The following summer, Canadian Military Headquarters asked for 350 CWACs to be sent overseas ; they arrived in Great Britain on 5 November 1942. In December 1943, three companies of CWACs were operational in London and one at Aldershot.

At the beginning of 1945, it was decided to transfer 156 CWACs to North-west Europe where they were assigned to various headquarters with administrative functions, or to signals units.

At the end of the war there were 3,000 CWACs serving overseas. Four of them were seriously wounded when a V-2 fell on Antwerp at the beginning of 1945. Lieutenant-Colonel Margaret Eaton was the Corps' commanding officer from April 1944 to October 1945.

Uniform

The emblem worn on the lapel of the service tunic and on the buttons was the helmeted head of the goddess Athena, the daughter of Zeus.

The uniform consisted of a khaki woolen jacket and skirt. The jacket was gathered in at the waist and had a pocket on the left side of the chest and two pockets below the waist. The ample skirt had to reach 5 inches below the knee. The khaki shirt with a collar was worn with a khaki tie.

In winter women soldiers were supplied with a cavalry-style khaki coat. The hand bag was made of brown canvas. An allowance was paid to each CWAC to purchase undergarments and linen.

Conditions of enlistment

Young women wanting to enter the corps had to be between 18 and 45, medically fit according to categories 'A' or 'B', weigh at least 7 stone, be at least 5-ft tall and of good morality.

They had to have a Grade VII school level or equivalent, and not be the mother of children less than six years-old.

Above.
During a meal in Great Britain in 1943. This young Lance Corporal of the Canadian Women's Army Corps poses obligingly for the reporter.
(PAC)

[*] After this date, CWAC rank insignia were the same as the rest of the army.

19. Canadian Film and Photo Units

These were photograph and film units from the War department attached to the Royal Canadian Army Service Corps.

Right.
**Shoulder badges
for the reporter teams
of the CFPUs.
Top, the printed
model and below
The embroidered
version.**
(L. Grimshaw collection)

17. Canadian Intelligence Corps

Officially constituted on 29 October 1942, this service consisted of personnel whose job was intelligence gathering, counter-intelligence and getting information about the order of battle and condition of enemy forces.

During the NW Europe campaign, Field Security Sections were attached to divisions or placed directly under Armies or Army corps. They were made up of a ranking officer (Intelligence Officer) and several NCOs who could speak several foreign languages fluently.

The main missions of the service were :
- Co-ordination with the resistance behind enemy lines.
- Searching for infiltrated agents.
- Enquiries into suspects among the civilian population.
- Interrogation of Prisoners of War
- Military censorship of mail and publications.
- Relations with the civilian authorities.

Above. **Photographers and camera operators from a Canadian Film and Photo unit posing for one of their comrades in Normandy during the summer of 1944.** *(DR)*

Below.
Holland, October 1944. This cameraman is wearing the Canadian Film and Photo Unit shoulder titles. The Formation sign is that of the 21st Army Group's lines of communications. *(PA 136214)*

Normandy, July 1944. Lieutenant Fafard, standing centre, and his Canadian Intelligence Corps section. *(Collection J. Garnier)*

18 Canadian Forestry Corps

This was set up in May 1940 with professionals of the wood industry: lumberjacks, carpenters, woodworkers, etc. Organised into 20 companies, the Corps was especially responsible for the construction of 131 platforms during the D-Day landings on 6 June 1944.

They were sent to Normandy and then to the Hürtgen Forest in Germany where they cut the wood needed by the Engineers for building bridges and barracks. In 1944, its strength was 4 055 officers and other ranks.

Above. **Croockham, Great Britain, 21 April 1945. Captured at Dieppe in August 1942, Lieutenant-Colonel C. Merritt, VC being interviewed by war correspondents after his release. The man with his back to the camera wears the 'War Correspondent' shoulder title.** *(PA 161938)*

20. Canadian Graves Registration Unit

This unit was attached to the rear maintenance areas and its function was to gather together the bodies of the fallen and to register them so that their graves could be found.

No matter what the rank or social status, it was prescribed that those killed in action were to remain where they had fallen, or gathered together in a cemetery.

The grave-digging parties were made up of Royal Canadian Engineer personnel supervising French civilian volunteers and German prisoners-of-war.

The first Canadian Military Cemetery was set up near Courseulles-sur-Mer (Calvados). The other cemeteries in Normandy are at Reviers to the north-west of Caen which has 2,044 graves and Bretteville-sur-Laize, to the south of Caen with 2,875 graves.
(DR)

PERMANENT GRAVESTONE FOR CANADIAN MILITARY CEMETERIES

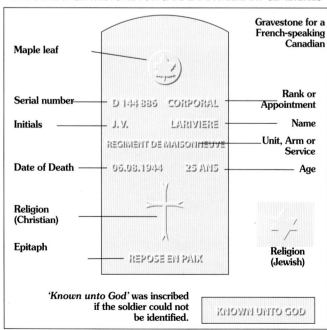

Maple leaf

Serial number — D 144 886

Initials — J.V.

Date of Death — 06.08.1944

Religion (Christian)

Epitaph — REPOSE EN PAIX

Gravestone for a French-speaking Canadian

CORPORAL — Rank or Appointment

LARIVIERE — Name

REGIMENT DE MAISONNEUVE — Unit, Arm or Service

25 ANS — Age

Religion (Jewish)

'Known unto God' was inscribed if the soldier could not be identified.

KNOWN UNTO GOD

21. La General List

This service gathered together officers and soldiers who were not assigned to a unit or a formation in the training centres and depots.

22. Beach Groups

The organisation of the Beach Groups was identical to that of the British Army. The signs were common to both armies.

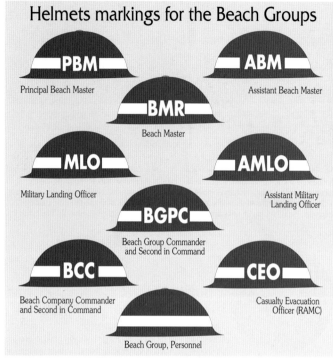

Helmets markings for the Beach Groups

PBM — Principal Beach Master
ABM — Assistant Beach Master
BMR — Beach Master
MLO — Military Landing Officer
AMLO — Assistant Military Landing Officer
BGPC — Beach Group Commander and Second in Command
BCC — Beach Company Commander and Second in Command
CEO — Casualty Evacuation Officer (RAMC)
Beach Group, Personnel

Source: Beach Organisation and Maintenance Combined Operations, Pamphlet No 2. Reprinted in Canada 1944.

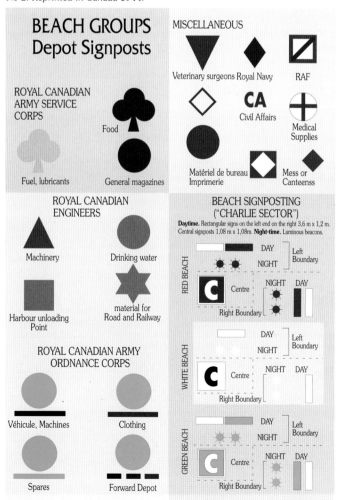

BEACH GROUPS Depot Signposts

ROYAL CANADIAN ARMY SERVICE CORPS
Food
Fuel, lubricants
General magazines

ROYAL CANADIAN ENGINEERS
Machinery
Drinking water
Harbour unloading Point
material for Road and Railway

ROYAL CANADIAN ARMY ORDNANCE CORPS
Véhicule, Machines
Clothing
Spares
Forward Depot

MISCELLANEOUS
Veterinary surgeons Royal Navy
RAF
Civil Affairs **CA**
Medical Supplies
Matériel de bureau Imprimerie
Mess or Canteenss

BEACH SIGNPOSTING ("CHARLIE SECTOR")
Daytime. Rectangular signs on the left end and on the right 3,6 m x 1,2 m. Central signposts 1,08 m x 1,08m. **Night-time.** Luminous beacons.

RED BEACH
DAY / NIGHT — Left Boundary
C Centre — NIGHT DAY
Right Boundary

WHITE BEACH
DAY / NIGHT — Left Boundary
C Centre — NIGHT DAY
Right Boundary

GREEN BEACH
DAY / NIGHT — Left Boundary
C Centre — NIGHT DAY
Right Boundary

23. The CANLOAN officers [1]

Holland 1944, CANLOAN Lieutenants W.A. Harvey and P. Turner, both survivors from the Arnhem operation. These Canadian officers were serving in the South Staffordshire Regiment, a unit of the 1st (British) Airlanding Brigade, 1st Airborne Division whose insignia they are wearing. The Title 'Canada' was worn between the Title and the Formation Badge. *(PAC 169958)*

Blazer badge worn after the war by CANLOAN veterans.

These were junior officers seconded to the British Army. After the two territorial defence divisions in Canada were disbanded, the army found it had too many officers.

The Canadian General Staff proposed and the British Command accepted, incorporating these officers in British infantry units, and Royal Army Ordnance Corps units for a small number of them. They were all volunteers and CAN-LOAN officers (the French-speaking officers had to be bilingual) could choose the regiment they wanted to serve in.

The Canadian Government took charge of their pay, allowances and pensions. The officers had to wear the emblems of the units to which they were assigned, but could display the title 'Canada' on their uniforms and wear Canadian battledress.

In April 1944 there were 673 Canadian officers in the British Army, most of them Lieutenants and Captains, of whom 90 were in the airborne regiments.

They took part in all the big operations in North-west Europe including the Normandy invasion on 6 June 1944.

CANLOAN casualties totaled 465: 128 officers killed in action or died from their wounds, 310 wounded and 27 prisoners of war. The following medals were awarded: one MBE, one DSO, forty-one MCs, one Silver Star (USA) and one Croix de Guerre (France) and one medal of the Order of the Bronze Lion (Holland).

24. Charities for assistance and recreation

The Canadian Legion

The Canadian Legion was an organisation run by veterans' associations. It managed mobile canteens for the soldiers as well as concerts and shows.

The Salvation Army

The Canadian Salvation Army ran rest camps and libraries and showed films.

The Knights of Columbus

This civilian organisation reserved hotel rooms for soldiers on leave and offered different welfare functions.

---

* Code-name (Sources obtained from the Canadian War Museum)

The Young Men's Christian Association

The famous YMCA supplied a lot of sports equipment and organised ice-hockey, American football, baseball competitions, etc. between units. It also held proficiency courses and taught the illiterate to read and write.

The Navy, Army and Air Force Institute

The British NAAFI was renamed the EFI (Expeditionary Forces Institute) after 6 June 1944. This co-operative was run by personnel from the three arms. Mobile shops were set up under tents, in specially adapted vehicles or in requisitioned premises. They sold all sorts of products such as cigarettes, toilet articles, notions, stationery, etc.

The organisation of the NAAFI was run by a civilian office of the British Treasury.

The centres and their supervisors were attached to all the Canadian units. The supervisors wore army uniform and had the rank of Captain but they remained civilians and had no command function.

NAAFI Insignia.

NAAFI canteen cutlery set. *(Private Collection)*

The Canadian Red Cross Society

The Canadian Red Cross Society had an important role looking after the wounded when they left the military hospitals. The society chartered ships to forward food parcels, clothes and basic items to prisoners of war of all nations held in Germany, as well as to the civilian population in the war-stricken regions.

Below.
A Canadian Red Cross parcel for Allied PoWs held in Germany. It had to go through Switzerland. Canadian PoW's Field service cap. The letters painted on the cap meant *Kriegsgefangene* -prisoner of war in German.
(RR)

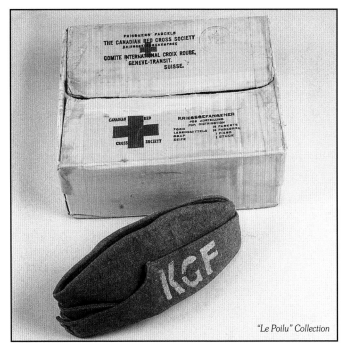

"Le Poilu" Collection

CHAPTER 2 HEADDRESS

1. Helmets

Canadian-made helmets
and their manufacturers' markings

The British-pattern Mk II Helmet was made in Canada by:

– Canadian Lamp Company, abbr. CL/C.
– General Steel Wares, abbr. GSW.
– Aluminium Goods Company, abbr. AG/C (usually reserved for the Royal Canadian Air Force)

The makers' initials were stamped on the lower rim of the helmet, near the nape of the neck, together with the year of production.

– D.P. and H (Department of Pensions and Health and Welfare) also produced some helmet shells.

Lining makers: Viceroy Manufacturing Co., marked on one of the fibre supports, with the production date and size.

Chinstrap manufacturers: Backstay Standard.

Motorcyclist Helmets

– Helmet, Crash, Motorcyclists, Plastic, produced in Canada by Backstay Standard (abbr. BS).

– Helmet Despatch Rider, Steel, Mk I (steel, dome-shaped), produced by Canadian Lamp Company (abbr. CL/C).

British-Made Helmets supplied
to the Canadian Army:

Mk III Helmet (nick-named the 'Tortoise'), distributed to Canadian assault units before D-Day.

Helmet, Royal Armoured Corps Steel, Mk I issued to the Armoured Regiments of the Canadian Armoured Corps as well as to Universal Carriers crews.

Helmet, Steel, Airborne troops
steel helmet for airborne troops.

Pulp Despatch Rider Helmet
motorcyclists helmet made of lacquered compressed fibre.

Helmet, Crash, Motorcyclist Steel
This was issued alongside the Canadian-made model.

Top.
Great Britain, 1942. King George VI reviewing the Régiment de la Chaudière. The regimental flash was painted on the left side of steel helmets. *(Photo Musée du Régiment de la Chaudière)*

Above:
The Regiment de Maisonnneuve in Great Britain during the winter of 1943-44. The second man from the left is wearing a Mk II helmet bearing the regimental flash, a Fleur de Lys, symbol of Québec.
(J. Garnier)

Helmet flashes

Forbidden in Canada (1943 instruction), these flashes were permitted by Canadian Military Headquarters in London which had overall control over Canadian forces overseas. These insignia were in the form of decals or small painted designs, and remained optional although mostly considered an asset to unit pride.

Helmet flashes were positioned on the left side of the helmet, even

Information taken from 'Tin Lids, Canadian combat helmets' by Roger V. Lucy, Canadian Military Artifacts 1997, with the author's kind permission)

Opposite, right.
Mk II CL/C 1942 helmet. The paint finish was light brown (first version) until 1942.

Below.
Mk II helmet with two-tone, green and brown, camouflage netting, adopted in 1943.

Below, right.
A. Detail of the inside of the Mk II CL/C helmet. The lining was made of rubberised canvas.

B. Inner lining variant in patent leather. This GSW made helmet is painted the second paint finish - olive drab - which was introduced after 1942. There was a relatively common practice of painting the soldier's name and number on the underside of the rim. Sometimes the unit's initials or name were found also.

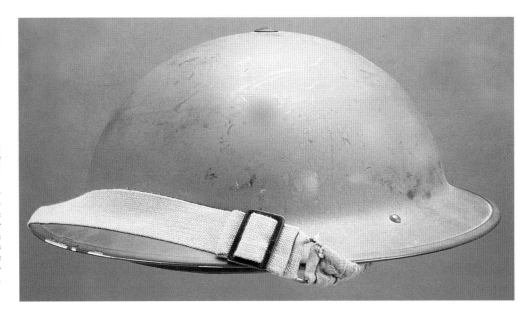

A

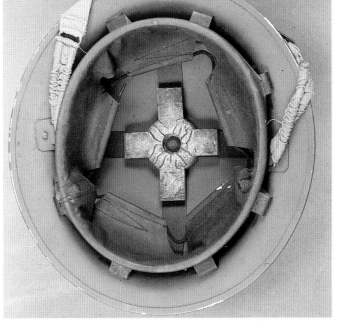

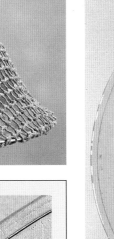

Helmet manufacturer's markings

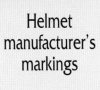

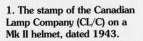

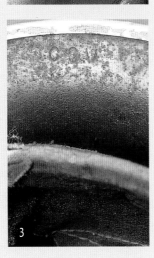

1. The stamp of the Canadian Lamp Company (CL/C) on a Mk II helmet, dated 1943.

2. The stamp of the Aluminium Goods Company (AG/C) on a Mk II helmet.

3. The stamp of General Steel Wares (GSW) on a Mk II helmet.

B

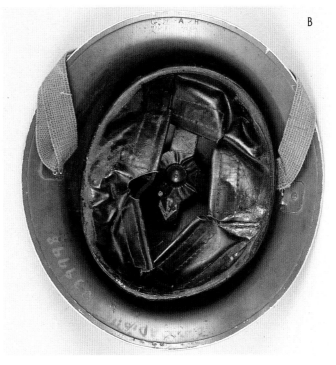

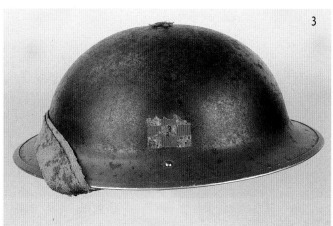

Regimental Helmet Flashes

1. Mk II helmet. Maroon-white-red flash of the Régiment de la Chaudière.

2. Mk II helmet of the 3rd Canadian Infantry Division. Flash attributed to Queen's Own Cameron Highlanders of Canada.

3. Mk II helmet. Flash of the Calgary Highlanders Regt.

4. Mk II helmet. Flash of the Fusiliers Mont-Royal. The position was particular to the whole of the infantry of the 2nd Canadian Infantry Division: see page 157, in the Dieppe chapter.

5. Mk II helmet with its original netting. Flash of the Régiment de Maisonneuve.

6. Mk II helmet, Flash of the Régiment de Maisonneuve.
(Private collections)

if this was not always strictly obeyed.

The symbols were:
- Regimental insignia or traditional colours.
- For the infantry regiments of the 2nd Infantry Division: a royal blue oblong under a geometric figure particular to the unit (see chapter on Dieppe, page 157).
- Unit and Formation Markings: Code numbers on a coloured background normally painted on vehicles and machines, as shown on the organisation charts on pages 10-17 and in the example opposite.

Examples of helmet flashes specific to support units

Royal Canadian Artillery.
The colours of the artillery and the code number determine the type of unit. Here 47 indicates a Light Anti-Aircraft Regiment.

Royal Canadian Engineers

NB. The helmets with flashes illustrating this chapter were all found in Normandy and come from private collections.

42

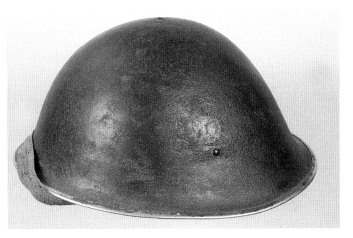

Above, left:
Flash of the Regina Rifle Regiment (3rd Infantry Division) on a British-made Mk III helmet.

Above, right:
Mk III Helmet. Flash of the Canadian Scottish, 3rd Infantry Division. The emblem is that of the battalion, the sixteenth levied by the Regiment during WWI. *(Private Collection)*

Above:
Detail of the Regina Rifle Regiment insignia, here a decal. The Regina Rifles' British parent unit was the King's Royal Rifle Corps.

Right:
This British Mk III helmet was handed out first to assault troops, including Canadian troops, on 6 June 1944 according to availability.

Bottom, right:
Manoeuvres in Great Britain, May 1944. The men from the *Régiment de la Chaudière* are wearing the British Mk III helmet with regulation markings. (PAC)

Below:
Caen, July 1944. Lieutenant W. Moisan of the Régiment de la Chaudière. The regimental flash is in maroon, white and red. *(Régiment de la Chaudière Museum)*

2. Helmets for Airborne, Armoured Corps troops and motorcyclists

Above:
British airborne troops helmets issued to the 1st Canadian Parachute Battalion.
1. Helmet, Steel, Airborne Troops. First version dating from 1942, worn to the end of hostilities.
2. Helmet, Steel, Airborne troops Mk I. The fibre strip along the inside edge was removed and replaced with an anti-magnetic ring.
3. Helmet, Steel Airborne Troops Mk II. The leather chin strap has been replaced by a webbing one. Produced from the end of 1943.

Left.
Helmet Steel, Airborne Troops Mk II *(Photo André Prince, Canada)*

Below.
Helmet Royal Armoured Corps, Steel Mk I. British-made helmet issued to the crews of armoured vehicles as well some Universal Carrier crews.

Above, left:
Helmet, Crash, Motorcyclists Plastic, made in Canada and distributed from 1944. The moulded plastic shell has been reinforced with a strip screwed to its lower part.
(Public archives of Canada, N°197148, courtesy of Clive M. Law, Military Artifact.

Above, right:
Pulp Despatch Rider Helmet. British-made motorcyclist helmet, issued to the Canadian Army. The shell was made of compressed varnished fiber.
(Le poilu)

Right, from left to right:
Motorcyclist's British-made steel crash helmet. The decal flash was that of the 1st Hussars (2nd Canadian Armoured Brigade).
(Private collection)

Motorcyclist's steel crash helmet, Canadian-made by CL/C (the chin strap was wider, the shock-absorbing pad inside the helmet was made of rubber instead of felt.
(Private Collection)

Left:
Mk I Royal Armoured Corps Steel Helmet, worn here by Major-General R.F.L Keller, commanding the Canadian 3rd Infantry Division.
(PAC)

Right:
Canadian motorcyclist wearing the British Despatch Rider Helmet made of compressed fiber.
(J. Garnier)

45

Left:
February 1945. Assembled before the attack on Goch, Germany, the 10th Armoured Regiment (Fort Garry Horse, 2nd Armoured Brigade) was engaged in support of the infantry of the Royal Regiment of Canada (2nd Infantry Division). The infantry in Full Marching Order have climbed on the tanks. The troops are wearing the Mk II Helmet or the khaki beret. *(IWM)*

Bottom, left, from top to bottom:
1. The Field Service Cap was chosen in 1939 with Battledress. Although replaced by the Khaki Beret in 1943, it was still worn in 1944-45 by some service troops.
2. The Khaki Beret was introduced in 1943 and worn slightly tilted to the left, the insignia had to be worn directly above the left eye.
3. Khaki Beret bearing the insignia for an officer of the Regina Rifles.

Bottom, right:
Lining markings of a beret made by Dorothea Hats Limited in 1944. The C and broad arrow at bottom are the Canadian Army property marking.

3. Service and Off-Duty Headgear

Cloth headgear worn in the theatre of operations with battledress were:

● Officers above the rank of Lieutenant-Colonel:
- Khaki Beret
- Service dress peaked cap.
- Special headwear (see below).
- Traditional headgear.

● Other personnel:
1. Black Beret: Canadian Armoured Corps.
2. Khaki Beret, Infantry [1] except for the units wearing headgear 3 and 4: all arms and services
3. Maroon beret: 1st Canadian Parachute Battalion.

N.B. The berets were made of a single piece of wool. The lower part was bound with leather through which ran a tape; this was then tied above the nape of the neck for adjustment. The black cotton lining featured a stamped lozenge with the maker's name, the size and the date.

4. Tam O'Shanter, the traditional head-dress of the Canadian Scottish Regiments.

---

1. Including the Irish Fusiliers of Canada, as their Caubeen was only worn off-duty.

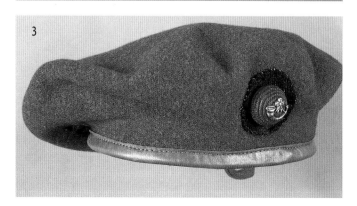

Lieutenant-Colonel A.S. Gregory of the Regina Rifles. The Khaki beret bears the officer's pattern badge. *(RR)*

Above:
Black Beret worn by a trooper of the 24th Tank Battalion (the Voltigeurs de Quebec) disbanded in Great Britain in August 1943. Note the 'tank' sleeve badge.

Above:
The Black Beret was adopted in 1938. It was worn by all personnel of the Canadian Armoured Corps.

Below:
Maroon Beret of the 1st Canadian Parachute Battalion.

Above:
Made in Canada after samples supplied by the British Royal Army Ordnance Corps (RAOC), the Maroon Beret was distributed at the end of April 1943 to all personnel having followed the training course for paratroopers at Camp Shilo (Manitoba). After the 1st Canadian Parachute Battalion left for Great Britain to join the 3rd Parachute Brigade of the 6th Airborne Division, damaged, worn or lost berets were replaced by the British RAOC.

CANADIAN ARMY BERETS

1

Black Beret: Canadian Armoured Corps

2

**Khaki Beret: Infantry (except units wearing the maroon beret or Tam O'Shanter) and all arms and services
The khaki beret was adopted in 1943.**

3

Maroon Beret: 1st Canadian Parachute Battalion

4

**Tam O' Shanter:
Canadian Scottish infantry**

How to wear the Beret

Instructions of June and November 1943.

1. The beret is worn with the rim 1 inch above and parallel with the eyes.

2. It is pulled down towards the right and slightly to the rear.

3. The badge is pinned 1 inch above the rim and directly above the left eye. In April 1944, it was stated that if necessary a small piece of cardboard could be placed inside the beret behind the badge in order to keep it straight. (Order dated April 1944 from Lt.Col. Bradbrooke, 1st Canadian Parachute Battalion.)

4. Service Dress Caps

This type of hat was worn only with the officers' service dress (trousers and tunic). Service dress caps made by hat-makers in town were different from those supplied by the Royal Army Ordnance Corps. Officers under the rank of Colonel were not permitted to wear the Service Dress Cap with Battledress.

Above:
Service Dress Cap worn by Colonels and Brigadiers.
(Le Poilu)

Below: **General HDG Crerar during the campaign of the Autumn of 1944. He is wearing the Service Dress Cap for general officers.**
(Public Archives of Canada).

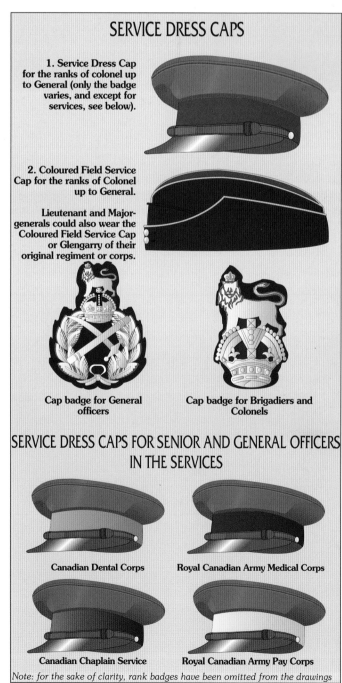

SERVICE DRESS CAPS

1. Service Dress Cap for the ranks of colonel up to General (only the badge varies, and except for services, see below).

2. Coloured Field Service Cap for the ranks of Colonel up to General.

Lieutenant and Major-generals could also wear the Coloured Field Service Cap or Glengarry of their original regiment or corps.

Cap badge for General officers

Cap badge for Brigadiers and Colonels

SERVICE DRESS CAPS FOR SENIOR AND GENERAL OFFICERS IN THE SERVICES

Canadian Dental Corps

Royal Canadian Army Medical Corps

Canadian Chaplain Service

Royal Canadian Army Pay Corps

Note: for the sake of clarity, rank badges have been omitted from the drawings

5. The Tam O'Shanter and Caubeen

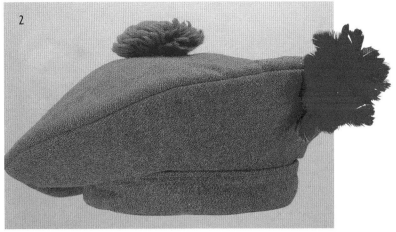

1

2

3

4

1. Tam O'Shanter with a green tuft and badges for the Highland Light Infantry of Canada.

2. Tam O'Shanter with the red plume particular to the Black Watch of Canada.

3. Tam O'Shanter sporting the cap badge of the 48th Highlanders of Canada, pinned onto a square of Davidson tartan.
(Overlord Collection)

4. Caubeen (Irish Bonnet), the traditional head dress of Irish regiments. It was worn leaning to the left, the cap badge was directly above the right eye fixed to a dark green silk rosette. In the field, the Caubeen was replaced by the Khaki Beret. Only soldiers on leave were allowed to wear it. The officers had a green, white and red plume worn above the cap badge (1943 Regulation)
(Overlord Collection)

Right:
The lining of a Tam O'Shanter (left) and Khaki Beret (right).
The name of the maker, the town where the company was located,
the head size and the light blue reception stamp can be seen. The Khaki
Beret, Black beret and Maroon Beret had two ventilation holes, on the right
side when the hat was worn.

Makers of cloth headgear

National Hat MFG Co
Grand Mère Knitting Co Ltd
Dorothea Hats Ltd Toronto
DMC. Cap MFG Co Ltd Winnipeg
William Scully Ltd Montreal
Hamilton Uniform Cap Co Ltd
The Principal Cap. Manuf. Co
Rogers-Rayman Industries Toronto
Adams Knitting Mills Toronto
Buffalo Cap
Beret Industries Ltd.
Bull Cap Winnipeg.

Tam O'Shanter
worn by Lt R.A.
Lindsay of the
Black Watch
of Canada
(2nd Canadian
Infantry
Division).
The cap badge
is replaced by a
red plume.
(RR)

Imperial and Metric Head sizes compared.	
6 1/2	53
6 5/8	54
6 3/4	55
6 7/8	56
7	57
7 1/8	58
7 1/4	59
7 3/8	60
7 1/2	61

6. WINTER HEAD-DRESS

Above:
Winter hats, cap and toque, worn normally in Canada and polar regions.

7. Coloured Field Service Cap

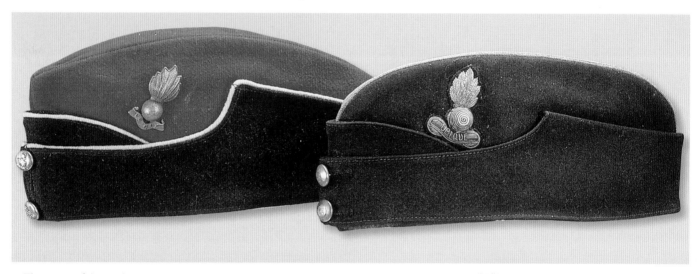

This type of hat, whose colours were chosen by the officer in charge of upholding unit traditions was the same shape as the Field Service Cap in khaki wool.

Regulated from 1943 onwards, its wear was optional, and at any rate only worn when on leave by personnel under the rank of Colonel. The Coloured Field Service Cap could only be acquired privately or with regimental funds. Made by hatters or regimental tailors, it was not part of the regulation issue and was not supplied by the RCAOC.

Insignia

Two buttons were placed on the front of the cap. They bore either the unit's distinctive design or were General Service brass buttons, with the Maple Leaf. Attached to the front left-hand side, the cap badge for officers was made of embroidered gold or silver thread. The soldiers wore their units metal badge. For officers, the braiding was of gold or silver thread (depending on which was specified) and for other ranks it was yellow or white cotton.

Above:
Officers' Coloured Field Service
Left: Royal Canadian Artillery ; right: Royal Canadian Engineers.

Right:
The traditional colours of the Régiment de la Chaudière were Maroon, silver (white) and scarlet. Originally these were the colours of the chasubles of the Canadian prelates chosen by the Pope to take part in the Conclave. *(Photo Musée du Régiment de la Chaudière)*

Coloured Field Service Caps. Cavalry/Canadian Armoured Corps
(Canadian War Dress Regulations May 1943)

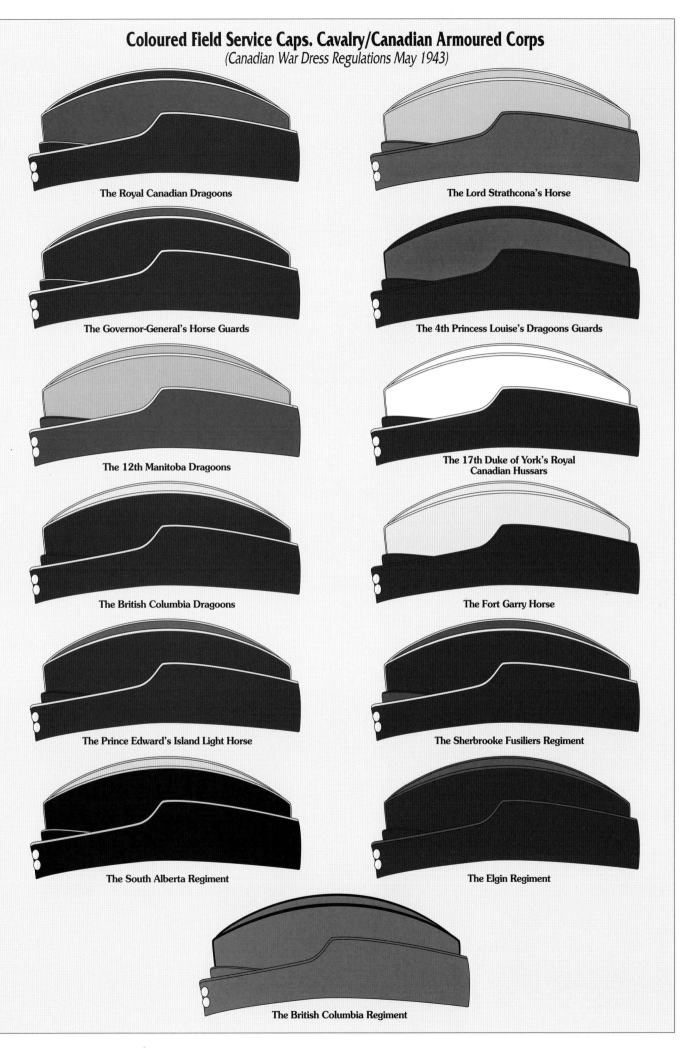

The Royal Canadian Dragoons

The Lord Strathcona's Horse

The Governor-General's Horse Guards

The 4th Princess Louise's Dragoons Guards

The 12th Manitoba Dragoons

The 17th Duke of York's Royal
Canadian Hussars

The British Columbia Dragoons

The Fort Garry Horse

The Prince Edward's Island Light Horse

The Sherbrooke Fusiliers Regiment

The South Alberta Regiment

The Elgin Regiment

The British Columbia Regiment

Coloured Field Service Caps - Arms and Services (1943 regulations, revised February 1944)

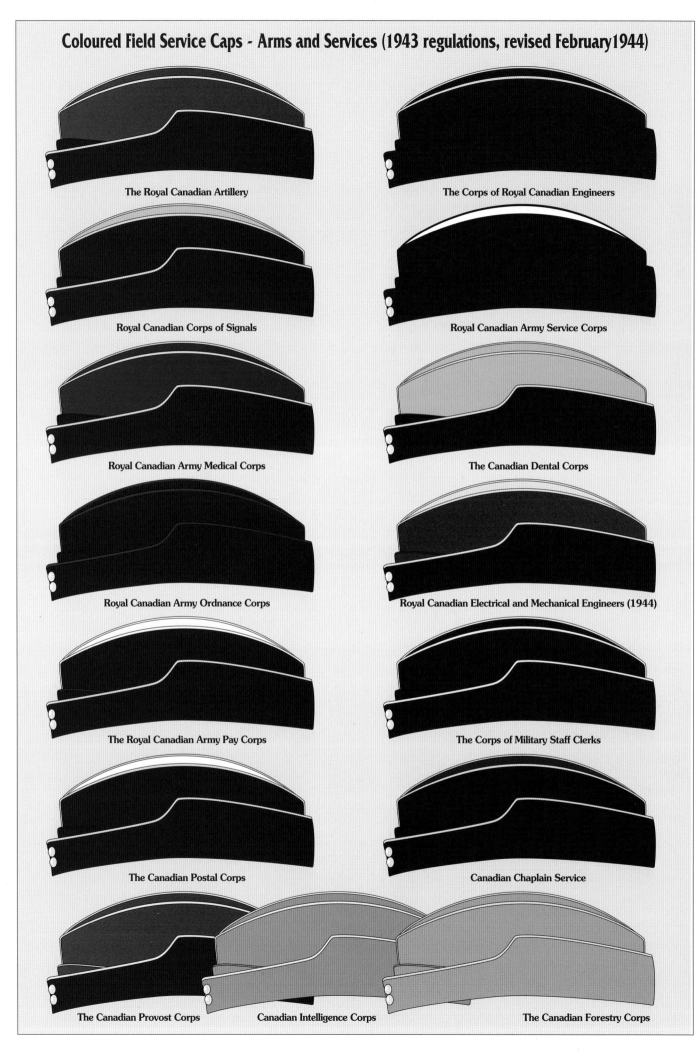

The Royal Canadian Artillery

The Corps of Royal Canadian Engineers

Royal Canadian Corps of Signals

Royal Canadian Army Service Corps

Royal Canadian Army Medical Corps

The Canadian Dental Corps

Royal Canadian Army Ordnance Corps

Royal Canadian Electrical and Mechanical Engineers (1944)

The Royal Canadian Army Pay Corps

The Corps of Military Staff Clerks

The Canadian Postal Corps

Canadian Chaplain Service

The Canadian Provost Corps

Canadian Intelligence Corps

The Canadian Forestry Corps

Coloured Field Service Caps - Foot Guards and Infantry

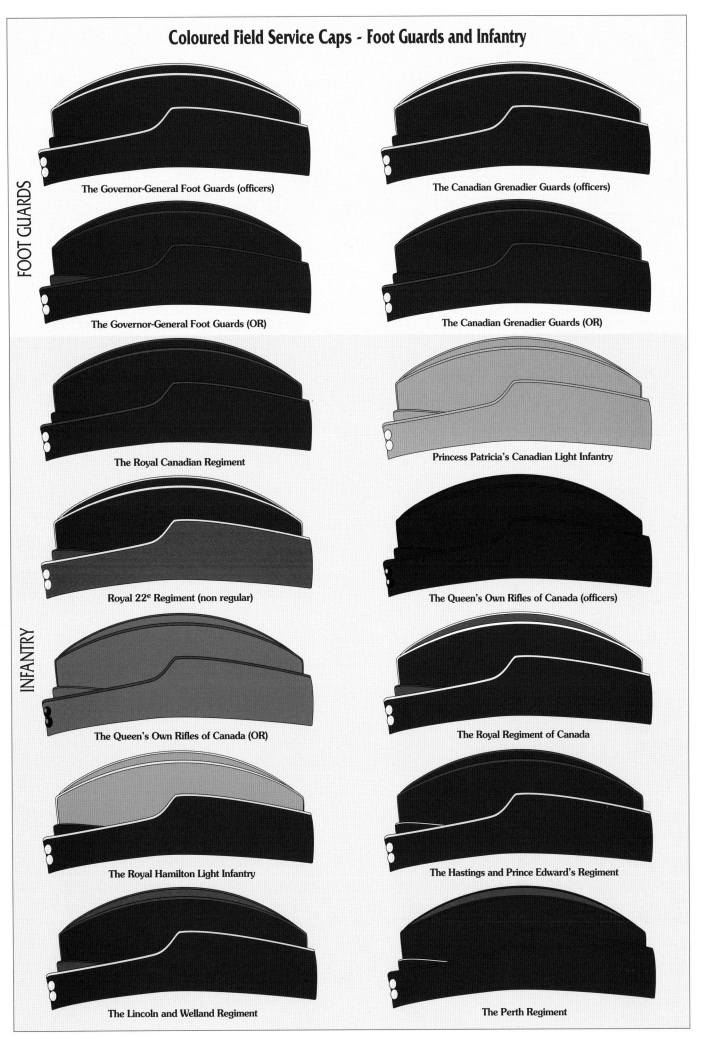

FOOT GUARDS

INFANTRY

The Governor-General Foot Guards (officers)

The Canadian Grenadier Guards (officers)

The Governor-General Foot Guards (OR)

The Canadian Grenadier Guards (OR)

The Royal Canadian Regiment

Princess Patricia's Canadian Light Infantry

Royal 22^e Regiment (non regular)

The Queen's Own Rifles of Canada (officers)

The Queen's Own Rifles of Canada (OR)

The Royal Regiment of Canada

The Royal Hamilton Light Infantry

The Hastings and Prince Edward's Regiment

The Lincoln and Welland Regiment

The Perth Regiment

Coloured Field Service Caps - Infantry

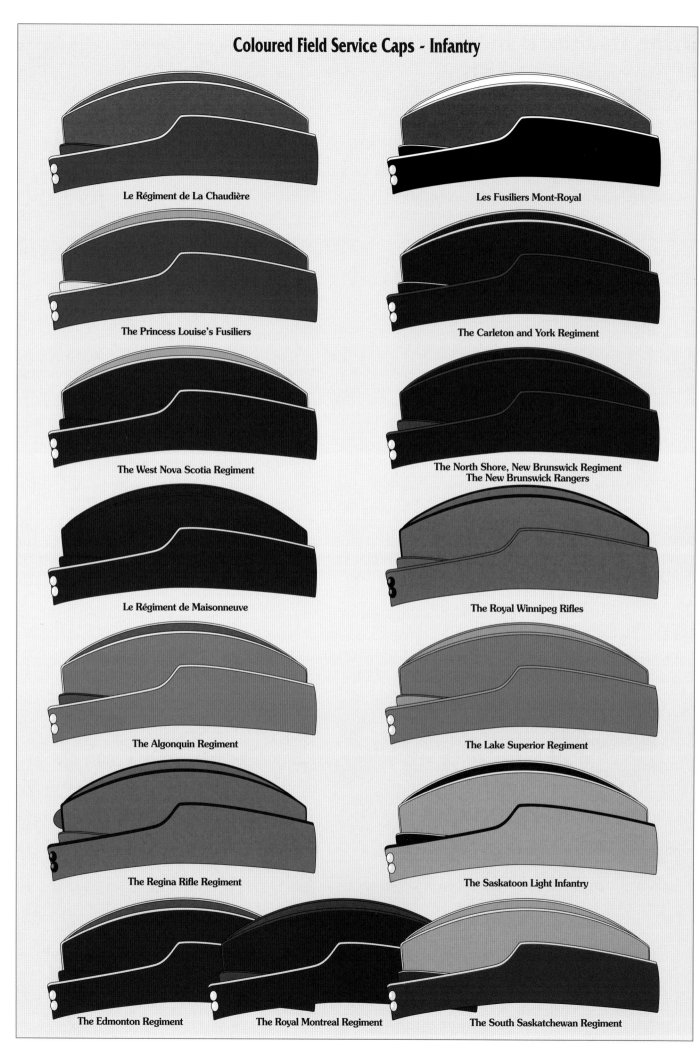

Le Régiment de La Chaudière

Les Fusiliers Mont-Royal

The Princess Louise's Fusiliers

The Carleton and York Regiment

The West Nova Scotia Regiment

The North Shore, New Brunswick Regiment
The New Brunswick Rangers

Le Régiment de Maisonneuve

The Royal Winnipeg Rifles

The Algonquin Regiment

The Lake Superior Regiment

The Regina Rifle Regiment

The Saskatoon Light Infantry

The Edmonton Regiment

The Royal Montreal Regiment

The South Saskatchewan Regiment

8. The Traditional Head-Dress of the Scottish and Irish Regiments

The Glengarry

This was the traditional head-dress of the regiments which recruited among the men of Scottish descent and was only worn by those officers above the rank of Lieutenant-Colonel. Although their regulation head gear was the Tam' O Shanter like all other ranks, Pipers and Drummers could, with special permission, wear the Glengarry during certain ceremonies.

Insignia

The cap badge was worn on the front left-hand side on a rosette or a simple black silk or rayon knot. The Black Watch wears its cap badge directly pinned to the Glengarry.

The Glengarry was made of wool cloth, the base of the cap was trimmed with black leather or ribbon. The cap was reinforced with canvas. The lining was made of Silesia cotton. There was a 1 1/2 inch split at the back, trimmed with black ribbon. On each side of the split there was a 12 inch strip of black ribbon. The free end of the ribbon was bevelled, the point thus formed pointing towards the outside.

A black ribbon rosette was placed on the left-hand side of the cap, measuring about 3 1/4 inches wide and 3 1/2 inches high ; the rosette was put about 1 1/2 inches from the front of the cap. The Black Watch's plain blue Glengarry did not have a rosette. A colored tuft was sewn on top of the cap.

Above, right:
A Glengarry worn by a private of the Cap-Breton Highlanders in going-out dress. (RR)

Above:
**Glengarries: left, Toronto Scottish ;
Centre, Calgary Highlanders ;
Right, Stormont, Dundas and Glengarry Highlanders.**

The Glengarries of the Canadian Scottish Regiments

1

2

3

4

5

1. Glengarry worn by the following regiments:
Black Watch of Canada
(Royal Highland Regiment) ;
Lanark and Renfrew Scottish Regiment ;
Cameron Highlanders of Ottawa [1] ;
Queen's own Cameron Highlanders
of Canada [1].
2. The Highland Light Infantry of Canada.
3. Cape Breton Highlanders ; Argyll and Sutherland Highlanders of Canada ; Calgary Highlanders.

4. Glengarries worn by:
Stormont Dundas and Glengarry
Highlanders ; North Nova Scotia
Highlanders ; Essex Scottish ;
48th Highlanders of Canada ;
Seaforth Highlanders of Canada;
Canadian Scottish Regiment ;
Lorne Scots.
5. The Toronto Scottish
Regiment.

[1]. With black cloth bow.

All badges worn by the Army had to be approved by National Defence Headquarters. Units committed overseas could obtain dispensations granted through Canadian Army Overseas Routine Orders. Regulation badges were issued by the Royal Canadian Army Ordnance Corps.

Normandy, 10 June 1944. Major E. Shelly of Civil Affairs, chatting to a little girl and her refugee grandmother. On his BD blouse, he is wearing the 'Canada' title and the Formation Signs of the 21st Army Group Lines of Communication.
(IWM)

1. Cap Badges

Every armoured or infantry regiment had its own insignia. The arms and support services had an insignia which was common to the whole corps.

How the Cap Badge was worn

The Cap Badge was worn fixed to the cap by two 'lugs' and a pin and on berets it was worn directly above the left eye; on the other hand, on Coloured Field Service Caps, Field Service Caps and Glengarries, it was affixed to the front left-hand side of the cap. The shape of the Tam O' Shanter meant that the badge had to be worn directly above the left temple.

The Caubeen was particular to the Irish Regiment of Canada and was worn tilted to the left, thus the cap badge was fixed directly above the right eye, on a dark green rayon rosette (see page 49).

Symbols

For infantry and armoured regiments, see page 25.

The Different Types of Badges

Cap Badges were copper, brass, white metal or bi-metal. Brass and white metal were the most commonly used. Private-purchase silver or silver bullion cap badges were sometimes worn by officers.

A plastic insignia was issued to the 1st Canadian Parachute battalion (see chapter on this unit, page 149).

ADGES

Above, left:
Infantry Corps Cap Badge worn on an instructor's Khaki beret.
(J. Garnier collection)

Above, right:
Major R.L. Houston, Royal Canadian Corps of Signals, was awarded the French Croix de Guerre with silver gilt Star for meritorious conduct during the campaign in North-west Europe. The cap badge is here pinned on the Corps of Signals dark blue badge backing. His Khaki Beret is private purchase.
(Canadian Army Overseas Photo)

Cap badge symbolism

1. Tudor Crown (Crown of the Kings of England) used during successive reigns from 1901 to 1952 (Edward VII, 1901-1910 ; George V 1910-1936 ; Edward VIII 1936 ; George VI, 1936-1952).

2. Queen's Crown (Victoria before 1901, then Elizabeth from 1952).

3. King George VI's monogram. He reigned during WWII.

4. Saint Andrew and his cross appeared on the badges of Scottish regiments.

5. The **harp** appears on the insignia of regiments with an Irish tradition.

6. The **Maple Leaf**, Canada's symbol. The regulation design, with its numerous serrations, was present on some badges, as well as on vehicles and machines.

7. Quebec's **Fleur de Lys.**

8. & 9. The **beaver** and **caribou** are native animals in Canada.

10. The **French horn**, with or without its cord, is a design specific to Rifle and Light Infantry regiments.

11. The **thistle** is one of Scotland's symbols.

12. The **flaming grenade** is specific to Fusilier and Grenadier regiments.

13. The **lion passant** of England is not to be confused with the Plantagenet leopards.

(RR)

GENERIC INSIGNIA

Left:

1. 21st Army Group. This sign was worn by Canadian personnel or units assigned to Army Group HQ.

2. 1st Canadian Army

3. 1st Canadian Army Artillery. 1st and 2nd RCA Groups.

4. Canadian Military Headquarters.

5. Lines of Communications Troops of the 21st Army Group.

6, 7 and 8. The 'Canada' titles worn on both sleeves of the battledress tunic when the word 'Canada' did not appear on the unit shoulder title.

ARMY ASSETS

Opposite page:

1. 25th Armoured Delivery Regiment (Canadian Armoured Corps). The Elgin Regiment was a crew and armoured vehicles replacement unit.

2. Lorne Scots. Its companies were used to provide security at division and brigade headquarters. The cap badge was worn on a square of Campbell of Argyll tartan.

3. Royal Montreal Regiment. Defence Battalion, 1st Canadian Army Headquarters.

4. 1st Corps.

5. Royal Canadian Artillery, 1st Corps.

6. 1st Corps Troops: 1st Armoured Car Regiment (Royal Canadian Dragoons)

7. 1st Light Anti-Aircraft Regiment (Lanark and Renfrewshire Regiment.) This regiment was affiliated to the Black Watch of Canada. The cap badge and backing were identical to these of the Black Watch.

8. II Corps.

9. Royal Canadian Artillery, II Corps.

10. II Corps Troops: 18th Armoured Car Regiment (12th Manitoba Dragoons)

11. II Corps Defence Company (Prince Edward Light Horse)

Makers of Cap Badges

The major Canadian badge companies of the time were W. Scully, Birks, McKenzie-Clay, Gaunt and Co. and Rodden Bros.

Badge Backings

The badge backing was a piece of cloth in the corps' or regiment's traditional colours worn behind the Cap badge (see table right). The badge backing was not compulsory, except for Highland and Scottish regiments and was left to the discretion of the corps commander.

2. Cloth Badges

Apart from hat badges, there was a wide range of regulation badges which enabled identification of the soldiers' corps or regiment, and formation. Other marks specific to certain corps could be added to them.

Shoulder Titles

Shoulder Titles were pieces of arc-shaped cloth bearing the name in full or the initials of the regiment, the arm or the service.

In Armoured and Infantry units, the title colours were chosen by a committee of regimental officers and those tasked with the upkeep of traditions.

(Continued page 67)

BADGE BACKINGS

	Royal Canadian Signals		Royal Canadian Army Ordnance Corps
	Canadian Infantry Corps		Royal Canadian Electrical and Mechanical Engineers
	Rifles		Royal Canadian Army Pay Corps
	Regina Rifles		Canadian Dental Corps
	Highland and Scottish Regiments (except Black Watch): regimental tartan		Corps of Military Staff Clerks
	Canadian Chaplain Service		Canadian Postal Corps
	Royal Canadian Army Service Corps		Canadian Provost Corps
	Royal Canadian Army Medical Corps		Canadian Forestry Corps

THE ELGIN REGIMENT

THE ROYAL MONTREAL REGIMENT

LORNE SCOTS CANADA

1

2

3

ROYAL CANADIAN DRAGOONS

LANARK AND RENFREW SCOTTISH CANADA

5

4

6

7

XII MANITOBA DRAGOONS CANADA

PRINCE EDWARD ISLAND LIGHT HORSE CANADA

8

9

10

11

CAP BADGES

1. Canadian Armoured Corps [1].
2. Royal Canadian Artillery [2].
2a. Grenade with seven flames (RCA).
3. Royal Canadian Engineers.
3a. Grenade with nine flames (RCE).
4. Royal Canadian Corps of Signals.
5. Canadian Infantry Corps.
6. Royal Canadian Army Service Corps.
7. Royal Canadian Army Medical Corps.
7a. RCAMC. Bullion embroidered badge for officers.
8. Canadian Army Dental Corps.
9. Royal Canadian Ordnance Corps.
10. Royal Corps of Canadian Electrical and Mechanical Engineers.
11. Royal Canadian Army Pay Corps.
12. Corps of Military Staff Clerks.
13. Canadian Postal Corps.
14. Canadian Chaplain Service (Christian denomination).
15. Canadian Chaplain Service (Jewish denomination).
16. Canadian Provost Corps.
17. Royal Canadian Mounted Police (CPC, 1st Company).
18. Canadian Women's Army Corps.
19. Canadian Intelligence Corps.
20. Canadian Forestry Corps.
21. General List, officers.
22. General List, Other Ranks.

SHOULDER TITLES

1. Canadian Armoured Corps.
2. Royal Canadian Artillery. Generic insignia and examples of shoulder strap slip-ons. 1st Survey Regiment, 1st Anti-Tank Regt., 4th Medium Regt (4.5 & 5.5-inch gun).
3. Royal Canadian Engineers
3a. Variant.
4. Royal Canadian Corps of Signals, 2nd Division, First type.
4a. Royal Canadian Corps of Signals, Shoulder title.
5. Canadian Infantry Corps.
6. Royal Canadian Army Service Corps.
7. Royal Canadian Army Medical Corps.
8. Canadian Army Dental Corps
9. Royal Canadian Ordnance Corps.
10. Royal Corps of Canadian Electrical and Mechanical Engineers.
10a. Variant for the 2nd Division.
11. Royal Canadian Army Pay Corps
12. Corps of Military Staff Clerks.
13. Canadian Postal Corps.
14 & 15. Canadian Chaplain Service. Title common to all confessions.
16. Canadian Provost Corps.
17. Royal Canadian Mounted Police (CPC).
18. Canadian Women's Army Corps
19. Canadian Intelligence Corps
20. Canadian Forestry Corps.

1. Insignia worn by depot and training centres personnel as well by men assigned to equipment testing.
2. Cap Badge identical to that of the British Royal Artillery since George V's 1926 decision to reward the action of this arm during WWI. The motto *Ubique* replaced *Canada*. The flaming grenade was normally worn on the Khaki Beret and on the Coloured Field Service Cap. It was placed in exactly the same manner as that of the 9-flame grenade of the Royal Canadian Engineers.

Major E.C. Scott of the Royal Canadian Artillery was awarded the French Croix de Guerre with silver gilt Star for meritorious conduct during the campaign in North-west Europe. On the beret, the Artillery's seven-flame grenade replaced the large-sized badge (No 2 on the plate opposite).
(Canadian Army Overseas Photo)

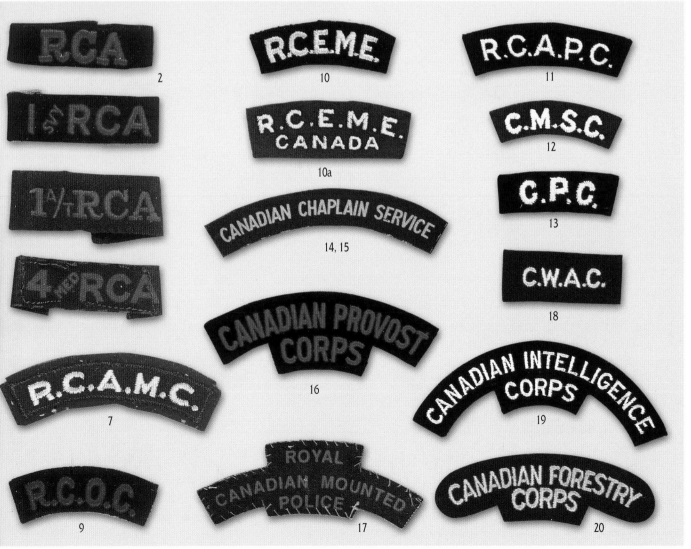

61

1st INFANTRY DIVISION

1. Divisional sign.
1a. Variant with '*Canada*'.
2. 4th Reconnaissance Regiment, Princess Louise IVth Dragoon Guards.
3. Saskatoon Light Infantry, MG (Support Battalion).

1st Infantry Brigade
4. Royal Canadian Regiment.
5. Hastings and Prince Edward Regiment.
6. 48th Highlanders of Canada.

2nd Infantry Brigade
7. Princess Patricia's Canadian Light Infantry.
8. Seaforth Highlanders of Canada.
9. Loyal Edmonton Regiment.

3rd Infantry Brigade
10. Royal 22ᵉ Régiment.
11. Carleton and York Regiment.
12. West Nova Scotia Regiment.

2nd INFANTRY DIVISION

1. Divisional sign.
1a. Variant for officers.
2. 8th Canadian Reconnaissance Regiment, 14th Canadian Hussars.
2a. Regimental flash.
3. Toronto Scottish Regiment, MG (Support Battalion).

4th Infantry Brigade
4. Royal Regiment of Canada.
5. Royal Hamilton Light Infantry.
6. Essex Scottish Regiment.

5th Infantry Brigade
7. Black Watch (Royal Highland Regiment of Canada) [1]
8. Régiment de Maisonneuve.
9. Calgary Highlanders.

6th Infantry Brigade
10. Fusiliers Mont-Royal.
11. Queen's Own Cameron Highlanders of Canada.
12. 12th South Saskatchewan Regiment.

The shoulder titles presented here were worn after the end of 1942, after the Dieppe affair on 19 August. See Chapter on the Dieppe Raid on page 154.

1. The Cap badge was worn only on the Glengarry. It was replaced by a red plume on the Tam O' Shanter.

63

3rd INFANTRY DIVISION

1. Divisional sign.
2. 7th Reconnaissance Regiment,
(17th Duke of York's Royal Canadian
Hussars).
3. Cameron Highlanders of Ottawa, MG
(Support Battalion)

7th Infantry Brigade

4. Royal Winnipeg Rifles.
5. Regina Rifle Regiment.
6. 1st Battalion Canadian cottish
Regiment.

8th Infantry Brigade

7. Queen's Own Rifles of Canada.
8. Le Régiment de la Chaudière.
9. North Shore (New Brunswick)
Regiment.

9th Infantry Brigade

10. Highland Light Infantry of Canada.
11. Stormont, Dundas and Glengarry
Highlanders.
12. North Nova Scotia Highlanders.

Below.
Major Lamoureux, January 1945.
(Régiment de la Chaudière Museum)

4th ARMOURED DIVISION

1. Divisional sign.
2. 29th Armoured Reconnaissance Regiment (South Alberta Regiment).
3. 10th Independent Machine Gun Company, New Brunswick Rangers (Support Company).

4th Armoured Brigade

4. 21st Armoured Regiment, Governor General's Foot Guards.
5. 22nd Armoured Regiment, Canadian Grenadier Guards.
6. 28th Armoured Regiment, British Columbia Regiment.
7. Lake Superior Regiment.

10th Infantry Brigade

8. Lincoln and Welland Regiment.
9. Algonquin Regiment.
10. Argyll and Sutherland Highlanders of Canada.

5th ARMOURED DIVISION
1. Divisional sign.
2. 3rd Armoured Reconnaissance Regiment, Governor General's Horse Guards.
3. 11th Independent Machine Gun Company, Princess Louise Fusiliers (Support Company).

5th Armoured Brigade
4. 2nd Armoured Regiment Lord Strathcona's Horse Royal Canadians.
5. 5th Armoured Regiment, 8th Princess Louise's New Brunswick Hussars.
6. 9th Armoured Regiment, British Columbia Dragoons.
7. Westminster Regiment

11th Infantry Brigade
8. The Perth Regiment.
9. The Cape Breton Highlanders.
10. The Irish Regiment of Canada.

On his black Canadian Armoured Corps beret, Trooper Jed Redman is wearing the British Columbia Dragoons Cap Badge (9th Armoured Regiment)
(Xavier Sieur collection)

3. Shoulder Titles

The Royal Canadian Artillery was the only regiment not to adopt shoulder titles, it replaced them with shoulder loops bearing the number of the regiment and initials indicating its function (**SVY** for Survey, **AT** for Anti-Tank, **MED** for Medium Regiment - medium calibre artillery - etc., see the examples on page 61).

Shoulder titles were adopted gradually during the war. Some regiments however - Foot Guards, Princess Patricia's Canadian Light Infantry and the Canadian Provost Corps - already had this type of badge at the time Canada entered the war. The units of the 1st and 3rd Infantry Divisions already had them when they arrived in Great Britain, as did the 4th Armoured Division at the time it was set up. The 2nd Infantry Division adopted the titles at the end of 1942 [1]. The 5th Armoured Division was the last to abandon the combined divisional insignia (formation sign and names or initials of the regiment), from the summer of 1944. At the time it was transferred to the North-west European front, its units as a whole had standard shaped shoulder titles.

1st Independent Canadian Armoured Brigade

1 - Formation sign.
2 - 11th Armoured Regiment (Ontario Regiment).
3 - 12th Armoured Regiment (Three Rivers Regiment).
4 - 14th Armoured Regiment (Calgary Regiment).

1. See page 157

2nd Independent Canadian Armoured Brigade

1 - Formation sign.
2 - 6th Armoured Regiment (1st Hussars).
3 - 10th Armoured Regiment (Fort Garry Horse).
4 - 27th Armoured Regiment (Sherbrooke Fusilier Regiment).

ARMS AND SERVICES SPECIAL ARM FLASHES

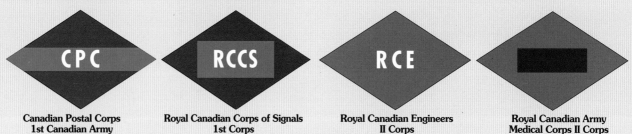

Flashes patterns combining the divisional sign and identification of divisional support elements, in this case for the 3rd Infantry Division. The background colour was that of the divisional sign: French grey for the 3rd Div., scarlet for the 1st Division, etc.

1. RCE (Royal Canadian Engineers), 3rd Infantry Division.
2. RCCS (Royal Canadian Corps of Signals), 3rd Infantry Division.
3. RCASC (Royal Canadian Army Service Corps), 3rd Infantry Division
4. RCAMC (Royal Canadian Army Medical Corps), 3rd Infantry Division.
5. RCOC (Royal Canadian Ordnance Corps), 3rd Infantry Division.
6. CDC (Canadian Dental Corps), 3rd Infantry Division.
7. CPC (Canadian Provost Corps), 3rd Infantry Division.

Below: **Similar flashes worn before shoulder titles were adopted, at the top of the Battledress tunic sleeves. These identified support units assigned to the 1st Canadian Army, and to I and II Canadian Army Corps. The Royal Canadian Artillery adopted a special design instead of initials (see patch No 3 page 58)**

(After Canadian Army Formation Signs, *by C.A. Edwards)*

Canadian Postal Corps 1st Canadian Army

Royal Canadian Corps of Signals 1st Corps

Royal Canadian Engineers II Corps

Royal Canadian Army Medical Corps II Corps

Left.
Examples of battle patches:

1. and 2. The Perth Regiment and the Westminster Regiment were units in the 5th Canadian Armoured Division (dark red rectangle). These patches were worn until July 1944 when the division finally standardised its shoulder titles. In the case of these two regiments, the new titles are illustrated on page 66, figs. 7 and 8.
3. Royal Canadian Corps of Signals/3rd Infantry Division. The RCCS was one of the last corps to adopt shoulder titles.

4. Royal Canadian Army Medical Corps, 2nd Armoured Brigade

BRIGADE BARS

1st Brigade (Senior)	2nd Brigade (Second)	3rd Brigade (Junior)

The different types of shoulder titles

The insignia embroidered on a felt background were British- or Canadian-made. The insignia printed on canvas were British-made, according to specifications issued by the Royal Canadian Army Ordnance Corps.

4. Formation Signs (Battle Patches)

These were geometrical shapes indicating to which unit the soldier belonged. Lozenges arranged horizontally were reserved for army and army corps units and to the Independent Armoured Brigades. Rectangles identified divisions. Before shoulder titles were introduced, the formation signs of certain units also bore the initials and the distinctive colours of the arms and services.

5. Brigade Stripes

The brigade bars were strips of cloth sewn above the Formation Sign and worn by officers assigned to the Brigade headquarters. This scheme was not however systematically respected in all the big units.

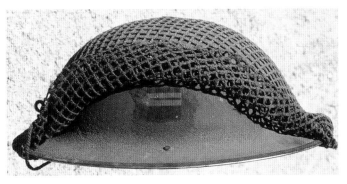

Above: **Mk II Helmet (made by GSW) with the insignia of the 1st RCOC Reinforcement Unit.** *(Author's Collection)*

Below: **Soldiers of the Régiment de la Chaudière guarding German PoWs after the end of hostilities. The grey-blue cloth stripe of the occupation forces has been sewn under the divisional sign.** *(J. Garnier)*

WARTIME REINFORCEMENT UNITS

 1st Division Reinforcement Unit

 1st Royal Canadian Engineers Reinforcement Unit

 2nd Division Reinforcement Unit

 1st RCCorps of Signals Reinforcement Unit

 3rd Division Reinforcement Unit

 1st RCArmy Service Corps Reinforcement Unit

 1st Canadian Armoured Corps Reinforcement Unit

 1st RCArmy Medical Corps Reinforcement Unit

 1st RCArtillery Reinforcement Unit

 1st RCOrdnance Corps Reinforcement Unit

Wartime reinforcement units were tasked with training of reinforcement personnel. Operating first in Canada, they were then transferred to the theatre of operations where they continued their activities in liaison with the units on the line.

Special Insignia: a yellow 2 1/2 inch cloth disk with the colours, signs or initials of the arm of the service.

These patches were worn on both sleeves of the Battledress blouse, and sometimes on the steel helmet. (see example, top left).

Above, left:
Canadian Forces Occupation of Germany, 1945-46.
Made up for the main part of units from the 3rd Infantry Division, the Canadian occupation troops in Germany kept the unit's French gray (blue-grey) formation sign;
a stripe of the same colour was added under the patch.
(Jocelyn Garnier and Alain Brogniez collections)

Above, right:
Canadian Army Pacific Force (CAPF). This unit was created after the end of hostilities in Europe in May 1945. It was made up of volunteer personnel from all units who wished to continue the war against Japan. The colours of the hexagon were those of the five divisions which had fought in Europe, the black symbolising the Independent Armoured Brigades.
(Ed Storey collection)

6. Rank Insignia, Lanyards, cloth armbands, proficiency badges and other service or good conduct badges

RANK IN THE CANADIAN ARMY — OFFICERS

		Rank	Appointment	
COMMISSIONED OFFICERS	GENERAL OFFICERS	Field Marshall	No Field Marshall in the Canadian Army at this time	
		General	Army	A
		Lieutenant General	Corps-	A
		Major General	Division	A
	SENIOR OFFICERS	Brigadier	Brigade	A
		Colonel	Staff Officer, Medical Officer (RCAMC)	A
	FIELD OFFICERS	Lieutenant-Colonel	Commanding Officer: Battalion, Regiment. Field Command.	A
		Major	Company commander, Squadron Commander. (Battalion, Regiment)	A
		Captain	Second in Command (Company, squadron - Mortar platoon commander or Carriers platoon commander)	A
	JUNIOR OFFICERS	Lieutenant	Platoon Commander (Infantry) or Troop Leader	A
		Second Lieutenant	Platoon Commander (Infantry) or Troop Leader	A

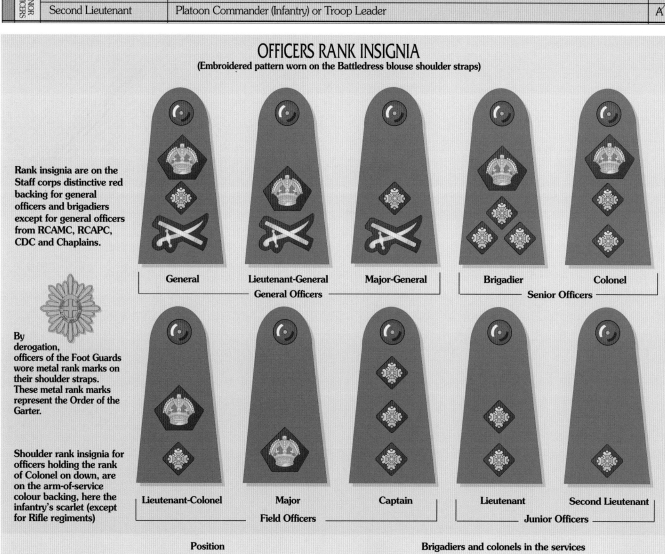

OFFICERS RANK INSIGNIA
(Embroidered pattern worn on the Battledress blouse shoulder straps)

Rank insignia are on the Staff corps distinctive red backing for general officers and brigadiers except for general officers from RCAMC, RCAPC, CDC and Chaplains.

By derogation, officers of the Foot Guards wore metal rank marks on their shoulder straps. These metal rank marks represent the Order of the Garter.

Shoulder rank insignia for officers holding the rank of Colonel on down, are on the arm-of-service colour backing, here the infantry's scarlet (except for Rifle regiments)

General — Lieutenant-General — Major-General — General Officers

Brigadier — Colonel — Senior Officers

Lieutenant-Colonel — Major — Captain — Field Officers

Lieutenant — Second Lieutenant — Junior Officers

General officers, brigadiers and colonels gorget patches worn on Battledress

* Only the button design denotes the exact rank.

Position

General Officers*

Brigadiers and colonels

5 cm

Brigadiers and colonels in the services

RCAMC

RAPC

CDC

Canadian Chaplain Service

BACKGROUND COLOURS
FOR OFFICERS' EMBROIDERED RANK INSIGNIA

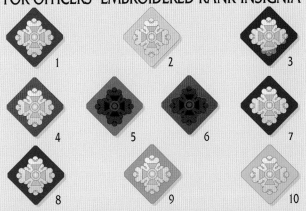

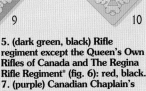

1. (red) Generals, brigadiers and colonels except for officers of those ranks in the RCAMC, RCAPC, CDC and Chaplains.
- Royal Canadian Artillery.
- Canadian Provost Corps.
- Royal Canadian Army Ordnance Corps.
2. (yellow) Cavalry/Canadian Armoured Corps.
- Royal Canadian Army Service Corps.
- Royal Canadian Army Pay Corps.
- Corps of Military Staff Clerks.
3. (blue) Royal Canadian Engineers.
- Royal Canadian Signals.
- Canadian Postal Corps.
4. (scarlet) Infantry, except Rifle regiments.
- General List.
- Canadian Officer Training Corps.

5. (dark green, black) Rifle regiment except the Queen's Own Rifles of Canada and The Regina Rifle Regiment* (fig. 6): red, black.
7. (purple) Canadian Chaplain's Service.
8. (dull cherry) Royal Canadian Army Medical Corps.
9. (emerald green) Canadian Dental Corps.
10. (green) Canadian Forestry Corps.

* Regiment affiliated to the British King's Royal Rifle Corps.
Note. The insignia used as an example here is the 'pip' star-shaped rank badge ; coloured backgrounds were also applicable to the other rank insignia described previous page.

THE LANYARDS

From 1939 to 1945, corps and regiments were permitted to adopt coloured lanyards, worn on the Battledress tunic. The officers used this cord for attaching their whistles and the soldiers for their knives.

Not every unit adopted a distinctive lanyard, which was often only worn when the soldier went on leave. The hand gun was attached to the regulation khaki lanyard.

Extract from the May 1943 War Regulations

'The colour of the whistle lanyard and the way in which it is worn on the uniform is left to the discretion of the commanding officer, on condition that all the officers (of the unit) abide with his instructions. Lanyards for the pocket knives and the officers' pistol are regulation khaki.

'The pocket knife lanyard and the whistle lanyard are of the type and colour determined by the quartermaster. However, the unit commander can allow the men to wear a pocket knife lanyard in the same colour as that of the officers' whistle lanyard, provided that these are bought personally. The Quartermaster only issues khaki lanyards.

'If a unit decides to adopt a whistle lanyard for its officers and a knife cord for other ranks in colours other than khaki, a sample of this accessory or a sketch, must be sent National Defence Headquarters for approval before distribution.'

Normandy, July 1944, Capt. H. Jones of the Regina Rifles, right, is wearing the black lanyard of the Rifle regiments on his left shoulder.

Coloured unit lanyards

1. 48th Highlanders of Canada (officers); Canadian Provost Corps (right sleeve)
2. Highland Light Infantry of Canada.
3. Irish Regiment of Canada.
4. Lake Superior Regiment.
5. Princess Louise's Fusiliers.
6. Queen's own Rifles of Canada.
7. Regina Rifle Regiment and Royal Winnipeg Rifles.
8. Le Régiment de La Chaudière.
9. 7th Reconnaissance Regiment (17th Duke of York's Royal Canadian Hussars).
10. 18th Canadian Armoured Car Regiment (12th Manitoba Dragoons).
11. Prince Edward Island Light Horse.
12. 1st Canadian Armoured Car Regiment (Royal Canadian Dragoons).
13. 14th Armoured Regiment (The Calgary Regiment).
14. Le Régiment de Maisonneuve (officers).
15. Saskatoon Light Infantry (Other ranks).
16. South Alberta Regiment.
17. Royal Canadian Artillery (right sleeve). 3rd Canadian Division Artillery personnel wear a red mixed with blue lanyard.
18. Royal Canadian Army Medical Corps.
19. Canadian Dental Corps
20. Royal Canadian Army Service Corps.

(Information taken from www.canadiansoldiers.com and from the works of Clive M. Law published by Service Publications.

WARRANT OFFICERS, SERGEANTS and CORPORALS RANK INSIGNIA

Staff Sergeant-Major

Warrant Officer Class I

Warrant Officer Class II

**Staff Sergeant,
Company Quarter-Master Sergeant**

Sergeant

Corporal

Lance-Corporal

REGULATION LAYOUT of INSIGNIA ON BATTLEDRESS BLOUSE SLEEVES

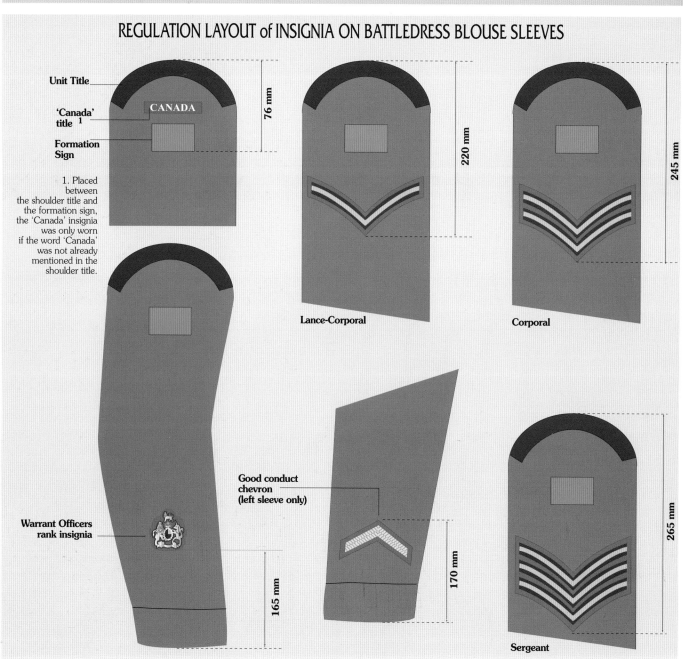

Unit Title

'Canada' title [1]

CANADA

Formation Sign

1. Placed between the shoulder title and the formation sign, the 'Canada' insignia was only worn if the word 'Canada' was not already mentioned in the shoulder title.

76 mm

220 mm

245 mm

Lance-Corporal

Corporal

Warrant Officers rank insignia

Good conduct chevron (left sleeve only)

165 mm

170 mm

265 mm

Sergeant

RANK INSIGNIA IN REGIMENTAL COLOURS

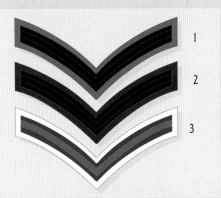

1. **Rifles Regiments:** (black on dark green).

2. **Queen's Own Rifles and Regina Rifles (Regiments affiliated to the British King's Royal Rifle Corps):** black on scarlet.

3. **Saskatoon Light Infantry (affiliated to the British King's Own Yorkshire Light Infantry):** green on white. The example here is that of a Lance-Corporal, but the colours were applicable to all rank insignia.

Warrant Officers and Other ranks

Warrant-Officers (WOs) were an intermediate class between officers and the NCOs and rank and file. Their warrant was granted by the War Office.

Unit strength was often indicated by using simple initials: OF for Officers, OR for Other Ranks including the Warrant Officers, NCOs and rank and file. Depending on his appointment, private soldiers was called as follows:

Infantry (other than Guards, Rifles, Fusiliers, parachutists and others): *Private.*
Foot Guards: *Guardsman.*
Rifles: *Rifleman.*
Fusiliers (Regiments): *Fusilier.*
Canadian Armoured Corps, cavalry, Armour: *Trooper.*
Royal Canadian Artillery: *Gunner.*
Royal Canadian Engineers: *Sapper.*
Royal Canadian Corps of Signals: *Signalman.*
Royal Canadian Electrical and Mechanical Engineers: *Craftsman.*
Royal Canadian Army Service Corps: *Driver.*

Special rank insignia for Sergeants in the Engineers and Artillery

Sergeant, Royal Canadian Engineers

Sergeant, Royal Canadian Artillery

RANK IN THE CANADIAN ARMY - WARRANT OFFICERS, SERGEANTS and CORPORALS

	Rank	Appointment	
NON-COMMISSIONED OFFICERS (NCOs)	Warrant Officer, Class I	Staff Sergeant-Major; Garrison Sergeant-Major (all arms); Master Gunner 1st, 2nd Class (RCA).	B
	Warrant Officer, Class I	Regimental Sergeant-Major (RSM). Unit administration, school, regimental bandmaster	B
	Warrant Officer, Class II	Company Sergeant-Major (CSM); Regimental Quarter-Master Sergeant (RQMS)	B
	Warrant Officer, Class III	Abolished in 1944	
	Staff Sergeant	Company Quarter-Master Sergeant (CQMS), Administration - supply	C
	Sergeant	Platoon second in command or Troop second in command (RAC); Lance-Sergeant: acting Sergeant	C
	Corporal	Infantry Section Leader, Gun section leader, tank commander	C
	Lance-Corporal	Bren LMG section leader, Mortar section leader).	C

Position of rank insignia on the Battledress

Right:
Holland, May 1945.
War in Germany has ended with the defeat of Nazi Germany. On this Ford Mk I Universal Carrier, these Canucks have chalked where they have been and their happiness to be going home. These Seaforth Highlanders of Canada are veterans of the Italian and Dutch campaigns. They are all wearing the traditional Tam O' Shanter of the Canadian Scottish regiments. The cap badge is pinned onto a McKenzie tartan backing. These backings, made from discarded kilts, were supplied as soon as the unit landed in Great Britain by the Seaforth Highlanders, the parent regiment. The regulation position of rank and unit insignia can be clearly seen. on the sleeves of the man standing on the left, and of the Sergeant.
(Private collection)

WINGS, PROFICIENCY, TRADE AND MISC. BADGES

awarded to Canadian personnel stationed in Great Britain[1]

Badge position on the blouse (see diagram at bottom left)

Insignia	Private	NCOs	WOs
1. Musketry Instructor, sharpshooter	D	B/E	C/D
2. Stretcher bearer	B/E	B/E	
3. Heavy machine gunner	D	D	
4. Artillery Instructor (NCOs)		D	D
5. Artillery Instructor (WOs)		D	D
6. Mechanic, Armourer, Bomb Disposal.	B	B	B
7. Signalman, Instructor (RCCS)	D	B	B
8. Physical Training Instructor		B/E	B/E
9, 10 and 11. Non-combatant Specialists: clerks, cooks, storemen, etc.	B/E	B/E	
12. Anti-Tank gunner (Infantry battalion)	D	D	
13. Rangetaker, (RCA)	D	D	
14. Light Mortarman	D	D	
15. Layer, (RCA)	D	D	
16. Surveyor, (RCA)	B	B	
17. Bren Gunner	D	D	
18. Driving Instructor	D	D	D
19. Driver	D	D	D
20. Musician	B	B	C
21. Bugler	B	B	C
22. Drummer	B	B	C
23. Piper	B	B	C
24. Trumpeter	B	B	C
25. Radio Operator	B	B	C
26. Radio repairs (RCOC)	B	B	C
27. Despatch Rider	D		
28. Bren Carrier Driver	D		
29. Motorcyclist	D		
30. Armoured Regiments and Instructor in the Canadian Armoured Corps	B	B	B
31. Qualified Paratrooper [2]	A	A	A
32. Armoured vehicle driver (worn above insignia No 30)	B		

PROFICIENCY BADGES WORN ONLY IN CANADA

33. Trained Soldier (six months' course)	C	C	C
34. Volunteer for Overseas Service (General Service), replaced by the ribbon of the Canadian Volunteer Service Medal (page 81) on leaving Canada.	C	C	C
35. Tradesman: Lance-Corporal, Lance-Bombardier, Private (Grade III) [3]			
36. Tradesman (Specialist): Lane-Sergeant, Corporal, Bombardier Tradesman: (Grade II)		B/E	B/E
37. Instructor, Cadre.		B/E	C/D
38. Tradesman ; Sergeant and higher ranks (Grade I) [3]		B/E	C/B

1. These were badges usually awarded after undergoing training courses in British Training centres and tolerated by the Canadian Overseas Forces Command.
2. A specifically Canadian badge.
3. These badges corresponded to a great variety of trades. Grade II Tradesmen could be, for instance, driving Instructors, signals instructors, radio technicians, etc.

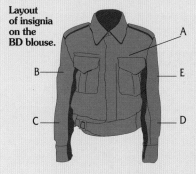

Layout of insignia on the BD blouse.

Private Maurice Caron
of the Régiment de la Chaudière
(3rd Division) wearing the insignia
of a qualified driver on his left sleeve.
(J. Garnier)

Above, from left to right:

– Battledress blouse of a Lieutenant-Colonel in the Canadian Scottish, 3rd Infantry Division. It bears seniority chevrons showing five years' service after September 1939 (red) plus one year before September 1939 (tan).
(R. Le Chantoux collection)

– Warrant Officer Class II's battledress blouse, West Nova Scotia Regiment, 1st Infantry Division. It shows seniority chevrons indicating four years' service after September 1939 (red) together with one year pre-September 1939 (tan).
(R. Le Chantoux collection)

– Battledress of a Private in the Essex Scottish, 2nd Infantry Division. On the bottom of the left sleeve, it bears, from top to bottom:
  – a good conduct chevron.
  – the unofficial qualification insignia for a 'Driver, Mechanical.'
  – two wound stripes (gilt metal).
The service ribbons are, from left to right, the 39/45 Star, the Defence medal, the Canadian Voluntary Service Medal with Maple Leaf indicating that the recipient was a volunteer for overseas service.
(Overlord Sarl collection)

Regulation Badges Position (Recapitulation)

	Battledress blouse	Great-coat	Denim overalls/ tank suit	Denison Smock
Rank insignia	●	●	1	2
Shoulder titles	●			
Formation Sign	●	●		
'Canada' Title	3	●		
Wings, Proficiency and trade badges	●			4
Good Conduct Chevrons	●			
Service Chevrons	●			
Wound Stripes	●			
Decorations (Service ribbons)	●			

1. Not attached permanently. For Warrant Officers and Other Ranks, worn on an arm-band worn on the right arm. For officers, on shoulder straps slip-ons.
2. Right sleeve only, for WOs and ORs.
3. Only for units whose shoulder title did not already include the word 'Canada'.
4. Parachutist's wings only. Above the left hand pocket.

GOOD CONDUCT AND SERVICE CHEVRONS

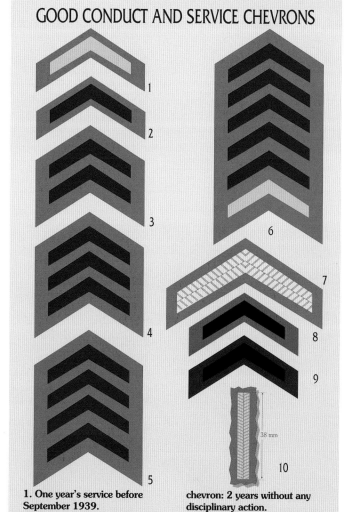

1. One year's service before September 1939.
2. One year's service after September 1939.
3. Two years' service.
4. Three years' service.
5. Four Year's service.
6. Five year's service plus one year before 9 September 1939.
7. Good conduct chevrons. - One chevron: 2 years without any disciplinary action.
- Two Chevrons: 5 years without disciplinary action.
8. Good conduct chevron for Rifle regiments.
9. Good conduct chevron for the Regina Rifles and the Queen's Own Rifles of Canada.
10. Wound stripe.

ARMBANDS

The 1943 Regulations specified several dozen armbands of different types. Only a small selection is shown here. Armbands were worn on duty only on the battledress blouse or greatcoat.

Except for the Red Cross armband which must be permanently sewn on, the other armbands were removable.

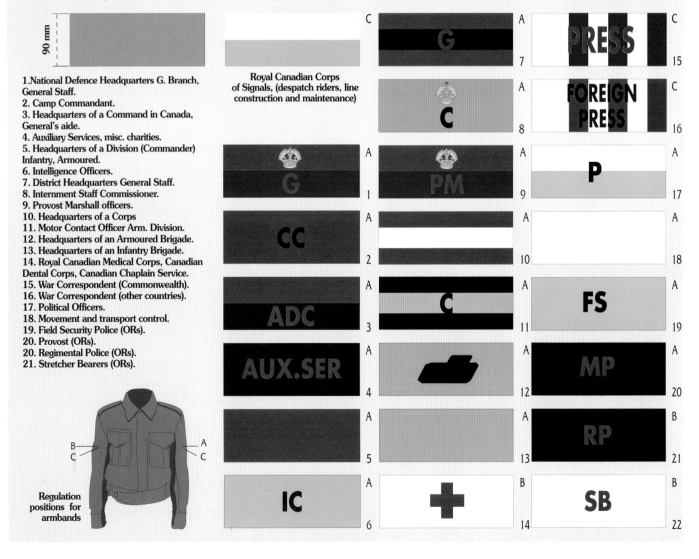

90 mm

1. National Defence Headquarters G. Branch, General Staff.
2. Camp Commandant.
3. Headquarters of a Command in Canada, General's aide.
4. Auxiliary Services, misc. charities.
5. Headquarters of a Division (Commander) Infantry, Armoured.
6. Intelligence Officers.
7. District Headquarters General Staff.
8. Internment Staff Commissioner.
9. Provost Marshall officers.
10. Headquarters of a Corps
11. Motor Contact Officer Arm. Division.
12. Headquarters of an Armoured Brigade.
13. Headquarters of an Infantry Brigade.
14. Royal Canadian Medical Corps, Canadian Dental Corps, Canadian Chaplain Service.
15. War Correspondent (Commonwealth).
16. War Correspondent (other countries).
17. Political Officers.
18. Movement and transport control.
19. Field Security Police (ORs).
20. Provost (ORs).
20. Regimental Police (ORs).
21. Stretcher Bearers (ORs).

Royal Canadian Corps of Signals, (despatch riders, line construction and maintenance)

Regulation positions for armbands

CHAPTER 4 DECORATIONS AND AWARDS

Decorations awarded to Canadian soldiers were the same that rewarded British soldiers with the exception of the Canadian Volunteer Service Medal.

Decorations for Bravery

- **Victoria Cross** (1): Exceptional behaviour under direct enemy fire (see table p. 81 for VCs awarded to Canadian soldiers)
- **George Cross** (2) and **George Medal** (12): Decorations for valour in civilian defence. They may be awarded to the military involved in air raid precautions, rescue, bomb disposal, etc.
- **Distinguished Service Order** (9): Remarkable conduct under fire in a commanding role.
- **Military Cross** (10), **Distinguished Conduct Medal** (11) and **Military Medal** (13): Remarkable individual behaviour under fire.

Successive awards of the same medal were represented by a bar. This bar was worn with the ribbon when the medal was worn in full. On the ribbon alone, the bar was replaced by a silver or silver metal rose (this device concerned decorations 1, 9, 10, 11 and 13.)

Orders

Order of the Bath (3), **Order of Merit** (4), **Order of Saint Michael and Saint George** (5), **Royal Victorian Order** (6), **Order of the British Empire** (7), **Order of the Companions of Honour** (8), **British Empire Medal** (14): distinctions awarded for outstanding service rendered to the British Empire.

Campaign Stars and Commemorative Medals

1914 Star (15), **1914-1915 Star** (16), **British War Medal 1914-1920** (17), **Victory Medal 1914-1918** (18). Commemorative and Campaign medals for 1914-1920.

1939-1945 Star (19). Ribbon alone created in August 1943: 18 days present in an operational sector or taking part in a particular

Note. The figures following each decoration refer to the table on page 79.

Above:
Holland, November 1944. Major Brady (7th Royal Canadian Artillery) being decorated with the Military Cross by Field-Marshall B. Montgomery.
(IWM)

operation, according to a list established by the War Office (Dieppe, for example).

Africa Star (20): operational service in Africa and in the Middle East between 10 June 1940 and 12 May 1943. Instituted in 1943.

Italy Star (21): operational service in Italy and Sicily between 11 June 1943 and 8 May 1945, instituted in 1945.

France and Germany Star (22): operational service in France, Belgium, Holland and Germany from 6 June 1944 to 8 May 1945.

Defence Medal (23): three years in Great Britain between 3 September 1939 and 2 September 1945 or one year's service overseas in a non-operational sector.

Canadian Volunteer Service Medal (24): the only specifically Canadian medal created during WWII. Ribbon worn alone after 1943. The Maple leaf device showed that the wearer was a volunteer for overseas service. 650 000 medals were awarded, of which 525 000 with bar.

War Medal 1939-1945 (25): 28 days' service in an operational sector. The ribbon can bear one or more oak leaves for being Mentioned in Despatches.

Coronation Medal

King George Coronation Medal (26): for personnel having taken part in the coronation ceremonies in 1937.

Meritorious Service, Long Service and Good Conduct Medal

Army Long Service and Good Conduct Medal (27)
Efficiency Decoration (28): 20 years' service for officers.
Efficiency Medal (29): 12 years' service for ORs.

Above:
Service ribbons worn on an officer's battledress blouse. From left to right: 39/45 Star, France and Germany Star, Defence Medal, Canadian Volunteer Service Medal, Canadian Efficiency Decoration.
(R. Le Chantoux collection)

Right:
Captain L. Dumais, MI 9, Fusiliers Mont Royal, commanding officer of the Shelburn maquis network in Brittany 1943-44. He had risen from the ranks, as shown by the ribbons of the Military medal and the Canadian Efficiency Medal reserved for warrant Officers and ORs. *(J. Garnier collection)*

ORDERS, GALLANTRY AND CAMPAIGN MEDAL RIBBONS

1 - Victoria Cross (Officers - OR)

2 - George Cross (Officers - OR)

3 - Order of the Bath (Officers)

4 - Order of Merit (Officers)

5 - Order of Saint Michael and Saint George (Officers)

6 - Royal Victorian Order (5 classes) (Officers)

7 - Order of the British Empire (5 classes) (Officers)

8 - Order of the Companions of Honour Officers

9 - Distinguished Service Order (Officers)

10 - Military Cross (Officers - WO)

11 - Distinguished Conduct Medal (WO - OR)

12 - George Medal (Officers - OR)

13 - Military Medal (WO - OR)

14 - British Empire Medal (OR)

15 - 1914 Star (Officers - OR)

16 - 1914 - 1915 Star (Officers - OR)

17 - British War Medal 1914 - 1920 (Officers - OR)

18 - Victory Medal 1914 - 1918 (Officers - OR)

19 - 1939 - 1945 Star (Officers - OR)

20 - Africa Star (Officers - OR)

21 - Italy Star (Officers - OR)

22 - France and Germany Star (Officers - OR)

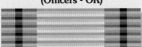

23 - Defence Medal (Officers)

24 - Canadian Volunteer Service Medal (Officers - OR)

25 - War Medal 1939 - 1945 (Officers - OR)

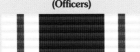

26 - King George VI Coronation Medal Officers (OR)

27 - Army Long Service and Good Conduct Medal (WO - OR)

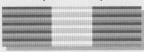

28 - Efficiency Decoration (Officers)

Keys
Officers: only for officers
Officers - OR: for Officers **and** Other Ranks
WO - OR: for Warrant Officers and Other Ranks

29 - Efficiency Medal (WO - OR)

79

1. Victoria Cross.
2. Military Cross.
3. 39-45 Star.
4. Africa Star.
5. Italy Star.
6. France and Germany Star.
These medals are shown here in their order
of precedence.

7. Canadian Volunteer Service Medal with the 'Dieppe'
clasp instituted in 1994 for veterans of '*Operation
Jubilee*' of 19 August 1942 (obverse).
8. Reverse side of the CVSM.

9. Defence Medal
10. Canadian Volunteer Service Medal with bar for
'Volunteer for overseas service.'
11. War Medal with oak leaf device for 'Mentioned in
Despatches.'

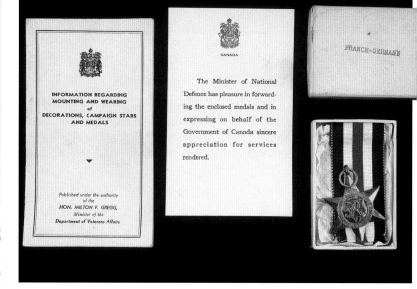

Right:
**Booklet and notice accompanying a Campaign Medal in its
original box.** *(Le Poilu collection)*

Below:
**Campaign medals were simply sent to the recipients with a
diploma ; there was no military ceremony.**

**Efficiency Medal
(12 years' service for Warrant Officers
and Other Ranks.**
(R. Le Chantoux collection)

AWARDS—CANADIAN ARMY (ACTIVE)				M
BRADY, John Campbell	B-144836	Pte	FILE NO. 405-B-51,794	
SURNAME (IN BLOCK LETTERS) CHRISTIAN NAMES	REG. NO.	RANK ON DISCHARGE	C.A.S.F. UNIT	

WAR SERVICE BADGE (CLASS) ELIGIBLE G.S.C No. 652480 (13-3-46) DD 2 DATE DESPATCHED:

ADDRESS:

CAMPAIGN MEDALS	REGISTRATION NUMBER AND DATE DESPATCHED
1939-45 Star	
France & Germany Star	5913 15/11/49
Defence Medal	
CVSM & Clasp	
War Medal, 1939-45	

(THE REVERSE TO BE USED FOR ESTATE PURPOSES)

REM. RAND LTD.   (N.D. 9048)   KARDEX SYSTEMS DIV. CAT. NO. K. 15332

7   8   9   10   11

Abbreviations used after the Name of the Recipient:

V.C.	Victoria Cross
G.C.	George Cross
C.H.	Companion of Honour
C.B.	Order of the Bath
C.M.G.	Order of Saint Michael and Saint George
C.B.E.	Commander of the Order of the British Empire
D.S.O.	Distinguished Service Order
O.B.E.	Officer of the Order of the British Empire
M.B.E.	Member of the Order of the British Empire
M.C.	Military Cross
D.C.M.	Distinguished Conduct Medal in the Field
G.M.	George Medal
M.M.	Military Medal
B.E.M.	British Empire Medal

Corporal George Topham V.C. of the 1st Canadian Parachute Battalion was awarded the Victoria Cross for his heroic conduct during the crossing of the Rhine on 24 March 1945. Although already wounded himself, he continued evacuating wounded comrades under intense enemy fire.

Below, right:
Normandy, July 1944. Lance-Corporal R.A. Geckles MM of the 1st Canadian Parachute Battalion being decorated with the Military Medal by Field-Marshall Montgomery.
(PA 193271)

Canadian Army Victoria Crosses, 1942-1945 *

NAME	RANK	UNIT	DATE, PLACE AND CIRCUMSTANCES
C. C. I. Merritt	Lt Colonel	South Saskatchewan	19 August 1942, Dieppe France (Prisoner of War)
J. W. Foote	Captain	Royal Hamilton Light Infantry	19 August 1942, Dieppe France (Prisoner of War)
P. Triquet	Captain	22e Royal Régiment	14 December 1943, Casa Berardi, Italy.
J. K. Mahoney	Major	Westminster Regt (Motor)	24 May 1944, River Melfa, Italy, seriously wounded
D. V. Currie	Major	29th Armd. Regt (South Alberta)	18 August 1944, Saint-Lambert sur Dives, Normandy, France.
E. A. Smith	Private	Seaforth Hders of Canada	22 October 1944, River Savio, Italy
A. Cosens	Sergeant	Queen's Own Rifles of Canada	26 February 1945, Mooshof, Holland, Posthumous Award
F. A. Tilston	Major	Essex Scottish	1 March 1945, Hochwald Forest, Germany. Seriously wounded. Both legs amputated.
F. G. Topham	Corporal	1st Canadian Parachute Bat.	4 March 1945, Rhine Crossing, Germany, seriously wounded.
Reminder			
J. R. Osborn	*Warrant Off.*	*Winnipeg Grenadiers*	*Hong Kong, 19 December 1941.*

*Except Navy and Air Force.

CHAPTER 5 CLOTHING

1. Battledress

Battledress was the standard uniform for all Army personnel, officers and other ranks in the theatres of operations.

Certain personnel (motorcyclists, armoured vehicle crews, paratroopers, etc.), drew special clothing which did not however dispense them from wearing battledress when not performing their duties. Two sets (blouse and trousers) were supplied to each man: one for training and combat, and one for military ceremonies ('Best' Battledress). This was taken on campaign as a change of dress.

Officers' Battledress

As with the rest of their kit, officers bought their uniforms. There were three possibilities for them:
1. Buy the standard pattern from the quartermasters,
2. Buy the standard pattern BD and have it altered (an open collar with lapels to show the shirt and tie, for example) for a more elegant turn-out,
3. Have a uniform tailor-made. The uniform had to be tailored from approved cloth and be identical in cut to that of Other Ranks.

Canadian Battledress

Canadian-made BD was made from September 1939, according to the British 1937 pattern. The first batches were issued in October of the same year. Except for its shade - a greeny bronze colour - Canadian battledress was identical in its cut and shape to its English counterpart.

'Blouses, trousers, anklets, field service caps and other field headgear (apart from Coloured Field Service Caps) which are part of the Battledress and worn by officers, will be the same as those of other ranks ; they may be obtained on indent from the Quartermaster. Officers' battledress will be the same cut and cloth as the ORs'. The officers can buy this uniform from their unit's quartermaster, or have it tailored in Serge, Drab, No 31, which is also available from the quartermaster. The officers who, in accordance with previous regulations, had a battledress made of fine woollen cloth, Whipcord, etc. will keep this uniform until it is worn out ; it will then be replaced by clothing identical in cut and cloth to that of the ORs.' (War Regulations, May 1943).

Above:
Canadian Battledress (1) was tailored on the same lines as the British '37 Pattern (2). On the right, the British Economy Issue battledress blouse (3), supplied from 1943.
(J. Bouchery)

Right:
On the left, Walking Out Dress as specified in 1942. This uniform was only allowed in Canada. It was not taken overseas. On the right, combat dress at the beginning of the war.
(J. Garnier)

Below:
A tailor's workshop making battledresses in Canada.
(DR)

Features of Canadian Battledress
Made according to the British '37 Pattern

BLOUSE

● All the buttons except for those on the shoulder flaps were fly-fronted.
● Pleated breast pockets.
● Two inside pockets.
● On the inside back, a cotton canvas strip fitted with three buttonholes allows for attaching the blouse to the trousers.
● Front tab for tightening the waist, with a steel and nickel slide buckle.

TROUSERS

● Buttons for the left thigh pocket and the hip pocket covered with a flap
● Four belt loops, buttoned towards the top.
● Three outside buttons around the waist, to fasten blouse and trousers.
● Buttoned tabs for tightening around the ankles to facilitate putting on the anklets.

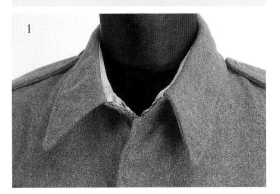

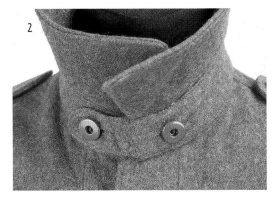

Above, from top to bottom:
1. Closing the collar of the blouse with hooks and eyes

2. 1943 Modification: collar is closed by a buttoned tab.

Below:
Label sewn at the waist, on the outside of the trousers from 1943 onwards. Before, these marks were ink-stamped on the lining of one of the pockets.

Examples of Battledress Blouse Markings
(on one of the inside pockets)

- Reception stamp (top),
the head of an arrow inside a C (for Canada).
- Maker's stamp (here DU-VAL).
- Size, here 16 followed by the measurements.
- Height: 6 ft 0 in.
- Breast: 39-40
- Date of production.

Sometimes there was also a 'V' indicating that the clothing had been impregnated against vesicant gases, which gave off a particular smell and made the uniforms sticky.

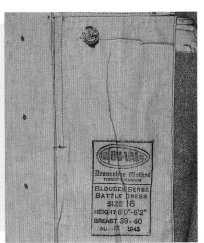

(Xavier Sieur and Jean Bouchery collections)

83

2. Two-piece Denim Overalls

Working uniform made up of a blouse and trousers. This was worn for training and dirty chores. A second set was issued as a spare depending on the circumstances.

The cut and sizing of the denim uniform was such that it could be worn over the wool battledress for work, exercises or for winter fighting.

The two-piece 'overalls' were made from cotton denim, to the same pattern as battledress, but with apparent plastic buttons (removable thanks to a split metal ring, which made washing easier).

Above and right:
Soldiers from the Régiment de Maisonneuve in Great Britain wearing the denim uniform on manoeuvres. *(J. Garnier)*

3. Shirts and ties

Above:

Regulation soldier's shirt. At the end of 1944, collar-attached shirts were issued to be worn with a tie when on leave. Unlike the British shirt, the Canadian model opened right down to the bottom and was put on like a jacket. In the summer, the shirt could be worn alone, with sleeves neatly rolled up.

Above, right:

1. **The black tie was worn by soldiers from the end of 1944, at the same time as the collar-attached shirts were introduced. It was only worn by those on leave.**

2. **Tie bought privately by an officer. It was worn with the field uniform, when on leave and for military ceremonial. The knot had to be kept in place, between the collar tips, with the help of a gilt tie-pin.**

3. **Woollen officers tie, British-issue.**

Collar size equivalents

Imperial sizing	Continental Sizing
14 1/2	37
15	38
15 1/2	39
16	41
16 1/2	42
17	43
17 1/2	44

Opposite Page, from top to bottom.
Wearing regulation braces. Brace buttons were sewn on inside the trousers' waistband.

In a rear area, a Canadian soldier wearing the regulation shirt is sorting out loaves of bread.

Nijmegen, Holland, 26 March 1945. A portrait of Private Simoneau, of the Régiment de Maisonneuve. The black tie is worn here with the collar-attached shirt issued at the end of 1944.

4. Cardigans and other winter clothing

(Collection J. Garnier)

1. Cardigan.
2. Scarf/Cap Comforter.
3. Handkerchief.

4. Woollen Scarf.
5. Wollen Gloves.
(Private Collection)

5. Underclothes

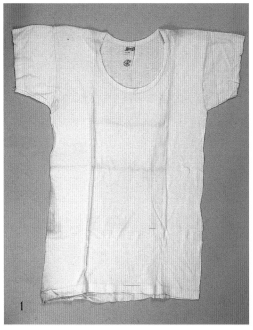  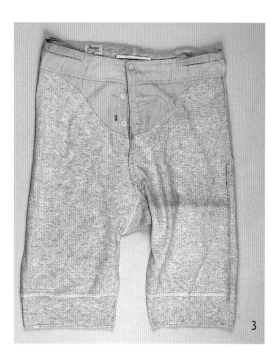

1. Cotton vest. 2. Wool and cotton long-johns. 3. Wool and cotton underpants.
Wool and cotton long- and short-sleeved vests were also issued for the cold season.
(Private Collection)

6. Footwear

The standard Ankle boot

Footwear worn with Battledress

Officers and Class I Warrant Officers wore brown leather ankle boots, or black leather boots in the case of kilted Highland and Scottish regiments, Rifle Regiments and units of the Canadian Armoured Corps (including reserve Armoured Regiments), except in the following circumstances:

a. Brown or black low lace-up shoes, without toe cap, could be worn during evenings and off-duty.

b. When felt or rubber boots or any other form of special footwear was stipulated.

ORs, except Class I WOs, wore black leather issue ankle boots at all times, except when felt or rubber boots or any other kind of special footwear was stipulated. However in evenings, simple black lace-up shoes with or without toe cap could be worn.

Above:
The Canadian boot closely resembled its British counterpart of the Great War without the toe cap. Called 'Boot, Ankle, Militia, GS,' it had a short tongue and seven pairs of eyelets. The sole was stitched with Goodyear welt, a steel strip being inserted under the arch of the foot, between the inner sole and outer sole. A leather tap was sometimes added. On this example, the maker (LaFayette 1943) is mentioned on the inner sole with the size 6 E (M). This indication is repeated in yellow ink at the top of the cuff.

The sole is stitched and held by metal pins. The rounded metal toe cleat is held on by four screws. The heel is reinforced with square-headed nails and with a U-shaped cleat held by four large square-headed nails. The cleat is stamped with EPF and the size (6-7 1/2).
(Author's Collection)

Wearing Anklets

Anklets were worn with Battledress at all times by all personnel except:

a. When off-duty.

b. When on duty in offices, depots, workshops, in the kitchens or in the canteen.

c. If the unit commander dispensed the soldiers from wearing anklets when on duty in barracks, at bivouac or in other manoeuvre areas. Anklets were however worn for all ceremonies.

d. When rubber over-boots were worn, unless the unit commander ordered anklets to be worn because of the weather.

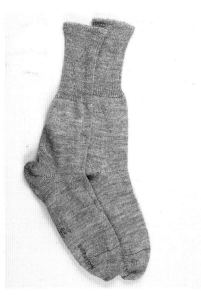

Above, left:
Grey knit woollen socks. A spare pair was often carried in the Haversack.
(Private Collection)

Above, right:
Canadian ankle boots for armoured vehicle crews. The rubber sole was meant to facilitate access to and work on the machines They were issued according to availability.
(Author's Collection)

Right:
**1. Talc for foot care.
2. Dubbin grease for taking care of footwear on campaign. This product contained a substance which made the boots impervious to gas. It was normally carried with a shoe rag, inside the entrenching tool carrier (see p.101).
3. Polish used on the boots worn for military ceremonies or for Walking Out Dress.
4. Shoe brush.**

Bottom, right:
Royal Canadian Army Ordnance Corps personnel, among other things, repaired boots.
(J. Garnier collection)

Below:
Webbing anklets were reinforced with leather on the inside. There were four sizes (1 to 4). The tips of the straps were reinforced with plastic tabs, instead of brass, on the later models.

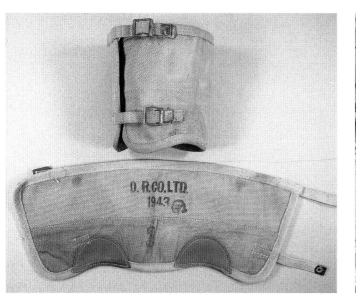

Shoe Size Equivalents

Boots came in three width sizes, mentioned on the inner sole, as well as the maker and the date of production.

S	*(Small)* =	Narrow
M	*(Medium)* =	Medium width
L	*(Large)* =	Wide

Canada/UK	Continental Europe
6	$39^{1/2}$
7	41
8	42
9	43
10	$44^{1/2}$
11	46

The Canadian intermediary sizes are indicated in fractions.

Left:
Boots with buckles and laces for motorcyclists. A piece of steel was screwed on at the instep in order to prevent damage to the solde from kick-starting the bike's engine.

Below, left:
Canadian Snow Boots. *(Author's Collection)*

Below, right:
Winter 1944-1945. Soldiers from the Régiment de la Chaudière wearing snow boots.
(Photo Musée Régiment de la Chaudière)

Above:
Boots had to be carefully polished before any military ceremony or before going out on leave. *(J. Garnier collection)*

Right:
19 July 1944, near Caen. German prisoners guarded by men from the Lorne Scots Regiment, a unit responsible for providing security at corps and division headquarters. The man on the right is wearing the high boots with cuffs. *(IWM)*

Smooth leather ankle
boots worn
for Walking Out.
(X. Sieur collection)

BOOT NAILS

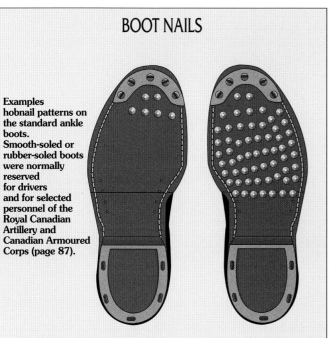

Examples
hobnail patterns on
the standard ankle
boots.
Smooth-soled or
rubber-soled boots
were normally
reserved
for drivers
and for selected
personnel of the
Royal Canadian
Artillery and
Canadian Armoured
Corps (page 87).

Above:
Officers' grained brown leather
boots, an example of what was
bought for field dress. They were
black for the Canadian Scottish

Regiments and the Canadian
Armoured Corps.
Below:
Canadian rest and sports shoes
(Plimsolls). *(Xavier Sieur collection)*

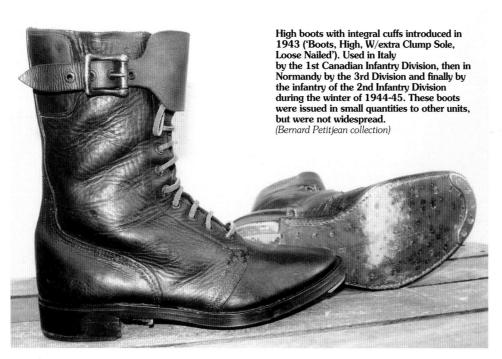

High boots with integral cuffs introduced in
1943 ('Boots, High, W/extra Clump Sole,
Loose Nailed'). Used in Italy
by the 1st Canadian Infantry Division, then in
Normandy by the 3rd Division and finally by
the infantry of the 2nd Infantry Division
during the winter of 1944-45. These boots
were issued in small quantities to other units,
but were not widespread.
(Bernard Petitjean collection)

Rally Magazine, 1944-1945.

7. Greatcoat and coat

Corporal wearing the issue greatcoat during the winter of **1944-45 in Great Britain.**
(Jocelyn Garnier collection)

Above:
Standard pattern ('General service') greatcoat button. Certain corps and regiments had buttons embossed with their own insignia.

Below:
Detail of the ink markings on the lining of the greatcoat.

SIZE - 4
Height 5' 5" - 5' 6"
Breast 39-40

8. General issue Protective Clothing

Right:
Groundsheet made of rubberised canvas. On the edges there were eyelets which enabled the soldiers with a bit of cord to pitch up a rough shelter. The Groundsheet was part of field kit . It was usually folded under the haversack flap.
(Reconstruction, Xavier Sieur collection)

Far right, bottom:
Holland, winter 1944-45. Infantryman from the Stormont, Dundas and Glengarry Highlanders in combat dress. The leather jerkin (a wool-lined leather sleeveless jacket) was a commonplace and practical piece of warm clothing.
(Reconstruction, Xavier Sieur collection)

Previous page:
Three-quarter length wool coat for officers and motorcyclists.
(Private collection)

Below centre and far right:
Wool-lined Leather Jerkin .
(Private collection)

Below, left:
This raincoat, made of black rubberised cloth, was issued to some units in limited numbers. It was worn by the Nova Scotia Highlanders in June 1944. The reception stamp, the maker's name and the date are on the inside.
(Private collection)

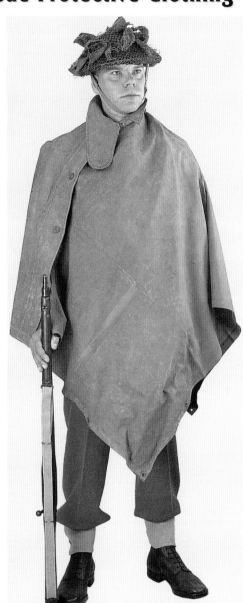

Above:
The Rubber Proofed Coat, 1942 Pattern. This motorcyclist's raincoat was British-made.

9. Miscellaneous specialised clothing

Coveralls

Below, from left to right:

1 and 2. British Tank Suit. For winter wear, this was made of waterproof canvas lined with flannel.

3 and 4. British Denim Tank Suit, made of grey-green cotton cloth. Issued to armour crews according to availability. This was worn especially in Normandy.

5 and 6. Canadian Khaki Work Suit. These coveralls for mechanics were sometimes issued to armour crews.

7 and 8. Canadian Tank Suit. Black canvas coveralls for tank crews, it was also issued to personnel carrying out dirty work.

Below:
Cotton cloth cap accompanying the Black Canadian tank Suit.
(Reconstruction, private and J. Bouchery collections)

Right:
Holland, October 1944.
The Firefly 'Adanac' of the Fort Garry Horse was the only tank still left intact since D-Day. The crew is wearing the British Denim Tank Suit.
(PA 138414)

Below, right:
During manoeuvres in Great Britain during the winter of 1943-44, crews members of training Ram tanks are wearing Canadian khaki coveralls except for the man crouching on the right who is wearing the Canadian Black Tank Suit.
(RR)

Following Page from left to right:

Manoeuvres in Great Britain: two tankmen in black overalls.
(RR)

Major Currie, VC, South Alberta Regiment is wearing the British-made wool-lined Tank Suit.
(RR)

- Ram crew member wearing the Black tank Suit.
(RR)

British Tank Suit
British Denim Tank Suit

Canadian khaki coveralls

Canadian Black Tank Suit
(J.-L. Bricon collection)

10. Duty and combat uniforms

PRÉPARATION AU COMBAT

CASQUE
Hessiau noué et garnissage naturel pour rompre l'éclat de la calotte et l'ombre sous le bord.

VISAGE, COU ET MAINS
Noircir avec crème de camouflage, suie, blanco noir ou cacao.

ÉQUIPEMENT
de toile *Blanco* noir no 1A ou 3. Peinturer en noir tout le cuivre.

MUSETTE
Tenir le hessiau en place avec de la ficelle. Y faire des nœuds et ajouter du garnissage naturel afin de supprimer la forme carrée.

MASQUE À GAZ
Blanco noir.

FUSIL
Noircir le métal luisant avec de la peinture mate. – Couvrir de hessiau la plaque de la crosse luisante.

BRODEQUINS
Enduits de dégras.

Fig. i

1. Le casque brille encore sous le filet.
2. Couvre-casque en hessiau foncé, nœuds, et ficelle entrelacée autour en boucles de 2".
3. Insuffisant: la calotte et le bord sont encore apparents.
4. Excessif: le bord reste apparent et l'abondant feuillage brille.
5. Parfait: la forme de la calotte et l'ombre disparaissent.
6. La forme carrée et le dessus luisant paraissent.
7. Des ficelles croisées tiennent la garniture naturelle sur le rabat.
8. Employer le filet personnel quand on observe.
9. Un petit écran d'hessiau et de garniture naturelle assure un excellent couvert contre un bon arrière-plan. Faire feu au-dessous.

Fig. ii

Extract from a Canadian bilingual manual on individual camouflage dating from March 1944.

Below:

1. Roll Call Order.

2. Drill Order. Drill and ceremonial dress

3. Walking Out Dress (1945)

Black and very plain, low shoes bought privately were accepted. At any rate, walking out dress was determined by the unit commander (belts and anklets to be worn, for example), who also decided in the winter season, whether the greatcoat was to be worn. This Corporal from the Glengarrians is wearing his blouse with the collar open and a shirt and black tie. He is wearing the Military Medal with the ribbon of the Canadian Volunteer Service Medal, with the Maple Leaf device for overseas service.

4 and 5. Battle Order. Regulation field dress. The haversack, with groundsheet folded under its flap, is placed on the soldier's back.

6. Full Marching Order. The Small Pack (haversack) is carried on the left hip, in the place of the entrenching tool. The 1918 pattern Large Pack is on the back. The blanket was rolled around the bag and held in place by straps or a cord. The groundsheet was used to cover the blanket if necessary. Depending on orders, the Large Pack contained the folded greatcoat or leather jerkin, and spare boots. Full Marching Order was normally only observed during training and on campaign and, exceptionally, when unit transport could not keep up with the troops.
(Reconstruction, Xavier Sieur collection)

7 and 8. Infantry Lieutenant (Platoon commander in regulation figthing order). The officers' individual equipment is presented in detail in Chapter 6, page100.
(Reconstruction, author's collection)

Roll Call Order — 1

Drill order — 2

Walking Out Dress — 3

Battle Order. — 4

BATTLE ORDER for Infantry troops (except mechanised Infantry)
Break-down of a soldier's clothing and equipment
(typical example, items could vary according to weather conditions or CO's orders)

CARRIED BY THE MAN

- **Helmet and net**
- **Face veil (individual camouflage net)**
- **Battledress**
Blouse, service book, trousers, braces, handkerchief, individual dressing, jacknife and lanyard, Identity discs.
- **Underwear**
vest, drawers, shirt, socks.
- **Boots, anklets**
- **Haversack** (+ 2 webbing braces): groundsheet, cardigan, mess tin, cooker and fuel, knife, fork and spoon, toiletry roll, 1 ration, mug.
- **Waterbottle** filled with tea, lemon drink or water
- **Respirator and accessories, gas cape**
- **Webbing belt**

– **Entrenching tool**
Shoe dubbin, brush & rag
– **2 basic pouches** [1]
2 grenades.
50 rifle rounds
2 Bren magazines
– **Bayonet and frog**
– **No 4 Rifle** and sling

Total weight per man (excluding shovel, GS): 30 kg.

Possible additions
- 1 pair of Bren magazines pouches
- 1 cloth bandoleer with 50 rifle rounds.
- 1 shovel or pick, General Service, wire-cutters.

1. Contents according to assignment within Infantry section.

IN BATTALION TRANSPORT

- Large pack
- Kit Bag
- Greatcoat
- Leather Jerkin
- 1 set of Battledress
- 2 sets of Denim overalls
- Plimsolls
- 1 pair of ankle boots
- Spare underwear
- Cap Comforter
- Housewife
- Gas protection clothing
- 2 blankets (5 per man in wintertime, in a second Kit bag)
- Small personal belongings.

Left:
On this left-hand side view, the way the various elements of the Battle Order were attached can be clearly seen. The large shovel (Shovel GS) has been slipped between the haversack and the soldier's back. *(Militaria Magazine)*

11. Officers's field uniform

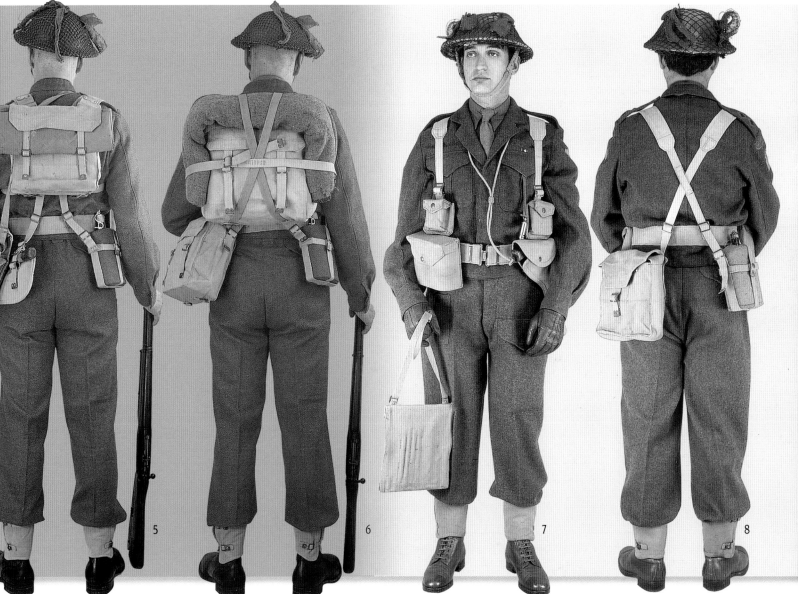

Battle Order.

Full Marching Order

Officers' field uniform

12. Camouflage Clothing

Left:
The Netherlands, 1945. Infantrymen wearing British snow camouflage clothing. They belong to the Lincoln and Welland Regt, 10th Infantry Brigade, 4th Armoured Division.

Right:
Canadian snow over-boots issued during winter 1944-45. They are being worn by the men on the right and centre on the photograph opposite.
(Courtesy Michel Perrier)

Below, left:
Winter 1944-45. A Canadian patrol in full British snow camouflage kit making its way through a German forest.

Bottom, left:
The British Snow Camouflage Suit called for a smock and trousers made of strong white material, worn over Battledress. It was issued from December 1944 onwards to some Canadian infantry units.
(Reconstruction)

Right:
A note from Lieutenant-Colonel Mathieu (Régiment de la Chaudière) dated 30 July 1943 dealing with the regimental tailor's fees for uniform alterations.

Great-Britain, 25 April 1944. HM the King George VI inspecting the 9th Infantry Brigade with General Crerar and Brigadier D.G. Cunningham, the brigade CO. On the right, several officers of the Highland Light Infantry are clad in McKenzie kilts. These were bought privately and allowed for ceremonial wear. *(PA 115515)*

96

13. Traditional Scottish Clothing

Canadian Scottish Regimental Tartans

Regiment	Tartan [1]
1. **Highland Light Infantry of Canada** **Seaforth Highlanders of Canada**	MacKenzie
2. **48th Highlanders**	Davidson
3. **Canadian Scottish**	Hunting Stuart
4. **Cameron Highlanders of Ottawa** **Queen's Own Cameron Highlanders of Canada**	Cameron of Erracht
5. **Lorne Scots**	Campbell & Argyll
6. **Toronto Scottish**	Hodden Grey (Elcho)
7. **Essex Scottish**	Mc Gregor
8. **North Nova Scotia Highlanders**	Murray of Atholl
9. **Stormont, Dundas and Glengarry** **Highlanders**	McDonnel of Glengarry
10. **Black Watch of Canada** **Lanark and Renfrew** **Cape Breton Highlanders** **Argyll & Sutherland Highlanders of Canada** **Calgary Highlanders**	42nd Government [1]

1. The '42nd Government' tartan was only a military pattern and had no clan antecedents.

Above:
Aurich, Germany, June 1945. Lt-General G.G. Simonds inspecting the Cameron Highlanders of Canada. The Company Sergeant-Major (CSM) on the right is wearing a kilt made from Cameron of Erracht tartan. *(RR)*

Uniform of Canadian Scottish Regiments

1. In the theatre of operations, all personnel wore standard Battledress with the khaki Tam O'Shanter (see page 49). The cap badge was pinned to a piece of the regiment's tartan.

2. Units present in the theatre of operations could not wear kilts.

3. However, for parades in rear areas, Pipers and Drummers were authorised to wear the kilt together with the Glengarry.

For officers, the regimental tartan tie was only allowed with Service dress. It was forbidden with Battledress.

97

Normandy Coast, June 1944. Reinforcement units landing. The men are carrying Full Marching Order, which particularly included the Large Pack, around which was attached the individual blanket rolled up in the waterproof groundsheet.
(IWM)

CHAPTER 6 EQUIPMENT

The 1937 Pattern Individual Equipment

Canadian individual equipment was copied directly from the British 1937 Pattern. Manufacture started at the beginning of 1940 and mass distribution began in October of the same year.

This equipment was made up of waterproofed cotton webbing. Assembling the web equipment - on and around the belt - was done with the help of buckles and brass hooks. As to manufacture, the Canadian pattern differed from its British equivalent by its yellower colouring and the brown paint which covered the metal parts.

The equipment comprised a certain number of basic parts which, with the addition of special items, enabled five different sets to be made up which covered the needs of all Army personnel.

1. An webbing set for Infantry as well as for personnel armed with the Sten Gun or the Bren Light Machine Gun (described page 99)

2. A webbing set for personnel armed with a rifle not assigned to an

(Cont'd page 101)

The 1939 Regulations

1. Infantry webbing set.
2. Rear view, showing haversack.
3. Webbing set for personnel armed with a rifle not assigned to an infantry unit.
4. Full Marching Order with the 1908 Large Pack, rear view.
5. Webbing set for officers.
6. Webbing set for personnel armed with a revolver or automatic pistol (except Canadian Armoured Corps - CAC).
7. Webbing set for armoured vehicles crews (CAC) with the special thigh holster (early pattern)

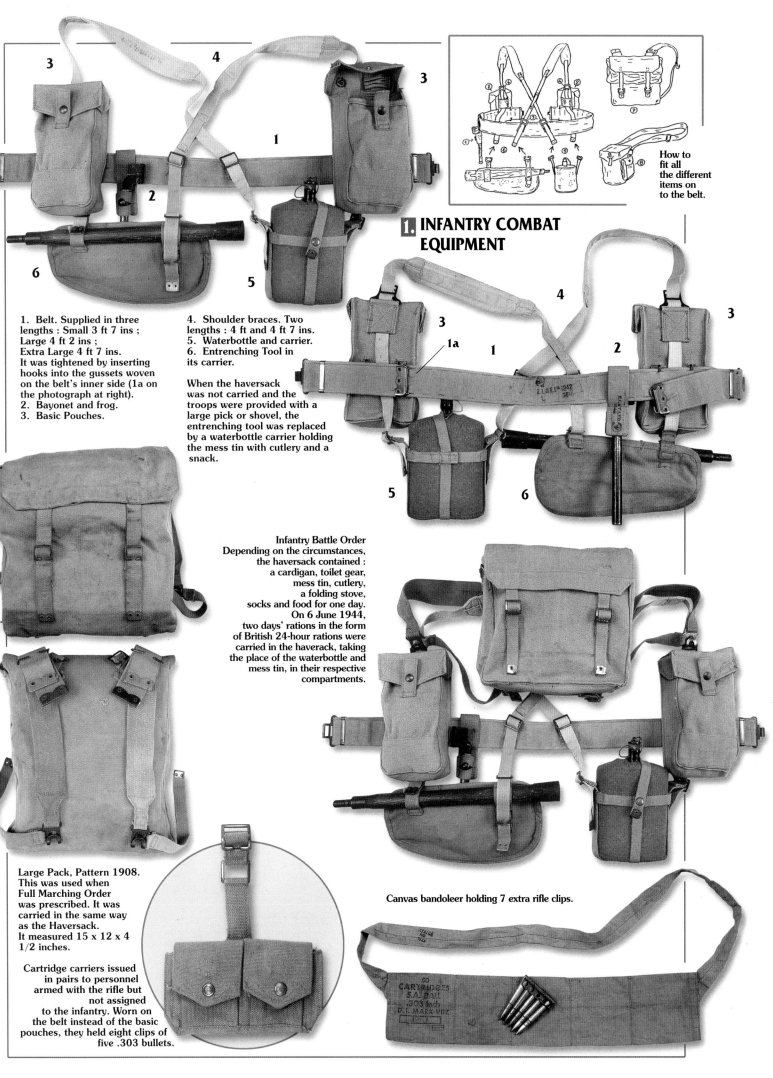

1. INFANTRY COMBAT EQUIPMENT

1. **Belt.** Supplied in three lengths : Small 3 ft 7 ins ; Large 4 ft 2 ins ; Extra Large 4 ft 7 ins. It was tightened by inserting hooks into the gussets woven on the belt's inner side (1a on the photograph at right).
2. **Bayonet and frog.**
3. **Basic Pouches.**

4. **Shoulder braces.** Two lengths : 4 ft and 4 ft 7 ins.
5. **Waterbottle and carrier.**
6. **Entrenching Tool** in its carrier.

When the haversack was not carried and the troops were provided with a large pick or shovel, the entrenching tool was replaced by a waterbottle carrier holding the mess tin with cutlery and a snack.

Infantry Battle Order
Depending on the circumstances, the haversack contained : a cardigan, toilet gear, mess tin, cutlery, a folding stove, socks and food for one day. On 6 June 1944, two days' rations in the form of British 24-hour rations were carried in the haverack, taking the place of the waterbottle and mess tin, in their respective compartments.

Large Pack, Pattern 1908. This was used when Full Marching Order was prescribed. It was carried in the same way as the Haversack. It measured 15 x 12 x 4 1/2 inches.

Cartridge carriers issued in pairs to personnel armed with the rifle but not assigned to the infantry. Worn on the belt instead of the basic pouches, they held eight clips of five .303 bullets.

Canvas bandoleer holding 7 extra rifle clips.

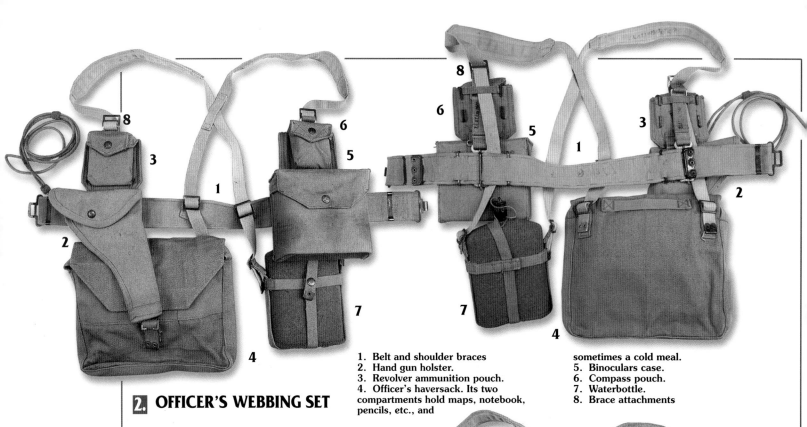

1. Belt and shoulder braces
2. Hand gun holster.
3. Revolver ammunition pouch.
4. Officer's haversack. Its two compartments hold maps, notebook, pencils, etc., and

sometimes a cold meal.
5. Binoculars case.
6. Compass pouch.
7. Waterbottle.
8. Brace attachments

2. OFFICER'S WEBBING SET

Detail of the Canadian Army property mark, an arrow inside a C (for Canada). It was normally stamped on all issue equipment and uniforms.

3. WEBBING SET FOR PERSONNEL ARMED WITH A REVOLVER OR PISTOL

(Except Canadian Armoured Corps)

1. Hand gun holster.
2. Revolver ammunition pouch.
Note. The pouch for automatic handgun magazines will be found in the *Armament* Chapter, page 117.
3. Brace attachments, see below.

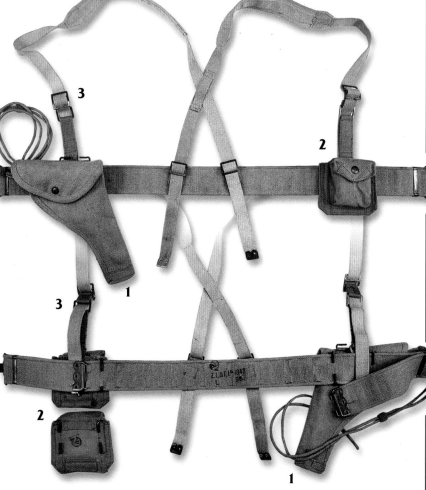

Brace attachments, rear and front view.
These enabled equipment to be worn with shoulder braces when the Basic pouches were not part of the set: i.e. in the case of officers' webbing sets and webbing sets for personnel armed with a handgun (except tank crews).

CANADIAN ARMOURED CORPS PERSONNEL
The special hand gun holster (1943-45) was worn on the right with the ammunition pouch on the left.

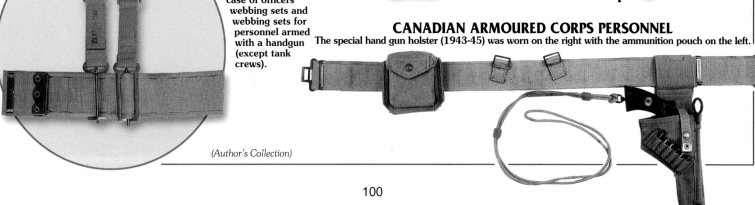

(Author's Collection)

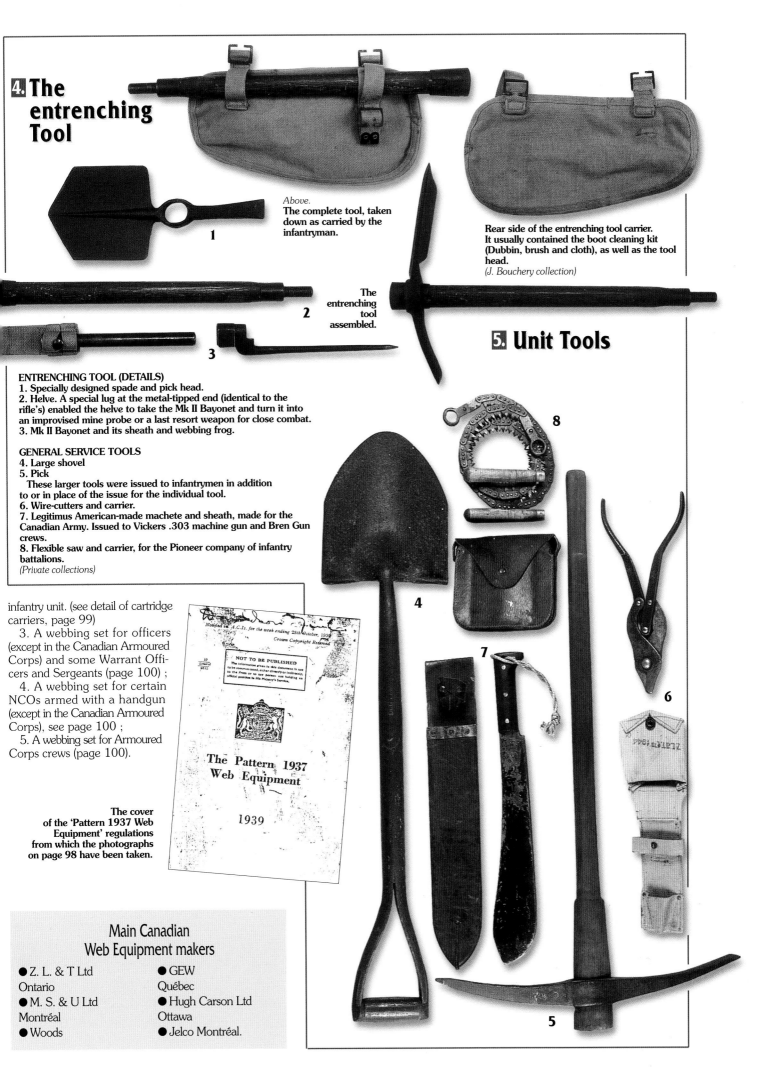

4. The entrenching Tool

Above.
The complete tool, taken down as carried by the infantryman.

1

Rear side of the entrenching tool carrier. It usually contained the boot cleaning kit (Dubbin, brush and cloth), as well as the tool head.
(J. Bouchery collection)

2

The entrenching tool assembled.

3

5. Unit Tools

ENTRENCHING TOOL (DETAILS)
1. Specially designed spade and pick head.
2. Helve. A special lug at the metal-tipped end (identical to the rifle's) enabled the helve to take the Mk II Bayonet and turn it into an improvised mine probe or a last resort weapon for close combat.
3. Mk II Bayonet and its sheath and webbing frog.

GENERAL SERVICE TOOLS
4. Large shovel
5. Pick
   These larger tools were issued to infantrymen in addition to or in place of the issue for the individual tool.
6. Wire-cutters and carrier.
7. Legitimus American-made machete and sheath, made for the Canadian Army. Issued to Vickers .303 machine gun and Bren Gun crews.
8. Flexible saw and carrier, for the Pioneer company of infantry battalions.
(Private collections)

8

4

7

6

5

infantry unit. (see detail of cartridge carriers, page 99)

3. A webbing set for officers (except in the Canadian Armoured Corps) and some Warrant Officers and Sergeants (page 100) ;

4. A webbing set for certain NCOs armed with a handgun (except in the Canadian Armoured Corps), see page 100 ;

5. A webbing set for Armoured Corps crews (page 100).

Notified in A.C.Is. for the week ending 25th October, 1939
Crown Copyright Reserved

NOT TO BE PUBLISHED
The information given in this document is not to be communicated, either directly or indirectly, to the Press or to any person not holding an official position in His Majesty's Service.

The Pattern 1937 Web Equipment

1939

The cover of the 'Pattern 1937 Web Equipment' regulations from which the photographs on page 98 have been taken.

Main Canadian Web Equipment makers

- Z. L. & T Ltd
  Ontario
- M. S. & U Ltd
  Montréal
- Woods
- GEW
  Québec
- Hugh Carson Ltd
  Ottawa
- Jelco Montréal.

6. The Battle Jerkin

The British-made battle jerkin was issued to certain Canadian assault units for 6 June 1944.
(Private collection)

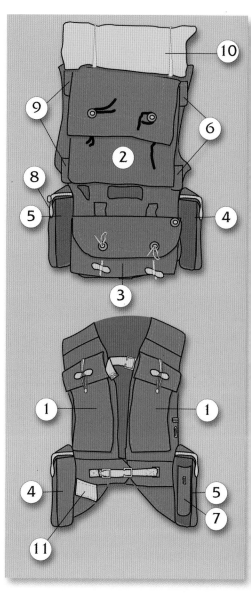

Right.
How equipment was placed in the Battle jerkin.
1. Ammunition.
2. Rations, mess tin. Cardigan. Toilet gear, socks, stove, beret/off-duty headgear.
3. Entrenching tool head.
4. Grenades.
5. Waterbottle.
6. Sleeve for a machete or the 2-in mortar tube.
7. Bayonet
8. Commando knife.
9. Sleeve for entrenching tool helve.
10. Groundsheet, or gas cape.
11. Revolver holster attachment.

7. Individual Light Armour Protection

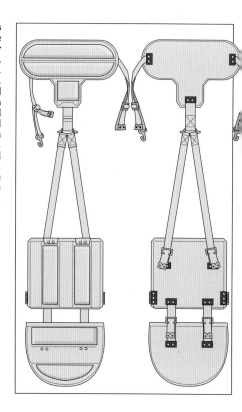

This was British-made by Briggs Motor Bodies, and Harrison Bros. and Howson. 3 200 were supplied to the 1st Canadian Army and issued mainly to the 2nd Infantry Division in July 1944. It weighed in all 2 1/2 lbs. The manganese steel plates were 1mm thick.

Left.
6 August 1944. D Company of the Régiment de Maisonneuve passing through the ruined village of Bons-Tassilly (Calvados). The officer leading the column is wearing the individual light armour protection.
(PAC 135955)

8. The Kit Bag

EQUIPMENT AND BAGGAGE IDENTIFICATION CODES *

In order to organise the loading, unloading and directing of baggage to the appropriate units, a system of coloured bar codes and serial numbers was set up by the War Office on 10 May 1944 (Note N° 5697).

Three horizontal stripes were painted and translated the last two figures of the unit's code number. The colour for the tens was painted above and below the central stripe indicating the digits.

Code colour/number

1		1
2		2
3		3
4		4
5		5

Example : the officer's bag (fig. 2 on the right) has two yellow stripes =3, and one central blue stripe = 2. The white unit code is 1132.
Through cross-checking it is known that the Régiment de la Chaudière's code was 743/1, although no official list giving the codes has come to light until now.
Information taken from the article in *Militaria Magazine* N°181 by Ed Storey.

* Only for Canadian and British armies.

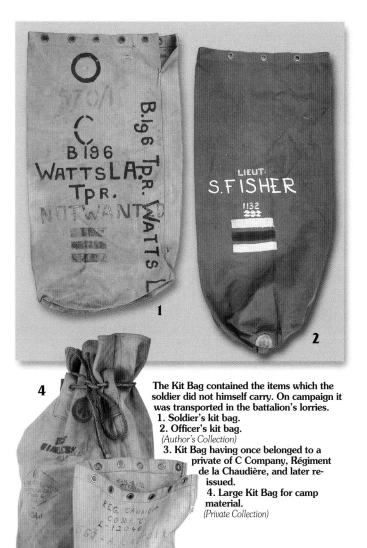

1

2

4

3

The Kit Bag contained the items which the soldier did not himself carry. On campaign it was transported in the battalion's lorries.
1. Soldier's kit bag.
2. Officer's kit bag.
(Author's Collection)
3. Kit Bag having once belonged to a private of C Company, Régiment de la Chaudière, and later re-issued.
4. Large Kit Bag for camp material.
(Private Collection)

Far left.
Great Britain, August 1944. Volunteers for the Canadian Armoured Corps leaving for a training centre. They are carrying infantry equipment ; the Kit Bag contains the rest of their equipment and clothing. On their black beret, the men are wearing the Canadian Armoured Corps Cap Badge.
(PA163407)

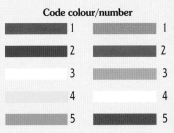

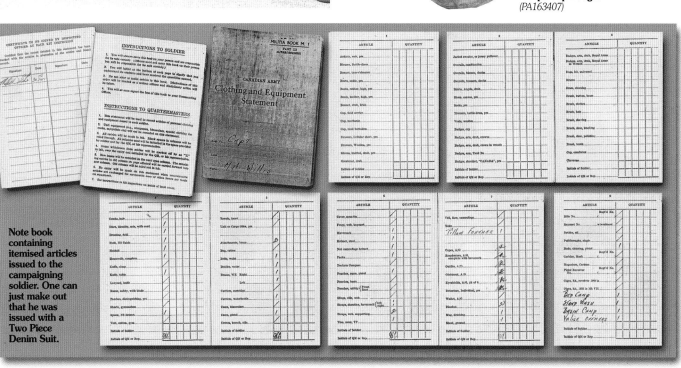

Note book containing itemised articles issued to the campaigning soldier. One can just make out that he was issued with a Two Piece Denim Suit.

📕 Anti-gas Protection

1. British Light Service Respirator in use after 1943.
2. Respirator Bag, Canadian-made (found in Normandy).
3. Detection armband. In the case of attack by vesicant gas, the khaki turned to red. Each man was issued with two. The Canadian Army black property stamp is clearly visible.
4. Envelope of six acetate Mk II antigas eyeshields, carried in the respirator bag.
5. Tin of anti-fogging compound and rag.
6. Boxes containing eight tubes of decontamination ointment.
7. Throw-away wool and cotton pads for applying the ointment.
8. Tin of anti-gas shoe dubbin, usually carried in the entrenching tool carrier (page 101).
9. Gas attack warning rattle.
10. Gas Detector Paint for vehicles and machines.
11. Paper indicator which reacted with vesicant gas. (Detector, Gas, Ground, N°1)
12. Gas Instruction Manual, 1943.

Below.
Gas cape in camouflage printed oil cloth, note the large bulge on the back to accomodate the haversack. On officers' orders, the cape could be rolled up under the flap of the haversack if the groundsheet (page 91) had not been issued) or attached to the belt with a strap. In any case, it was often used as a raincoat.

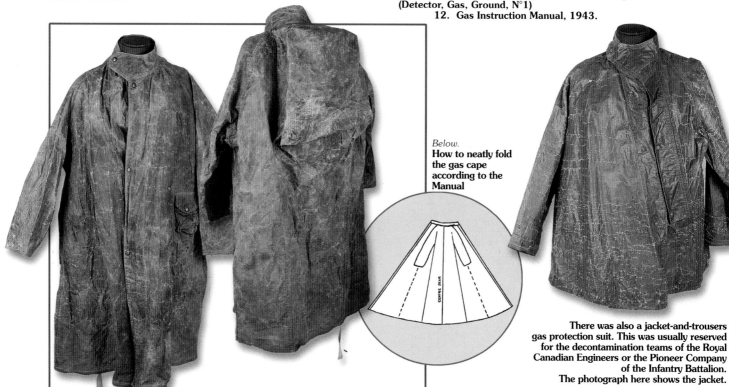

Below.
How to neatly fold the gas cape according to the Manual

There was also a jacket-and-trousers gas protection suit. This was usually reserved for the decontamination teams of the Royal Canadian Engineers or the Pioneer Company of the Infantry Battalion. The photograph here shows the jacket.

Protection and Decontamination Equipment

Equipment reserved for Decontaminating Teams.
1. Gloves.
2. Boots made of rubberised cloth.

Protective equipment
3. No 4 Rifle antigas cover.
4. Anti-gas wallet for personal documents.
5. Protective hood in oil cloth. There was also a green-brown camouflage helmet cover with integral neck flap.

Below.
Life jacket CO2 canister inflation system.
(P. Nonzerville collection)

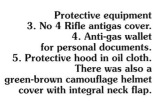

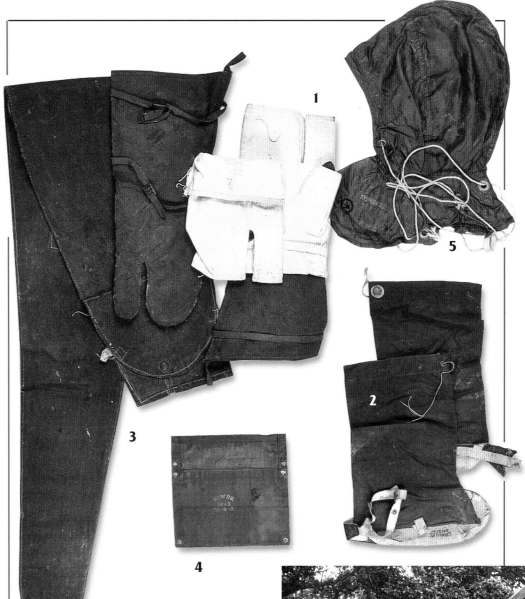

10. Life-jackets and life-belts

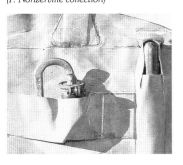

Above :
16 June 1944, Normandy.
Anti-gas capes were used as waterproofs.
(PA 169255)

Left :
Flotation Equipment used for airborne and amphibious operations (British-made).
1. Life-Jacket.
2. Life-Belt.

105

11. Face veil

A waterbottle carrier which has been renovated with Blanco, placed on the individual camouflage netting (Face Veil). The metal box contains a brush used to spread the Blanco over the webbing.

12. Jerrycans and Other Cans

Right, on the left. **British Jerrycan containing 4 1/2 gallons of fuel.** An identical jerrycan was used for carrying drinking water. The pressed metal ribbing was painted white and the word 'water' was stamped on the lower part. On the right : 2-gallon General Purpose Can. This was also used for condensing steam from the Vickers machine gun cooling sleeve.

13. Bivouac Equipment

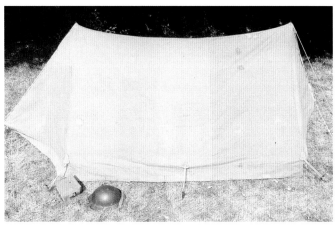

Above, left.
British two-man tent.
Length (apse not included) : 6 ft 6 ins.
Width : 5 ft 6 ins.
Height : 3 ft 6 ins. The entrance was fitted with a mosquito net.

Below.
Canadian camp water bucket and basin.

Below, right.
3 1/2 gallon water container.

Above, right.
1. Rubber-backed groundsheet.
2. Regulation Canadian woollen blanket.

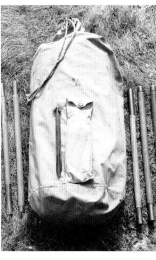

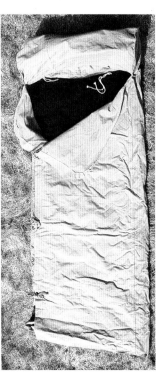

Above.
Two-man tent bag, with two taken-down poles, and pegs.

Right.
British issue sleeping Bag

1. Soldier's Pay and Service Book belonging to a French-speaking Canadian soldier.
His number was D- 448 249, so he was recruited in Quebec, at Montreal.
The book also mentions his measurements, vaccination, service, wounds, the address of his next of kin, in case of wounds, death and decorations, etc.
The unit to which he was assigned was only mentioned when he was mustered out.
The book had to be carried by the soldier at all times.

2. Tourists' guide to Paris handed out by charities to soldiers on leave.

3. Notebook.

4. Claude Lachevrotière, army number D- 193577 was born in 1923 and assigned to D Company of the Régiment de Maisonneuve.
He was killed 22 July 1944 near Saint-André-sur-Orne, to the south of Caen.

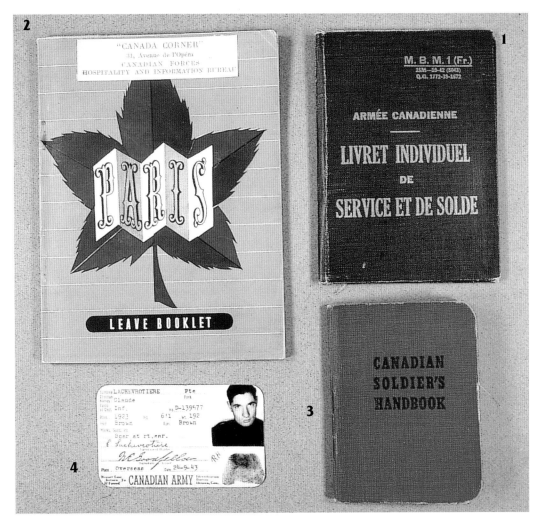

PERSONAL EFFECTS

14. Identity discs

These were made of compressed fibre and were worn round the neck.

They were inscribed with the army service number (except for officers), the initials and last name, religion (always abbreviated) and the three letters CDN indicating nationality.

In the case of death, the green eight-sided disc was buried with the body. In order to facilitate identification at a later date by the War Canadian Graves Unit, burial details would lay near the body, in a cigarette tin, the man's Cap Badge and shoulder title, or failing this an item of the man's equipment bearing the regimental number.

A spare green disk was placed in the gas mask bag.

On the ORs identity discs, the prefix letter of the regimental number indicated the number of the district where the soldier was recruited (Non Permanent Active Militia, see table page 108).

Identity tag belonging to a Driver from the Royal Canadian Army Service Corps (*Dvr.*) named Brady, enrolled at Toronto, Ontario.

Accepted abbrevations for religions on identity discs

— Church of England	C-E	— Christian Science	C-SCI
— Roman Catholic	RC	— Greek Catholic	GC
— United Church	UN-C	— Greek Orthodox	GO
— Presbyterian	PRES	— Jewish	J
— Baptist	BAPT	— Other Denomination	OD
— Lutherian	LUTH		
— Pencostal	PENT		

Identity discs belonging to an officer. Officers' army numbers were not inscribed on these discs.

Army Number Prefixes

Prefix	Military District	Province	Provincial HQ
A	1	Ontario	London
B	2	Ontario	Toronto
C	3	Ontario	Kingston
D	4	Quebec	Montreal
E	5	Quebec	Quebec City
F	6	Nova Scotia	Halifax
G	7	New Brunswick	Saint-John
H	8	Manitoba	Winnipeg
K	10	British Columbia	Vancouver
L	12	Saskatchewan	Regina
M	13	Alberta	Calgary
N	Recruited at St-Johns, Newfoundland.		
P	Recruited in the Non-Permanent Active Militia before 10 September 1940		
T	Militia Officer or Canadian Overseas Volunteer Firefighter		
U	Recruited in Great Britain		
W	Women (CWAC)		
Y	Recruited in Holland or in Europe		
Z	Chaplain Corps.		

WEARING IDENTITY DISCS

"1. Identity discs must be worn according to the picture.

2. Each disc must show number, rank, name, initials, religion as well as nationality (CDN).

3. The red disc must be attached to the green one by a separate string.

4. Company commanders must ensure that all ranks wear their identity discs at all times in the appropriate manner. RSMs will check that regimental personnel do likewise. Do not forget those who are on leave or on a training course."

J. B. Rousseau/Adjudant Régiment de la Chaudière. Order No 156 dated 30 July 1943.

(Régiment de la Chaudière Museum)

In this example, Driver J. Brady RCASC, army number B-144886, was enrolled in Military District No 2 (Ontario) HQ at Toronto.

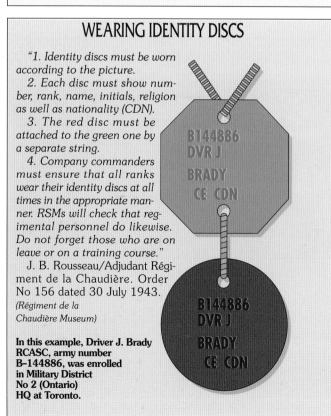

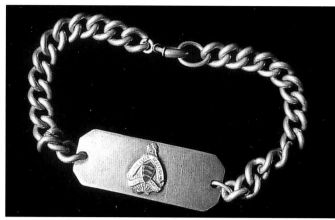

Private-purchase silver bracelet, bearing an Essex Scottish Regiment enameled badge, together with the soldier's Army number and name. Private Fox's number (A-22 510) indicated that he came from and was recruited in Military District No 1, in London (Prefix A), Ontario (Canadian Army Active Force).

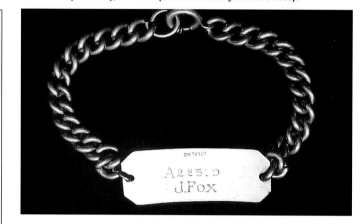

15. Mess Equipment and Cutlery

Following page, bottom.
1. Enamel mug.
2. Box of matches, sweets and salt.
3. Top half of the mess tin containing a 24-Hour Ration (*).
4. Bottom half of the mess tin.
5. Tea ration. The box contains powdered tea, milk and sugar
6. Powdered lemonade.
7. Biscuits and sweets, part of the 24-Hour Ration.
8. Folding stove with solid fuel tablets.
9. Chocolate and raisin bar.
10. Emergency ration, only to be consumed upon orders of the commanding officer. It contained 170 grams of high-calorie content chocolate.
11. Box containing two bottles of water purification tablets.
12. Jack-knife and its lanyard so that it could be worn at the waist.

*See detail of contents on page 28.

Below.
Items of cutlery dug up in Normandy in the combat area of the 2nd Infantry Division. Top right : standard issue spoon and fork.
(Private Collection)

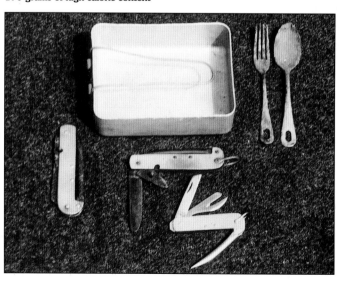

The holdall and its contents

1. Holdall.
2. Cutlery : Knife, fork, spoon.
3. Toothpaste and brush.
4. Shaving cream.
5. Razor blades.
6. Comb and button stick for polishing up the brass buttons.
7. Shaving brush.
8. Shoe laces.
9. Soap and soap-tin.
10. Hair brush.

Other personal effects.
11. Pack of cards.
12. Bath towel.
13. Wristwatch.
14. Pocket lamp, Mk. I with green, red and white filters.
15. Housewife. (see details page 110)
16. Razors (details page 110)
17. Eyeglasses case.
(Author's Collection)

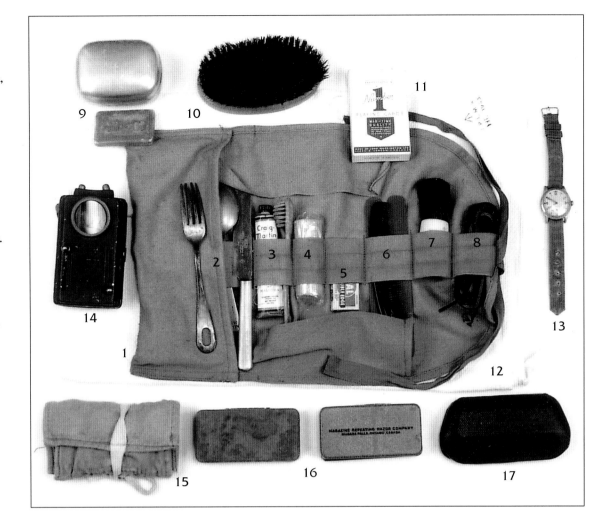

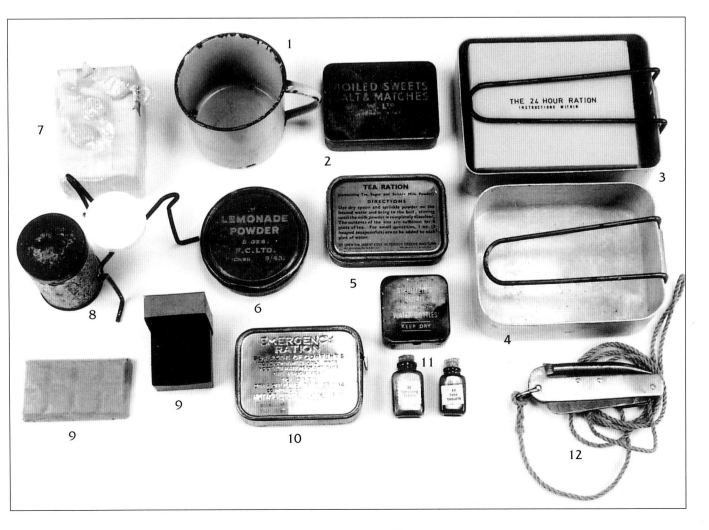

109

Tobaccania

1. Box of 50 cigarettes issued with the Compo Ration. The issue ration was seven cigarettes per soldier per day.
2. Standard issue cigarette pocket tin.
3. Privately-bought cigarette case with the Royal Canadian Army Medical Corps badge ; lighter bearing the Royal Canadian Artillery badge.
4. Packets of English cigarettes bought in soldiers canteens.

Below.
**Stationery sold at the NAAFI.
(Navy, Army, Air Force Institutes).**

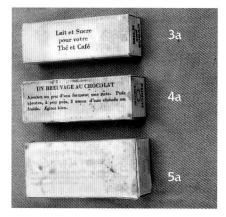

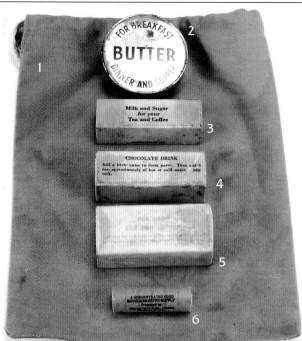

Below.
The housewife

1. Housewife.
2. Issue razor with mirror incorporated in the lid of the box.
3. Private purchase razor for military personnel.

Food Extras

Above, from top to bottom.
1. Food bag.
2. Butter.
3. Powdered milk and sugar for tea and coffee.
4. Concentrated chocolate for making a hot drink.
5. Pea soup for mixing with hot water.
6. High-vitamin content chocolate sweets.

3a., 4a and 5a.
The other side of the packets of powdered milk and sugar ; chocolate concentrate and pea soup respectively, written in French.

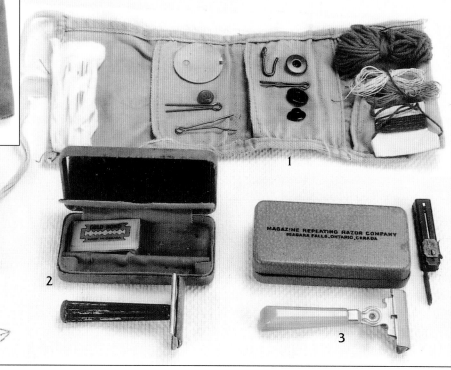

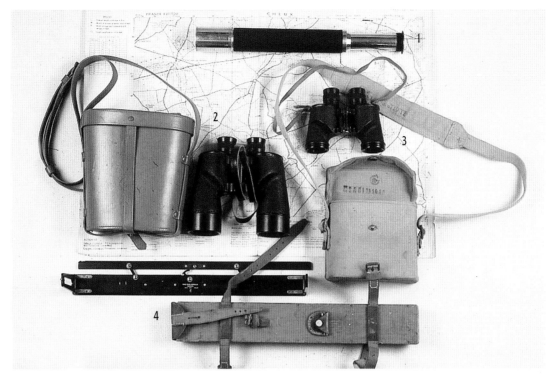

Right.
1. Telescope issued
to sharpshooters.
2. Mk II Binoculars (x 7)
with case
(for artillery laying).
3. Mk II Standard No 2
Binoculars (x7) with case.
4. Artillery slide rule
with case.

**Canadian Makers
of Optical Equipment**

— **Research Enterprises,
Ltd. (REL)**
— **Canadian Kodak
Corporation (CKC)**

Below.
1. **Flare gun with holster
(1939-45 version).**
2. **Flare gun with holster
(1914-1918 version).**
3. **Flares for the gun.**
4. **Mk II Compass with its
padded pouch.**
5. **Liquid level Mk III
Compass with leather case.**
6. **Issue Fob Watch.**

CHAPTER 7
MAPS, SIGNALLING, SIGNALS AND OPTICAL INSTRUMENTS

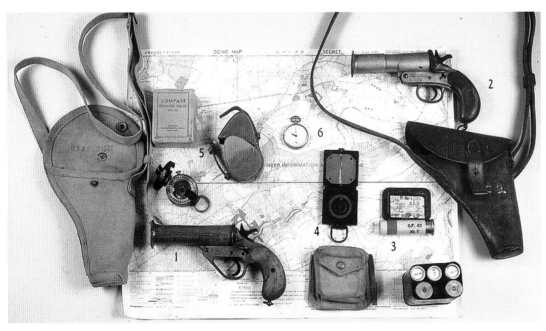

Below : (from left to right).
**Liquid level compass in its
delivery package.**

**Goggles for motor transport
drivers, AFV crews and
motorcyclists.**

(Private collections)

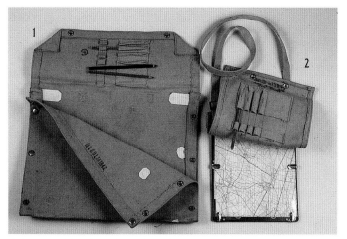

1. **Large-size Map Case for artillery observers or reconnaissance units.**
2. **Standard map case.** *(Private collection)*

MAP SYMBOLS

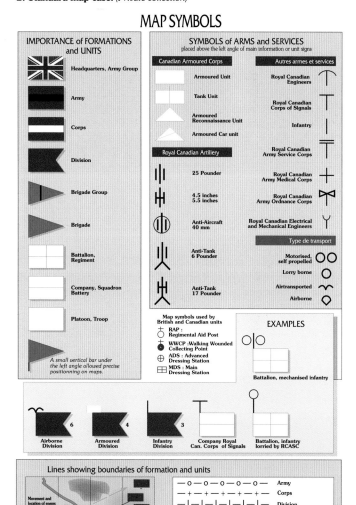

IMPORTANCE of FORMATIONS and UNITS

Headquarters, Army Group	
Army	
Corps	
Division	
Brigade Group	
Brigade	
Battalion, Regiment	
Company, Squadron Battery	
Platoon, Troop	

A small vertical bar under the left angle allowed precise positionning on maps.

SYMBOLS of ARMS and SERVICES
placed above the left angle of main information or unit signs

Canadian Armoured Corps

- Armoured Unit
- Tank Unit
- Armoured Reconnaissance Unit
- Armoured Car unit

Royal Canadian Artillery

- 25 Pounder
- 4.5 inches / 5.5 inches
- Anti-Aircraft 40 mm
- Anti-Tank 6 Pounder
- Anti-Tank 17 Pounder

Autres armes et services

- Royal Canadian Engineers
- Royal Canadian Corps of Signals
- Infantry
- Royal Canadian Army Service Corps
- Royal Canadian Army Medical Corps
- Royal Canadian Army Ordnance Corps
- Royal Canadian Electrical and Mechanical Engineers

Type de transport

- Motorised, self propelled
- Lorry borne
- Airtransported
- Airborne

Map symbols used by British and Canadian units
- RAP : Regimental Aid Post
- WWCP : Walking Wounded Collecting Point
- ADS : Advanced Dressing Station
- MDS : Main Dressing Station

EXAMPLES

Battalion, mechanised infantry

Airborne Division 6 | Armoured Division 4 | Infantry Division 3 | Company Royal Can. Corps of Signals | Battalion, infantry lorried by RCASC

Lines showing boundaries of formation and units

Movement and location of enemy units drawn in blue.
Movement and location of allied units drawn in red.

— o — o — o — o — o —	Army
— + — + — + — + — + —	Corps
— | — | — | — | — | —	Division
— · — · — · — · — · —	Brigade
— — — — — — —	Battalion or Regiment
— → — → — → —	Movement lines

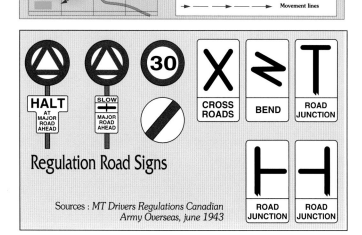

Regulation Road Signs

HALT AT MAJOR ROAD AHEAD | SLOW AT MAJOR ROAD AHEAD | 30 | CROSS ROADS | BEND | ROAD JUNCTION

ROAD JUNCTION | ROAD JUNCTION

Sources : MT Drivers Regulations Canadian Army Overseas, june 1943

13 August 1944, Normandy, on the Caen - Falaise road.
Two Lance-Corporals of No 2 Provost Company putting up a signpost on the side of the road.
(PA 116505)

Examples of road signs posted on the 1st Canadian Army's route across Europe

72 R.S.D. SALVAGE CASUALTY KITS

RSD- Returned Stores Depot where the personnel effects belonging to the wounded and the killed were centralised

SLOW ! BAILEY AHEAD

MAPLE LEAF UP

41 Serial A 1130 VICTORIA BRIDGE

ONYX ROUTE STARTS HERE

WARNING ROAD NARROWS

THIS WAS THE SIEGFRIED LINE

THE WASHING

After Canadian Road Signs, 1944-1945 by Peter A. Veldher.

Normandy 1944. Roadsigns posted by the 2nd Infantry Division. On the left, a bridge for tracked vehicles built by the Engineers over the River Orne, to the south of Caen. On the right, signpost indicating how to reach rear divisional HQ.
(After the Bayeux Memorial Museum Collection)

Above.
Fluorescent recognition panel worn by fighting troops during night operations.
Dimensions.
Greater length = 3ft
Shorter length = 10 ins.
Height = 1 ft 5 ins.

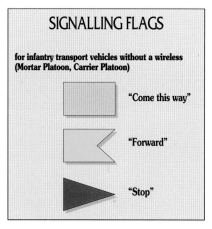

SIGNALLING FLAGS

for infantry transport vehicles without a wireless (Mortar Platoon, Carrier Platoon)

"Come this way"

"Forward"

"Stop"

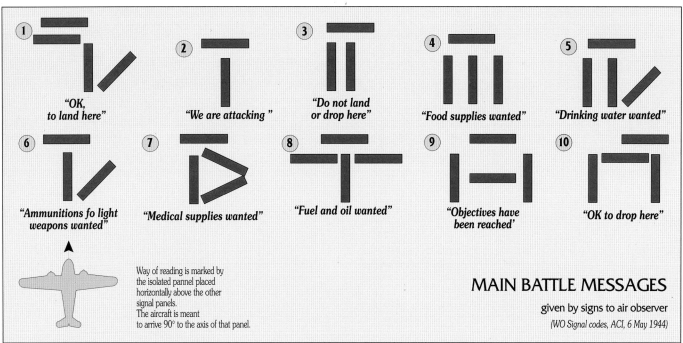

1 "OK, to land here"

2 "We are attacking"

3 "Do not land or drop here"

4 "Food supplies wanted"

5 "Drinking water wanted"

6 "Ammunitions fo light weapons wanted"

7 "Medical supplies wanted"

8 "Fuel and oil wanted"

9 "Objectives have been reached'

10 "OK to drop here"

Way of reading is marked by the isolated pannel placed horizontally above the other signal panels.
The aircraft is meant to arrive 90° to the axis of that panel.

MAIN BATTLE MESSAGES

given by signs to air observer
(WO Signal codes, ACI, 6 May 1944)

Above.
Battery-powered signalling lamp. A key enabled Morse signals to be sent.

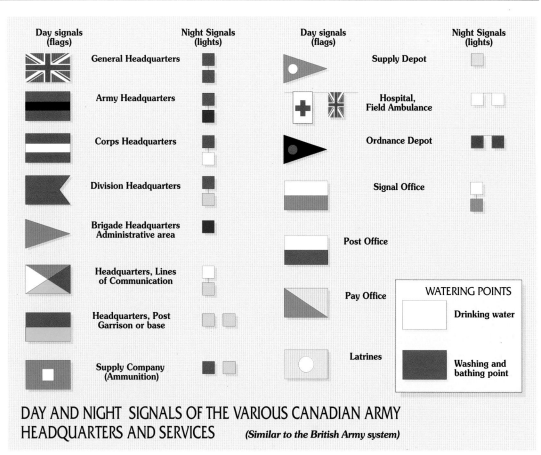

Day signals (flags)		Night Signals (lights)
	General Headquarters	
	Army Headquarters	
	Corps Headquarters	
	Division Headquarters	
	Brigade Headquarters Administrative area	
	Headquarters, Lines of Communication	
	Headquarters, Post Garrison or base	
	Supply Company (Ammunition)	

Day signals (flags)		Night Signals (lights)
	Supply Depot	
	Hospital, Field Ambulance	
	Ordnance Depot	
	Signal Office	
	Post Office	
	Pay Office	
	Latrines	

WATERING POINTS

Drinking water

Washing and bathing point

DAY AND NIGHT SIGNALS OF THE VARIOUS CANADIAN ARMY HEADQUARTERS AND SERVICES
(Similar to the British Army system)

Some Canadian Army radio sets

WIRELESS SET NO 38
Network: platoon - company
Voice Range: 1/2 Mile
Weight: 21 lbs 12 oz.

WIRELESS SET NO 18
Network: company - battalion
Voice Range: 5 Miles
Morse Range: 10 Miles
Weight: 31 lbs 9 oz.

WIRELESS SET NO 19
Network: regiment - brigade
Voice Range: 10 Miles
Morse Range: 15 1/2 Miles.
This set was mounted on vehicles
and armoured vehicles, including all
tanks in Armoured Regiments.
Made in Canada as well in other
Commonwealth countries, it replaced
the American SCR-508 sets.

**WIRELESS SET (CANADIAN)
NO 9 MK I (1943)**
Network: brigade - division.
Voice Range: 25 Miles
Morse Range: 50 Miles.
This set was in widespread use
and was mounted on vehicles or
ground stations. Operated by Royal
Canadian Corps of Signals personnel.

**WIRELESS SET (CAN.) NO 43
(1943)**
Network: division - army corps
Voice Range: 75 Miles
Morse Range: 100 Miles

CANADIAN MAKERS OF RADIO EQUIPMENT

— Northern Electric
— Canadian Marconi
— RCA Victor

Above.
**July 1944, Normandy. Private Ryan of the North Shore
New Brunswick Regiment, 8th Infantry Brigade,
3rd Infantry Division using the No 18 Wireless Set.**
(IWM B 6974)

THE ARMOURED REGIMENT TACTICAL RADIO NETWORK
(Wireless Sets No 19 and High-Power No 19)

Commanding Officer's Scout Car — Armoured Command Vehicle

Regimental Headquarters

Regimental Squadron

Recce. Troop

AA Troop

Intercommunication Troop (x 9)

Medical Officer

B SQUADRON

Squadron Commander

Squadron Commander's Scout Car

Armoured Recovery Vehicle

No 1 TROOP   No 2 TROOP   No 3 TROOP   No 4 TROOP

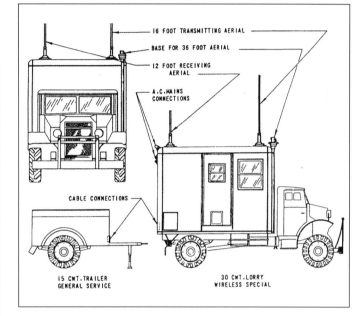

Above.
**Standard configuration of the Wireless Set (Canadian) No 43 Mk II on
a 30-cwt Lorry, Wireless, Special towing its 15-cwt General service trailer.**

Left.
**Distribution of radio sets within the Armoured Regiment.
The standard set used are the WS No 19 or No 19 HP
(high-powered) within the regiment-to-brigade network.**
(After South Albertas, A Canadian Regiment at War)

**March 1945, Germany. Three members of the crew of a Firefly posing
with their war booty, destined for the pot the following day.
The man on the left, Trooper E. Stewart, is wearing Mk II -7 binoculars,
the man in the middle a pair of standard Mk II -6s.
On the right, Corporal B. Levers.**
(© Cliff Allen, South Alberta's Regimental Association)

Right.
Field Telephone Set Mk 5

Above.
How to carry the Infantry Wireless Set 38 No 2 (platoon/company network).

Right.
Wireless set (Canadian) No 43 (1943).

Below.
Wireless set (Canadian) No 19.

Wireless set (Canadian) No 9 Mk I (1943).

Wireless Set No 38.

PHONETIC ALPHABET

(War Office note, 3 June 1944)

LETTERS

		S -	Sugar
		T -	Tare
A -	Able	U -	Uncle
B -	Baker	V -	Victor
C -	Charlie	W -	William
D -	Dog	X -	X-Ray
E -	Easy	Y -	Yoke
F -	Fox	Z -	Zebra
G -	George		
H -	How	**FIGURES**	
I -	Item	0 -	Zero
J -	Jig	1 -	Wun
K -	King	2 -	Too
L -	Love	3 -	Thuh-ree
M -	Mike	4 -	Fo-wer
N -	Nan	5 -	Fi-yiv
O -	Oboe	6 -	Six
P -	Peter	7 -	Seven
Q -	Queen	8 -	Ate
R -	Roger	9 -	Niner

WIRELESS SETS USED IN FRONT LINE UNITS AND FORMATIONS

TYPES (Wireless Set)	NETWORK	TRANSPORT	MAXIMUM RANGE Voice	Morse	WEIGHT
W. Set No 1	Brigade - division - artillery	Vehicles	3,2 km	8 km	106,6 kg
W. Set No 9	Brigade - division	Vehicles and AFVs	40 km	56 km	86,4 kg
W. Set No 12	HQ division - army corps Air support	3-ton 4WD lorries	25 km	100 km	300 kg
W. Set No 14	Battalion HQ - Tanks	Vehicles	1,6 km		36,45 kg
W. Set No 18	Infantry - company - battalion	Portable	8 km	16 km	14,4 kg
W. Set No 19A	Battalion - brigade	Vehicles AFVs	16 km	24 km	45 kg
W. Set No 21	Brigade - Artillery	Vehicles	8 km	12,8 km	22 kg
W. Set No 38	Platoon - Company	Portable	1 km		9,9 kg
W. Set No 46 waterproofed	Company - battalion Combined operations	Portable	12 km		10,8 kg
W. Set No 48	American-made, characteristics similar to W. set No 18				
W. Set No 68 (Set 18 variant)	Airborne troops Brigade-division Combined Operations	Portable	8 km	16 km	14,4 kg
W. Set No 76	Airborne troops- GHQ	Jeep or portable in 4 different loads		480 km	14,85 kg

CHAPTER 8

ARMAMENT

I. Edged Weapons

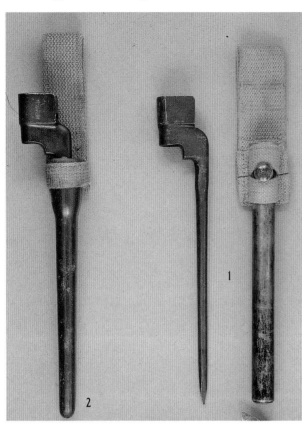

1943, in Great Britain, officers and a Warrant Officer of the Régiment de la Chaudière comparing the respective qualities of the Smith & Wesson issue revolver and the German P08.

1. Bayonet Mk II for No 4 Rifle made by Long Branch Arsenal in Canada.
2. Bayonet Mk II in its sheath, made by the American firm Victory Plastics.
3. Large Canadian jack-knife with spike.
4. Canadian combat knife made from the shortened bayonet of a Ross Rifle. The maker was Ross Rifle Co. of Quebec.
5. British Fairbairn dagger with its sheath. It had been slipped inside a webbing bayonet frog.
6. Issue British fighting knife.

7. Fairbairn dagger in an American M6 sheath.
8. Fairbairn dagger and its sheath decorated by cotton tresswork.
(The gift of a Canadian Veteran, private Collection)

These weapons were not standard issue, except in the 1st Canadian Parachute Battalion. They were privately bought or were occasional hand-outs.

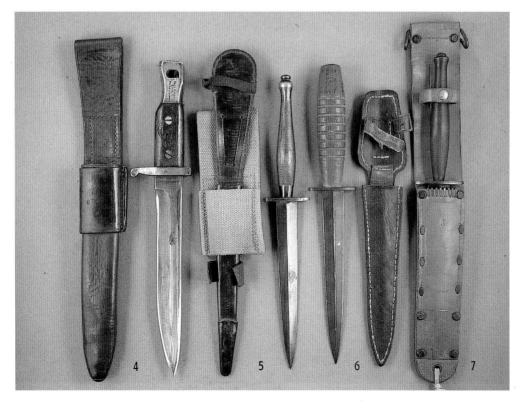

2. Handguns

Above. 1. Pistol Revolver No 2
Mk I*.
2. Ammunition for .38 Pistol
Revolver.
3. Automatic Pistol Colt M1911A1,
.45 caliber.
4. Smith & Wesson Revolver
K 38/200.
5. Browning FN-Inglis Automatic
Pistol, 9mm Parabellum, standard
Canadian Army issue. Pistols with
back ramp sight and slot in the butt
for a detachable stock were made
for China.
6. FN-Inglis pistol holster.
7. 13-round magazine.
8. Box of 64 9mm Parabellum
cartridges.
9. Pouch for two Browning or Colt
pistol magazines.

1. Pistol, Revolver No 2 MkI*

Calibre: .38 (9mm)
Weight: 1lb 12 oz.
Length: 10 ins
Practical Range: 33 yards
Muzzle velocity: 600ft/sec.
Capacity: 6 cartridges in the cylinder ;
Operation: Double action only. Spent shells extracted by swinging the barrel and the cylinder
Maker(s): (UK) Albion Motors, Enfield, RSAF.
Issued to: AFV crews, officers and miscellaneous personnel not armed with the rifle, Sten gun or Bren LMG (except for airborne troops). Replaced the Webley Mk IV as of 1942.

3. Automatic Pistol (Colt) M1911A1

Made in North America.
Calibre: .45 (11.43mm)
Weight: (fully loaded) 2 lbs 12 oz.
Length: 7 ins
Practical Range: 33 yards.
Muzzle velocity: 858 ft/sec.
Magazine: 7 cartridges.
Issued to: 1st Canadian Parachute Battalion.

4. Smith & Wesson K 38/200 Revolver

Calibre: .38 (9mm)
Weight: 2 lbs
Length: 10 ins
Muzzle velocity: 760 ft/sec.
Capacity: 6 rounds.
Operation: Simple or double action
Maker(s): USA for the Commonwealth Nations.
Issued to: Officers and heavy machine crews.

5. Browning FN-Inglis No 2 Mk I* Automatic Pistol

Calibre: .38 (9mm)
Weight: 2.2 lbs with mag.
Practical Range: 55 yards
Muzzle velocity: 1 320 ft /sec.
Magazine: 13 cartridges.
Ammunition: 9mm Parabellum (identical to that of the Sten and certain German weapons)
Maker(s): Inglis, Canada.
Issued to: Officers and AFV crews, miscellaneous personnel not equipped with a rifle or a Sten Gun. It gradually replaced the issue revolvers after October 1942.

PISTOL AND REVOLVER HOLSTERS

A. Holster for No 2 Mk I* revolver issued to AFV crews (1944-1945).

B and C. Standard holsters for pistols and revolvers.

D. Holster for FN-Inglis pistol. This holster was intended originally for an arms supply contract with China. It was distributed to the Canadian Army from October 1944. This holster features a magazine pocket.

E. Definitive version of the Browning FN-Inglis pistol holster.

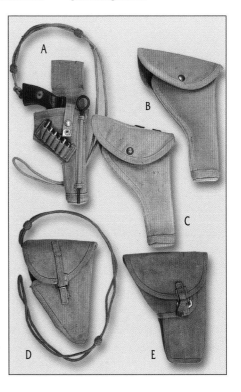

3. The No 4 Mark I* Rifle

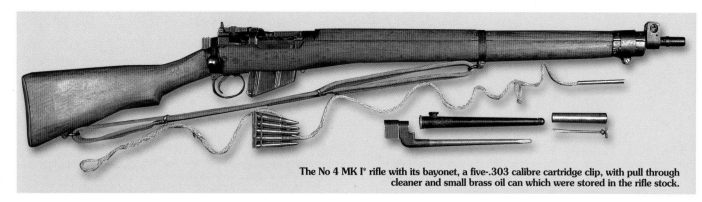

The No 4 MK I* rifle with its bayonet, a five-.303 calibre cartridge clip, with pull through cleaner and small brass oil can which were stored in the rifle stock.

The No 4 Mk I * Rifle

The Canadian Army's standard rifle.
Calibre: .303 (7.7mm)
Weight: 8 lbs 12 oz.
Length: 3 ft 9 ins
Max. range: 1 960 yards.
Practical Range: 295 yards.
Muzzle velocity: 2 458 ft./sec
Magazine: 10 rounds

Operation: Bolt action. Manual repetition.
Sights: simplified backsight with two apertures, for 890 ft and 5940 ft range.

Maker(s): from 1942-1945 S.A.L./C.A.L. at Long Branch, Canada.

Great Britain, 17 May 1944. During a visit from the Royal Family, 1st Canadian Parachute Battalion sharpshooters carried out a demonstration. The No 4 Mk I* (T) with telescopic sight has been fitted with the regulation American M-1907 leather sling. (PA 179 150)

The N°4 Mark I* Rifle was the Canadian Army's basic weapon. (PA 133104)

Left.
Details of the N°4 Mk I (T) Rifle with telescopic sight and the Canadian 'Telescope, Observing Sniper Mk I' with its case.
(D. Coste collection)

Right.
Holland, 1945.
This sniper from the Calgary Highlanders Regiment is armed with a No 4 Rifle made at Long Branch Arsenal (Canada) fitted with a 'Telescope Sighting No 32 Mk 4.'
The camouflage face veil is worn here like a turban.
He is also carrying a Kukri, the fearsome Gurkha knife on his left hand side.

1. Calibre .303 Cartridge chambered by the No 4 Rifle, the Bren Gun and the Vickers machine gun. (length: 3 ins ; weight: 1 oz ; initial velocity: 2460 ft/sec).
2. 5-cartridge clip for the rifle

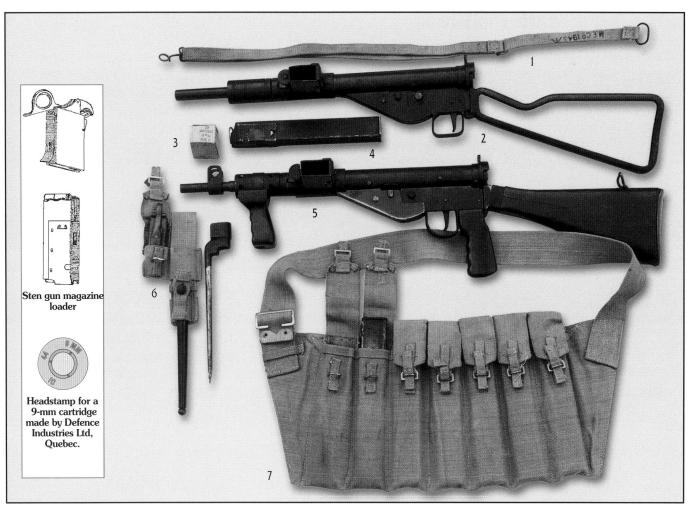

Sten gun magazine loader

Headstamp for a 9-mm cartridge made by Defence Industries Ltd, Quebec.

4. The Sten Machine Carbine

Below.
Germany, near Oldenberg in April 1945. A corporal from the Fusiliers Mont-Royal loading a Sten Gun Magazine.
(PA 163401)

The Sten Gun and its accessories.
1. Standard sling.
2. Mark II Sten gun with skeleton butt.
3. Packet of 9mm Parabellum cartridges.
4. Magazine.
5. Sten Mk V for Airborne troops. A lug at the end of the barrel enabled the Mk II bayonet

to be fixed.
6. Bayonet frog with pouch for the simplified magazine loader.
7. Sten gun magazine pouch for Airborne Troops.

Note. With the exception of the Mk V, the Sten Gun was manufactured by the Long Branch arsenal in Canada.

Calibre: 9mm Parabellum
Weight: 8lbs-10lbs depending on the version.
Length: 2 ft 6 ins.
Practical Range: 110 yards.
Muzzle velocity: 1 204ft / sec.
Rate of Fire: 550 rounds/min.
Magazine: Straight magazine with 32 cartridges

Operation: simple blowback action, single shot or full automatic.

Issued to: Corporal (Section Leader, Infantry) including Airborne troops. No 2 (loader) of the 2-in mortar team, CMP and RCS despatch riders, etc. One Sten Gun was issued to each Sherman tank crew.

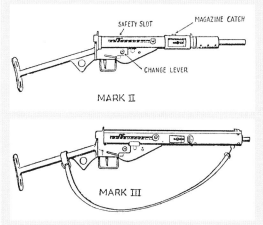

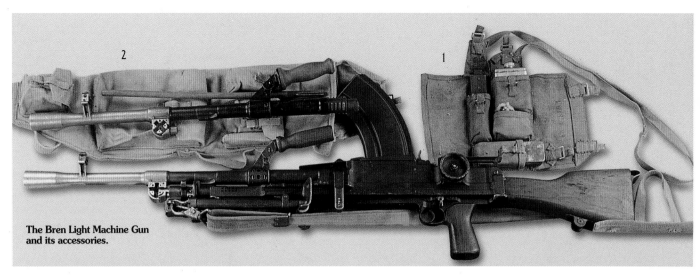

The Bren Light Machine Gun
and its accessories.

5. The Bren Light Machine Gun

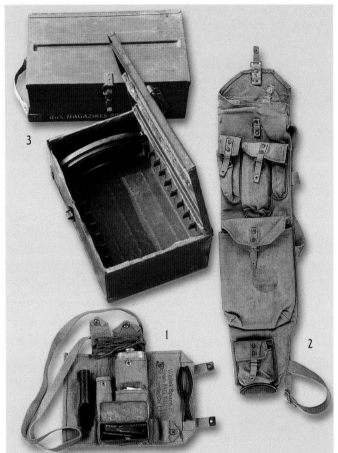

The Bren Light Machine Gun Mk I

Calibre: .303 (7.7mm)
Weight: 23 lbs.
Length: 3 ft 9 ins
Maximum Range: 1 650 yards
Practical Range: 660 yards
Muzzle velocity: 2 458 ft / sec.
Rate of Fire:
- **single shot:** 40 shots/min
- **burst:** 650 rounds/min.
Magazine: 30-round magazine box (practical load 28 rounds)
Operation: gas-activated, single shot or bursts.

Maker(s): John Inglis Co. Ltd., Toronto (1939-1945).
Quantities made: 186 802, of which a number were for other Commonwealth nations.

Use: Infantry Section automatic weapon used for 'fire and movement' (see scale of issue in the Infantry Battalion Chapter, page 25).
It was also used in the majority of front-line units.

Top and above;
1. Bren gun wallet carried by the No 1 of the Bren Gun team.
2. Bag containing a spare barrel and spare parts, the cleaning rod and various tools. Carried by the No 2 (loader).
3. Metal case for 12 Bren Gun magazines, carried in unit transport

Right.
A. Contents of the Bren gun wallet.
1. Gas cylinder setting key
2. Oil can.
3. Cloth.
4. Spare parts box.
5. Broken case extractor.
6. Pull through cleaner with string, cleaning brush.
B. Extra Utility Pouches containing 2 magazines each (these could also hold grenades, 2-in mortar shells or other ammunition). They were worn on the chest, suspended from the neck by the upper strap and held on the body by the horizontal strap, on top of the standard webbing equipment.

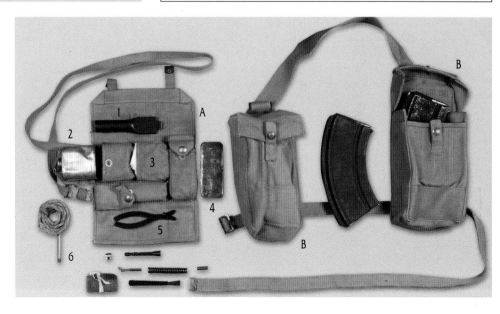

Right.
Normandy, 20 June 1944. A camouflaged Bren Gun pit.
(PA 131 432)

Below, left.
The .303 Vickers machine gun in action during the battle for Carpiquet, near Caen, on 4 July 1944. The gun is crewed by men of the Cameron Highlanders of Ottawa, the Machine Gun battalion of the 3rd Infantry Division.
(PA 129 037)

6. Heavy and light machine guns

Vickers Heavy Machine Gun

Calibre: .303 (7.7mm)
Weight: 93 lbs 8 oz. in fighting order
Practical Range: 880 yards
Trajectory elevation: Man standing at 660 yards.
Operation: short barrel recoil, water-cooled.
Rate of Fire: 500 rounds/min.
Ammunition: rimmed case. Nickel-silver jacketed bullet, lead core.
Ammunition packaging: wooden crates containing two boxes of one cloth 250-cartridge belt.

Crew: - Lance-Corporal/gunner (carrying the tripod).
- Loader (carrying the gun itself, sight, cooling jacket tube and spare parts)
– Ammunition number (carrying two 250-round cases of ammunition and the water condensing can)
Issued to: Mortar and Machine Gun Battalion of the Infantry division (36 guns, carried in Universal carriers), and to the Independent Mortar and Machine Gun Company of the Armoured Division (12 guns).

BESA Machine Gun

Czech-designed machine gun built under licence by BSA.

Calibre: 7.92mm (the cartridge was identical to the German 7.92 round).
Weight: 48 lbs 6 1/2 oz
Length: 3 ft 7 ins

Magazine: 225-round metal or cloth belt.
Rate of Fire: 450-750 rounds/min.
Operation: gas activated.
Issued to: secondary armament for British tanks and armoured cars.

Browning, .30 caliber, Machine Gun (USA)

Calibre: .7.62mm
Weight: (without mounting) 30 lbs 4 oz.
Maximum Range: 2 420 yards
Practical Range: 880 yards.
Feed system: canvas belt.
Operation: delayed blowback , short barrel recoil.

Browning, .50 caliber, Heavy Machine Gun (USA)

Calibre: 12.7mm
Weight: (without mounting) 83 lbs 9 oz.
Rate of Fire: 500 rounds / min
Maximum Range: 2 860 yards
Practical Range: 1 320 yards
Feed system: cartridges loaded on belt made up of expendable metal links
Operation: gas-activated, barrel recoil

Both used as secondary armament in American-made vehicles.

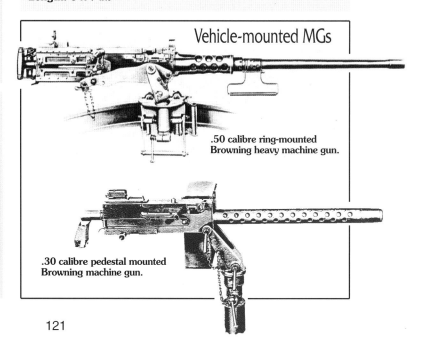

Vehicle-mounted MGs

.50 calibre ring-mounted Browning heavy machine gun.

.30 calibre pedestal mounted Browning machine gun.

Normandy, 20 June 1944. Lance-Bombardier W.J. Pelrine of the 14th Field Artillery Regiment ready to fire the .50 Calibre Heavy Machine Gun mounted on his self-propelled M7 howitzer. *(PA 114 583)*

8. Flame-throwers

The Ack-Pack here is being used by a British infantryman during a training session. *(IWM)*

7. The PIAT

Great Britain, January 1944, Canucks from the Toronto Scottish (MG) 2nd Infantry Division, undergoing PIAT (Projector, Infantry, Anti-Tank) training. *(PA 177 100)*

PIAT Anti-Tank Gun
Weight: 35 lbs 3 oz.
Length: 3ft 1 1/2 ins.
Practical Range:
Anti-Tank: 110 yards
Houses, strongpoints: 380 yards.
Rate of fire: 5-6 shots/min.
Shell: 2 lbs 8 ozs. Green rocket, red crosses on the body of the charge.

Would pierce the armour of any tank in service.
Operation: Rocket propelled by incorporated cartridge. System automatically re-armed when projectile expelled.
Issued to: see page 25 (Infantry Bn.) The PIAT was also used by most of the forward units.

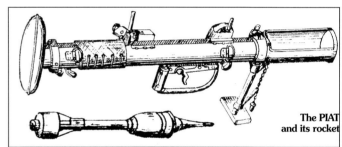

The PIAT and its rocket

1. Ack Pack

Carried on the operator's back.

Total weight: 48 lbs 7 oz.
Tank capacity: 4 gallons.
Range: 150 feet.
Operation: Jet ignited by .303 cartridges.
Duration of jet: 2 seconds.
N° of jets: 10.

2. Wasp

Mounted on a Universal Carrier.

Total weight: 1 600 lbs.
Tank capacity: 79 1/2 gallons.
Range: 110 yards.
Operation: Electrically fired, each jet lasts 2 secs.
Issued to: (depending on availability) Medium Machine Gun Battalion, or MMG Company in the Armoured Divisions.

10. Anti-Personnel and Anti-Tank Mines

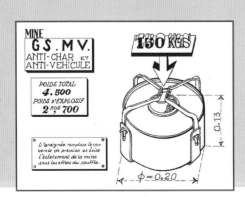

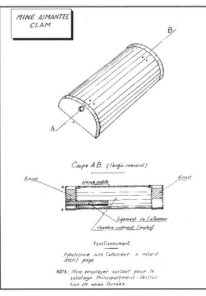

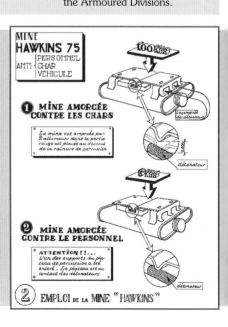

9. Grenades

Above.
1. No 36 Mills bomb (grenade).
2. Grenade No 82 'Gammon Grenade', a 2-lb plastic ball of malleable explosive paste contained in a cloth sack. After unscrewing the top of the plastic, the soldier threw the grenade, which was primed by means of a cord weighted with lead which unrolled by itself. The detonator set off the charge on impact.

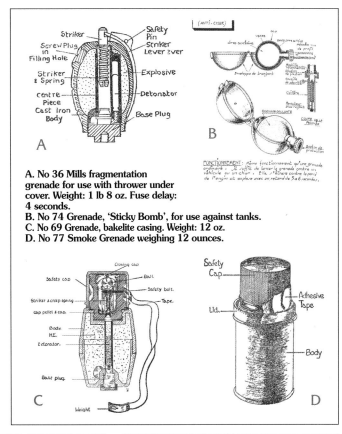

A. No 36 Mills fragmentation grenade for use with thrower under cover. Weight: 1 lb 8 oz. Fuse delay: 4 seconds.
B. No 74 Grenade, 'Sticky Bomb', for use against tanks.
C. No 69 Grenade, bakelite casing. Weight: 12 oz.
D. No 77 Smoke Grenade weighing 12 ounces.

Below.
1. Hawkins Anti-tank mine, set off by pressure.
2. Clam Magnetic Mine, for use against all vehicles.
3. Smoke Grenade.
4. Release-type firing device.
5. Fuse-crimping pliers.
6. Grenade No 82 ('Gammon bomb,' Plastic Charge).
7. Mills No 36 Defensive Grenade.
8. No 69 Offensive Grenade.
9. No 73 Phosphorus incendiary grenade.
10. Tube of primary explosives
11. Cone of primary explosives
12. Plastic and 808 explosive, available also in rolls.
13. Delayed action ignition pencils.
14. Box of detonators.
15. Bickford cord and cigarettes for ignition.

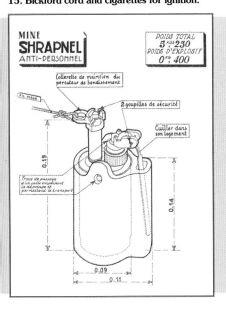

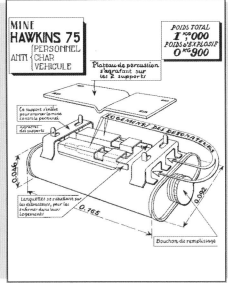

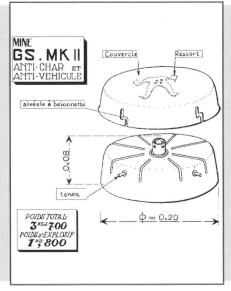

11. Mortars

2-inch Mortar

Calibre: 2-in. (50.8mm)
Weight: 23 lbs 7 oz.
Practical range: 275 yards.
Rate of Fire: 4 bombs/min.
Shells
- Explosive: 2 1/2 lbs, brown with red and green stripe.
- Smoke: 2lbs. green, red stripe. Gave off 2 minutes-worth of

smoke, with an average of 55 yards of screen.
Crew: 2. The gunner (an NCO) carried the gun, the loader the ammunition.
Used for close support within the infantry platoon.
Made in Canada.

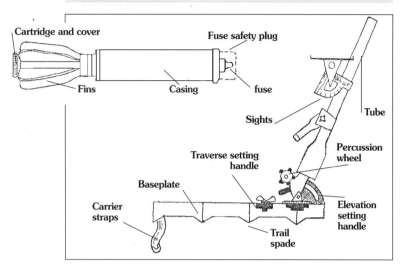

Cartridge and cover — Fuse safety plug — Fins — Casing — fuse — Sights — Tube — Traverse setting handle — Percussion wheel — Baseplate — Carrier straps — Trail spade — Elevation setting handle

Great Britain, November 1942. Men from the Lake Superior Regiment learning to fire the 2-in mortar. *(PA 113 637)*

4.2-inch Mortar

Calibre: 4.2 inches (106.7mm).
Total weight in fighting order: 468 lbs.
Practical range: 1 100 to 4 125 yards depending on the charge.
Rate of fire: 8-10 shots/min.
Shell weight: 19 1/2 lbs.
Piece divided into three loads: tube, tripod, baseplate..

Crew: 4 (1 L/Corporal or Corporal, in command and 3 loaders)
Transport: Llloyd Mortar Carrier and its trailer.
Support weapon in Mortar and Machine Gun battalions in the Infantry Divisions (16 mortars) as well as in the Independent MMG Companies of the Armoured Divisions (4 mortars).

February 1943 in Great Britain. A Fusiliers Mont-Royal 3-inch mortar crew during a field exercise. The men here are wearing the denim two-piece overalls. *(RR)*

3-inch Mortar

Calibre: 3 inches (76.2 mm)
Weight: 132 lbs.
Practical Range:
125 yards to 2,750 yards depending on the charge.
Rate of Fire: 5 bombs a minute.
Shell weight: 10 lbs
Piece divided into three loads:

Tube, tripod, baseplate.
Transport: Universal carrier.
Used as support weapon in the Infantry and Motor Battalions (Mortar platoons)
Made in Canada.

Great Britain, April 1944. A 3-inch mortar crew on manoeuvres. *(PA 197 534)*

CHAPTER 9 CANADIAN VEHICLES

1. Bicycles

Airborne Folding Bicycle

Transporting the Folding Bicycle
1. Ready for use. A special portage frame could be fitted over the front wheel.
2. Folding. Two articulated joints fitted with butterfly screws enable the frame to be folded in half. With the help of a quick-release lever, the handlebars folded over parallel to the frame. On certain models the pedals could be positioned so that they did not stick out.
3. Ready for transportation. The folded parts were held together other with straps. The bike could be air-dropped by itself or in the same way as the leg bag, with the paratrooper.
This type of bike was issued to airborne troops but also to land forces.
(Reconstruction, private collection)

The Canadian Army's BSA Standard Bicycle was the same as that used by the British Army.
Tyres: 28 x 1 3/4. Brakes operated with rods and links.

Normandy, June 1944. The Airborne Folding Bicycle was not only issued to airborne troops but as with the Standard Bicycle, also to infantry and service units. Here, a Private of the Highland Light Infantry repairing a tyre.
(A 133100)

2. Army Motorcycles

Norton Model 1G-H

Engine: Norton Single-cylinder 4-stroke air cooled engine.
Power rating: 490cc.
Gearbox: Four gears changed by foot selector.
Weight: 367 lbs.
Speed: 65 mph.

Use: Liaison, traffic direction, escort.
(Reconditioned. private collection)

Norton Model 1G-H during manoeuvres of the South Alberta Regiment in Great Britain.
(Photo CND)

James Model ML 125 cc

Engine: Villiers single-cylinder four-stroke air-cooled.
Power rating: 125 cc.
Gearbox: 3 manually-operated gears.
Weight: 140 lbs.
Speed: 40 mph.

Use: light motorbike for airborne troops, and also used for liaison over short distances by land forces. *(Reconditioned machine, private collection)*

Harley Davidson Motor Co Heavy Solo Motorcycle

Engine: V-2 (45°), four-stroke air-cooled.
Power rating: 23 bhp/737 cc.
Transmission: chain
Gearbox: 3 gears
Weight: (empty) 625 lbs.
Model presented: WLC 43 (export)
Main features compared with the US

Army model:
— Front and rear wheels interchangeable.
— Accelerator on the left.
— Forward and retard lever on the right.
Use: Liaison, escort, traffic direction (on good roads)

Chevrolet Personnel Heavy Utility 4 x 4 Truck

Bridge Classification: 3 (page 141)
Engine: General Motors 6-cylinder petrol.
Power Rating: 85 bhp
Speed: 50 mph.

Use: light transport for personnel (6 men). Used as a command post in the arms and the services. It was also converted into a light ambulance. *(PAC photo)*

3. Light Vehicles

5-Cwt, 4 x 4, Car "Jeep"

Length: 11 ft.
Width: 5 ft 2 1/2 ins.
Height: 5 ft 10 ins (with canvas top)
Engine: 4-cylinder, 60 bhp, 2.2 litre petrol.
Fuel tank capacity: 12 1/2 gallons.
Transmission: 3 forward, one

reverse gears.
- 2-speed transfer box.
Range: 280 miles on road.
Speed: 56 mph.
Use: all reconnaissance, liaison, command missions. Also adapted for carrying stretchers.
(PAC photograph, below)

Ford Motor Co 4x2 Station Wagon

Bridge Classification: 2
Engine: Ford V8 petrol.
Power Rating: 95 bhp
Max. Speed: 70 mph
Use: existed in 5- or 7- seat versions.

Issued to Army Headquarters for transporting senior officers, depending on road conditions.
(PAC photograph)

4. Medium Trucks

4x4 Ford 15-cwt, GS, Truck
Bridge Classification: 4
Engine: Ford V-8 petrol.
Power rating: 95 bhp
Max. Speed: 50 mph.

Use: General service lorry, all arms and services. Towed a 10-cwt trailer. Used alongside the Model C15A-GS Chevrolet.

(Photo Tank Museum, Bovington)

Chevrolet 4x4 15-cwt, Water bowser
Bridge Classification: 5
Engine: General Motors 6-cylinder petrol.
Power Rating: 85 bhp
Speed: 45 mph

Water tank Capacity: 200 gallons of filtered drinking water
Use: Supplying front-line units.

(PAC photograph)

Army vehicles payloads
Cwt (Hundredweight) = 50,80 kg

5-cwt	250 kg (jeep)
8-cwt	400 kg
10-cwt	500 kg
15-cwt	750 kg
30-cwt	1 500 kg

Note: above 30-cwt, weight is expressed in tons, roughly equivalent to the metric tonne: 1 016, 04 kg.

5. Heavy Trucks

Ford 4x4 3-Ton GS Lorry

Bridge classification: 8

Power rating: 95 bhp

Use: all arms and services. Troop transport and RCASC trains. Different bodies were available for converting it into a kitchen, mobile canteen, shop or medical station.

(Tank Museum, Bovington, photograph)

3-Ton Petrol bowser

Model: 3-ton 4 x 4 Chevrolet.
Bridge classification: 8
Weight: 7.2 tons
Engine: General Motors 6- cylinder petrol
Power rating: 85 bhp
Tank capacity: 800 gallons.
Use: Royal Canadian Army Service Corps for supplying units in the line.
(PAC)

6. Armoured Vehicles

Universal T-16 Carrier (Ford Motor Co, USA for Canada)

Bridge classification: 4
Engine: Ford V-8 petrol
Power rating: 100 bhp
Armour: max. 1/4 inch thick .
Speed: 30 mph.
Use: towing the anti-tank 6-Pdr guns

in infantry battalions, or carrying the
4.2 Mortar in the Medium Machine
Gun Battalions or Companies.
28,992 produced.
(PAC)

Windsor Universal Carrier (Ford Canada, Windsor factory)

Bridge classification: 5
Engine: Ford V-8 petrol
Power rating: 90 bhp.
Other characteristics and uses the same

as the Universal T-16 Carrier.
5,000 produced (1944-45).
(PAC)

Armoured 4x4 15-cwt Truck (General Motors Canada)

Bridge classification: 6
Engine: General Motors 6-cylinder petrol.
Power rating: 104 bhp.
Armour:
front: 1/2 inch ; sides: 1/4 inch.
Speed: 45 mph

Use: Infantry transport into forward zones. Equipment destined to make up for the lack of US half-tracks and scout-cars. Could also be fitted up for ammunition transport or as an ambulance.
(PAC)

(PAC)

Below:
Holland, 27 October 1944. Men from the Royal Hamilton (2nd Infantry Division) moving along aboard their 15-cwt Armoured 4 x 4 Trucks.
(DR)

White Motor Co. Armoured M3A1 15-cwt Truck

Bridge classification: 5
Engine: Hercules 6-cylinder petrol, front-wheel drive
Power rating: 110 bhp

Armour: 1/4 to 1/2 inch.
Max. road speed: 50 mph.
Use: personnel transport, reconnaissance, command. (PAC)

Following page, from left to right:
Summer 1944, a rare White half-track issued by Americans to the Canadian Army. *(PAC)*

Belgium, 26 September 1944. An International M9A1 half-track crossing the Albert Canal by means of a double trellis Bailey Bridge.
(PA 114574)

1939-1945 CANADIAN VEHICLE PRODUCTION

Vehicle	Quantity produced	Percentage
CANADIAN MILITARY PATTERN [1]		
8-cwt. 4x2	9 837	1,14
Heavy Utility 4x4	12 967	1,51
15-cwt. 4x2	34195	3,98
15-cwt. 4x4	69 227	8,08
30-cwt. 4x4	19 319	2,24
3-ton 4x2	6 000	0,70
3-ton 4x4	209 004	24,40
FAT 4x4	22 891	2,62
3-ton 6x4	4 123	0,48
3-ton 6x6	2 710	0,31
Trailers	19 663	2,29
Total	**409 936**	**47,75**
MODIFIED CONVENTIONAL [2]		
15-cwt. 4x2	88 096	10,28
30-cwt. 4x2	21 188	2,47
3-ton 4x2	197 073	23,00
Total	**306 357**	**35,75**
ARMOURED		
Universal Carriers	28 992	3,37
Windsor Carriers	5 000	0,58
Cars, Armoured	1 506	0,17
Cars, Light Recce	1 761	0,20
Scout Cars	3 255	0,38
Truck Armoured	3 961	0,46
Tank, Valentine	1 420	0,16
Tank, Cruiser, Ram	1 948	0,23
SO 25-Pdr. Sexton	2 122	0,25
Tank, Cruiser, Grizzly	189	0,02
Tank Command OP	84	0,01
Tank AA 20 mm Quad Skink	3	
Total	**50 241**	**5,85**
MISCELLANEOUS		
Station wagons, Staff Cars	81 942	9,55
Rear Engine 4x4 (India only)	9 494	1,10
Total	**91 436**	**10,65**
GENERAL TOTAL	**857 970**	**100**

1. Vehicles made only according to military specifications.
2. Vehicles of commercial pattern converted for military use. These were wheeled vehicles made in Canada in decentralised American factories: Ford and General Motors (through its subsidiary: Chevrolet) supplied directly with some parts by the American factories.

Like the US Army, the Canadian Army only used four- or six-wheel drive vehicles in the combat zone. A large part of Canadian production was delivered to other Commonwealth nations and to the Soviet Union.

A selection of vehicles used by the Canadian Army on campaign has been presented here. They were classified 'A' for combat vehicles and 'B' for transport.

All Canadian vehicles were right-hand drive

7. Command Vehicles

AEC 'Matador' 4x4 Armoured Command vehicle (High Power)

Bridge classification: 12
Engine: AEC 6-cylinder diesel, front wheel drive.
Power rating: 95 bhp
Armour: 1/2 inch
Max. road speed: 38 mph

Use: Royal Canadian Signals and Armoured Divisions Headquarters.
High power radio sets: W 53 Transmitter and R107 Receiver, and Set No 19.
(PAC)

8. Armoured Personnel Carriers

International Harvester Co. 15-cwt M14* Half-Track Truck.

Bridge classification: 8
Engine: IHC 6-cylinder petrol.
Power rating: 143 bhp
Armour: 1/4 - 7/16 inch
Max. road speed: 45 mph.
Use: personnel carrier (10 men), command vehicle, ambulance in the armoured regiments.

* The M14 was originally equipped with an AA mount with four .50 MGs. The British and Canadians removed the guns and used the vehicle only as a troop transport. *(PAC photos)*
Note. See also on p. 152 for the Ram 'Kangaroo' APC.

9. Reconnaissance Vehicles

(IWM)

(Photo Tank Museum Bovington)

Lynx II 4 x 4 Scout Car (Ford Motor Co., Canada)

Bridge Classification: 5
Engine: Ford V-8 petrol
Power Rating: 95 bhp
Crew: 2.
Armour: 7/16 - 1 3/16 inches.

Armament: 1 Bren Gun.
Radio: Set No 19.
Use: Armoured Car Regiments, Armoured Regiments, Reconnaissance Troop.

Humber Mk I 4 x 4 Scout Car

Bridge classification: 4
Engine: Humber 6-cylinder petrol
Power Rating: 79 bhp
Crew: 2
Armament: one Bren gun.

Armour: 3/16 in - 7/16 in.
Speed: 55 mph.
Use: Armoured Car Regiments, Intercommunication Troops, Armoured Regiments, Reconnaissance troops.

(PAC)

Humber Mk IV 4 x 4 Armoured Car

Bridge Classification: 7
Engine: Rootes 6-cylinder petrol.
Power rating: 90 bhp front-wheel drive.
Crew: 3
Armament: one 37-mm canon, one BESA 7.92-mm machine gun, one Bren Gun.
Armour: 3/8-7/16 inch
Max. Road Speed: 45 mph
Use: Infantry Division armoured car reconnaissance regiments.

Otter 4 x 4 Light Reconnaissance Car

Bridge Classification: 5
Built by General Motors Canada
Engine: General Motors 6-cylinder
Power Rating: 106 bhp
Crew: 2
Armament: one Bren Gun in the turret.
Armour: 5/16 - 1/2 inch
Speed: 45 mph
Use: Reconnaissance, convoy escort 1 761 produced in 1942.
(PAC)

Daimler Mk I 4 x 4 Armoured Car

Bridge classification: 7
Engine: Daimler 6-cylinder petrol.
Power rating: 95 bhp
Crew: 3
Armament: one 2-Pder (40 mm) gun, one BESA 7.92 coaxial machine gun.
Armour: 3/8 - 5/8 inch

Max. road speed: 50 mph
Vehicle fitted with forward-reverse transfer box ; so-driver's seat installed in the rear.
Use: Armoured Car Regiments.

Staghound T-17E1 4 x 4 Command Armoured Car

Bridge classification: 15
Built by General Motors
Engine: GM 6-cylinder petrol.
Power rating: 97 bhp
Crew: 4
Armament: one 37-mm gun,
two .30 calibre machine guns.
Armour: 1/2 inch max.
Max. road speed: 50 mph.
Use: Army Corps armoured
car regiments.
(PAC photo)

10. Light Tanks

'Stuart V' M3 A3 Light Tank

Bridge classification: 14
Built by American Car and Foundry
Engine: Continental (aircraft-style) 7 cylinder radial air-cooled petrol.
Power rating: 240 bhp
Armament: one 37-mm gun, three .30-calibre machine guns.
Armour: 1/2 inch- 2 3/4 inches
Radio: Set No 19
Use: Reconnaissance Troop in Armoured Regiments.

Tank, Light, 'Stuart VI' M5 A1

The main part of the supply of American light tanks was made up of M3A3s. Delivered in limited numbers, the M5 A1 differed from the M3 A3 as follows:
– 2 V8 Cadillac engines meaning that the rear deck was higher instead of being level.
– Hydramatic gearbox.
– Front glacis modified.
It was used for the same tasks as the M3 A3.

Above
The M3 A3 light tank, Stuart V.
(PAC)

Above, right.
The M5 A1 light tank, Stuart VI.
(IWM)

'Stuart V' M3 A3 Light Tank

Turretless tanks used as reconnaissance vehicles, forward observation posts or for transporting ammunition. Operated by : RCArtillery, Anti-Tank Regiments in Armoured Divisions.

Here the 4th Anti-Tank Regiment, 5th Armoured Division, Holland, May 1945. *(PAC)*

11. Medium Tanks

The M4 Sherman Tank

The American M4 Sherman cruiser tank was the main AFV of the Canadian Armoured Regiments. In 1944-45, after the Dieppe fiasco, there were no Churchill tanks in Canadian service.

Bridge Classification: 33
Engine:
– M4 A2 Sherman III: twin coupled 6-cylinder diesel engines (380 bhp)
– M4 A4 Sherman V: five Chrysler petrol engines coupled, 450 bhp. The extra space these needed explains the lengthening of the hull and the wider gap between the bogies. The Sherman V was the base for the 'Firefly' conversion.
Transmission: Five forward and one rear gears.
Crew: 5
Armament: one 75-mm gun with 98 shells ; one .50 calibre MG on the turret top, two .30 calibre machine guns (one co-axially in the turret and one on the hull)
Armour:
– Hull front: 2 1/4 inches ;
– Hull sides: 1 1/2 inches.
– Turret: 3 inches ; sides: 2 inches
Radio: one Set No 19
Max. Road Speed: 26 mph

M4 Firefly Tank

British modification of the American M4. The M4 A4 Sherman V became the Vc-1 and was principally used in the context of these modifications.
The principal modifications were:
– replacing the 75-mm gun by the British 17 Pdr (76.2 mm) A/T gun. The longer barrel made it necessary to re-balance the turret and move the Wireless Set No 19 in an outside bin at the rear of the turret.
– adding a hatch above the loader's position.
– replacing the co-driver's position by a shell rack. The crew was thus reduced to four men. Ammunition was 78 17-pounder shells.
Use: to reinforce Armoured Regiments, one Firefly per troop, then two during the campaign.

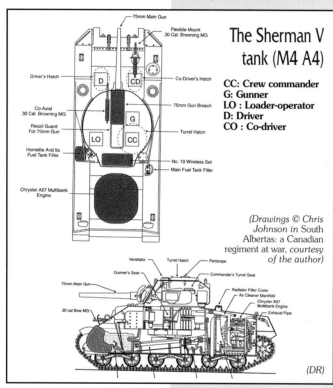

The Sherman V tank (M4 A4)

- 75mm Main Gun
- Flexible Mount .30 Cal. Browning MG
- Driver's Hatch
- D
- CD
- Co-Driver's Hatch
- Co-Axial .30 Cal. Browning MG
- 75mm Gun Breech
- G
- Recoil Guard For 75mm Gun
- LO
- CC
- Turret Hatch
- Hornelite And Its Fuel Tank Filler
- No. 19 Wireless Set
- Main Fuel Tank Filler
- Chrysler A57 Multibank Engine

CC: Crew commander
G: Gunner
LO : Loader-operator
D : Driver
CO : Co-driver

(Drawings © Chris Johnson in South Albertas: a Canadian regiment at war, *courtesy of the author)*

- Ventilator
- Turret Hatch
- Periscope
- Gunner's Seat
- Commander's Turret Seat
- 75mm Main Gun
- Radiator Filler Cover
- Air Cleaner Manifold
- Chrysler A57 Multibank Engine
- .30 cal Bow MG
- Exhaust Pipe

(DR)

Above: **A Sherman V in Holland, winter of 1944-45.**
(Public Archives of Canada

Below: **Normandy, 17 July 1944. The Sherman Vc 'Firefly'.** *(PAC 131391)*

12. Special tanks

M4 A4 Sherman, Duplex Drive

A British modification, this tank was for supporting infantry during landing operations.
Its features were:
– Special waterproof canvas skirt made rigid by inflating hoops with compressed air and which enabled it to float over short distances in a calm sea.
– Propulsion was by means of two propellers activated by the gearbox when the tank entered the water.
– When it reached the beach, the skirts were dropped and the tank could use its weapons.

Ram, Wasp Flame Equipment

Bridge Classification: 30

Engine: Continental 9-cylinder radial air-cooled (aircraft power plant) petrol.

Power rating: 400 bhp.

Use: A turretless Ram (Canadian-made Sherman) tank transformed into a flame-thrower by fitting tanks for the inflammable liquid. The hull machine gun was replaced by the flame-thrower. This AFV was used by the Royal Canadian Engineers to destroy blockhouses. Apart from its Wasp and 'Kangaroo' (see p. 152) variants, the Canadian turretless Ram was also used for transporting ammunition under the name of 'Wallaby' and for towing the 17–pounder anti-tank gun.

Above:
A Wasp Ram flame thrower in Holland in April 1945.

Valentine Bridge-laying Tank

Bridge Classification: 18
Engine: General Motors 6-cylinder 190 bhp diesel.
A Valentine tank modified for bridge laying by means of a metal gangway supported by folding arms.
Crossed gaps of 30 feet.
Used: by armoured regiments depending on availability.

M4A4 Sherman V Recovery Tank.

This was a breakdown tank made from an turretless M4A4 Sherman. It was fitted with a three-ton hoist, a winch with a capacity of 15 tons and various tools including oxy-acetylene welding gear.
Bridge classification: 33
Armament: One .30 calibre machine gun.
Crew: 2.
Use: in Armoured and Armoured Reconnaissance Regiments, as well as RCEME units.
(Public Archives of Canada)

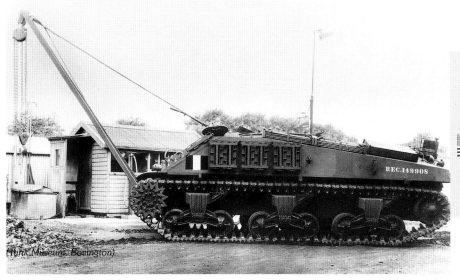

(Tank Museum, Bovington)

13. Self-Propelled artillery

Centaur IV

Bridge Classification: 30
Engine: Liberty V-12 395-bhp petrol.
Max. Speed: 27 mph
Crew: 5 of which 3 in the turret.
Armament: One 95-mm howitzer with 51 shells. Two BESA 7.92-mm machine guns.
Radio: one No 19 set.
Use: 1st Canadian Centaur Battery. An provisional unit used to support the British 6th Airborne Division

and the Dutch and Belgian units which were attached to it. Placed under the command of Major D.M. Cooper, the battery comprised an HQ and three troops of four Centaurs with 7 officers and 103 ORs. After the fighting along the River Dives and at Beuzeville (Operation Paddle) the battery was disbanded on 30 August. *(Public Archives of Canada-PAC)*

Source: The Royal Regiment of Canadian Artillery.
http://www. artillery.net.museum

(Tank Museum, Bovington)

Sexton 25-pounder Self-Propelled Tracked Gun

Canadian Ram tank hull
Bridge Classification: 30
Weight: (in fighting order) 58,630 lbs (25 1/4 tons)
Engine: (aircraft power plant) 9 cylinder air-cooled radial, petrol (400 bhp).
Crew: 6
Armament: One 25-pounder gun howitzer (see page 135), with 112 rounds ; 2 Bren guns with 1,500 rounds
Use: Field Artillery Regiments of the Armoured Divisions.

Priest M7 Self-Propelled Gun

Bridge Classification: 30
Weight: (in fighting order) 21 tons.
Length: 31 ft 4ins.
Width: 10 ft.
Height: 9 ft.
Engine: (aircraft power plant) 9-cylinder petrol air-cooled radial (400 bhp).
Crew: 7
Armament: One 105-mm howitzer

with 57 rounds and one .50 calibre MG with 300 rounds.
Shell weight: 31 lbs.
Max. Range: 6 1/4 miles (w/ charge No 7)
Rate of fire: 4 rounds/ min.
Set-up Time: 2 mins.
Use: Field Artillery Regiments- Self-Propelled - Royal Canadian Artillery.

Below, left:
Normandy, June 1944. The seven gunners of a 105-mm self-propelled howitzer. They belong to the 3rd Infantry division and were specially equipped with this SP gun for D-Day. The driver is wearing the special American armour crew's helmet which was delivered by the USA with the gun. *(PAC)*

Below, right:
Normandy 28 June 1944. An M7 105-mm self-propelled howitzer of the 13th Field Artillery Regiment, 3rd Infantry Division
(PAC 114577)

14. Field Artillery

25-pounder Howitzer Field Gun

Calibre: 87.63 mm
Weight: 3 960 lbs
Shell weight: 24 3/4 lbs (high explosive)
Max. range: 7 1/2 miles
Rate of Fire: 5 rounds/min. (normal)
Set-up time: 1-2 mins.
Gun Carriage: single, hollowed-out trail.
Transport: Towed by a Ford or Chevrolet tractor.
Crew: 6
Used by: Field Regiments (Royal Canadian Artillery)

Great Britain, 27 May 1944. A Ford CMP 25-pounder gun tractor with its limber. 5th Artillery Regiment (Royal Canadian Artillery).
(PAC)

Left.
A 25-Pounder assembly line in Sorel arsenal, Québec, during the year 1941.
(RR)

Mack manufacturing Co. 6-ton 6 x 6 Lorry

Bridge classification: 17
Engine: Mack 6-cylinder petrol
Power Rating: 156 bhp
Max. Speed: 35 mph
Use: as tractors for 4.5 or 5.5 in. artillery pieces.
Other version: 4- ton 4 x 4 Waukesha Medium Artillery Tractor.
(PAC photograph)

Mk I 4.5-inch Gun

Calibre: 114.3 mm
Total Weight: 7 tons
Shell Weight: 55 lbs (high explosive.)
Max. range: 11 1/4 miles
Rate of fire: 2 shells/ min.
Set-up Time: 3 mins.
Transport: towed by Mack 6-ton tractor
Crew: 10

Used by: Medium Regiments RCA, Army Reserve units.

5.5-inch Gun

Calibre: 139.7 mm.
Shell weight: 79 lbs
Total weight: 5 1/2 tons.
The other details were the same as for the 4.5-inch. gun.

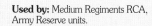

23 July 1944. Cleaning the barrel of a 5.5-inch artillery piece.
(PAC 131 382)

(DR)

Chevrolet 8440/CGT 4 x 4 Field Artillery Tractor

Bridge classification: 8/6
Engine: GM 6-cylinder petrol
Power rating: 85 bhp
Crew: 6 (One driver, one gun chief and four gunners)
Ammunition: 96 shells in ammunition bins and in the towed limber.
Use: Tractor for the 25-Pdr gun howitzer, in Field Artillery units
Other Model: Ford CMP (Canadian Military pattern), identical specifications except for the engine: Ford V-8.

(PAC photograph)

15. Anti-Tank Guns

6-Pounder, Anti-Tank Gun

Calibre: 57 mm
Weight: 2 640 lbs
Shell weight: 6 1/4 lbs
Av. Range: 0.6 miles
Muzzle velocity: 2 720 ft/sec.
Penetration: 3 1/3 inches at 550 yards at angle of attack of 30° (ACCBP projectile)
Rate of fire: 15 shells/min.

Set-up Time: a few seconds without splitting the trail.
Gun Carriage: Split Trail
Transport: Towed by Ford or Windsor Universal carriers. (page 128)
Crew: 4-5 men.
Used by: Anti-tank Platoons in Infantry Battalions, Anti-tank Regiments.
(RCA)

26 August 1944 in Normandy. The 3rd Infantry Division liberating Elbeuf after it was crossed by a patrol from the American 2nd Armored Division. This 6-pounder is crewed by men from the anti-tank platoon of one of the infantry battalions.
(PAC)

The fearsome 17-pounder gun seen from the side.
(DR)

Calibre expressed by the weight of the shell

1 pound = 0,453 kg	
2-pounder	40 mm
6-pounder	57 mm
17-pounder	76,2 mm
25-pounder	87,6 mm

17-Pounder Anti-Tank Gun

Calibre: 76.2 mm
Total weight: 4 400 lbs
Shell weight: 16 lbs 12 oz.
Practical range: 1/2 mile for a moving target ; 3/4 mile for a stationary target.
Muzzle velocity: 3 290 ft/sec with ordinary shot ; 3 960 ft/sec with the sabot-discarding projectile.
Penetration: 7 1/4 inches at 990 yards with a 30° angle of attack.

(APDS projectile)
Rate of Fire: (practical): 10 shells/min. ; (max): 20 shells/minute.
Set-up time: a few seconds without splitting the trail.
Transport: towed by Chevrolet or Ford tractors or turretless Ram tanks.
Used by: Anti-tank Regiments (Royal Canadian Artillery)

(RR)

Normandy, 22 June 1944. 17-pounder anti-tank gun drawn by a Ford or Chevrolet tractor.
(PA 169273)

Below:
The Archer anti-tank SP gun was a 17-pounder mounted on the chassis of a Valentine Mk IX or X Infantry Tank. Because it fired to the rear, the Archer crew needed to use very special ambush tactics. Despite this inconvenience, the Archer turned out to be a fearsome weapon during the few months of its operational career. *(DR)*

Archer 17-pounder Self-propelled Anti-tank Gun.

17-pounder gun mounted in a casemate on a Valentine tank chassis, firing towards the rear.
Total weight: 14 1/4 tons.
Engine: GMC 165 CVM 10 diesel.
Armament: One 17-pounder with 39 rounds.
Penetration: 3 1/2 inches at 990 yards with 30° angle of attack.

Armour: 2 1/2 inches
Max. road speed: 15 mph
Crew: 4
Used by Anti-tank Regiments (Royal Canadian Artillery) from the end of 1944, one troop per A/T battery in the Infantry Division.
(RR)

M10, M10 A1 Tank Destroyer

Bridge Classification: 33
Total weight: 21 1/2 tons
Length: 19 ft 7 ins
Width: 10 ft
Height: 8 ft 2 1/2 ins.
Transmission: Four forward gears and one reverse.
Engine: Twin coupled General Motor diesels (M10), one Ford V-8 petrol for

the M1 A1.
Armament: One 75-mm gun (54 rounds), one .50 machine gun in the turret (300 rounds)
Penetration: 3 1/2 inches at 990 yards with a 30° angle of attack.
Armour: 1/2 inch to 2 inches.
Fuel tank capacity: 126 galls (M10) ; 161 galls (M10 A1)
Range: 200 miles (M10), 156 miles (M10 A1)

Max. road speed: 25 mph.
Crew: 5
Used by: Anti-tank Regiments (Royal Canadian Artillery) of the Armoured Division.

M10 17-pounder Self -Propelled 'Wolverine'

British modification of the American M10 tank destroyer.

Bridge Classification: 33.
Principal transformations: American 75 mm gun replaced by the British 17-pounder with balancing weight mounted on the muzzle brake. This modification also meant a change to the front of the turret.

16. Anti-Aircraft Guns

The Crusader A/A was 40-mm Bofors gun mounted on the hull of a Crusader tank. Operational from 1943, 215 were made. The last shielded versions had a simplified roof with removable canvas top and were usually mounted on the Crusader Mk III hull.
(RR)

Vaucelles, Normandy, 4 August 1944. A 40-mm Bofors gun ready to fire.
(PAC 169336)

Bofors 40-mm Mk III

Opposite, center and above, center:
The 40-mm Bofors Gun and its ammunition, ready to move off, on the chassis of a Ford 4 x 4 3-ton truck.
(Public Archives of Canada)

Calibre: 40 mm.
Ammunition: Complete round with explosive, tracer, self-detonating or armour-piercing shell.
Shell weight: 4 lbs 9 oz.
Magazine: 4-round magazine.
Practical Range: 1 650 yards with open sights.
Muzzle velocity: 2 805 ft/sec.
Penetration: at 990 yards with a 30° angle of attack. (APDS projectile)
Rate of Fire: 120 shots/min (burst) or single shots.
Set-up time:
— Open sights : 2 minutes
— Indirect fire: 30 minutes.
Carriage: on two sets of removable

wheels with collapsible side trails.
Transport:
— towed by a 4 x 4 Chevrolet or Ford truck.
— could be mounted on a Crusader tank hull with an armoured shield.
Crew: 8 gunners
Used by: Light Anti-Aircraft Regiments (Royal Canadian Artillery). Note that the 40-mm Bofors had started to replace the 20-mm Oerlikon batteries, depending on availability.

Self - Propelled Bofors Vehicle.

Bridge Classification: 7
40-mm Bofors AA gun mounted on a Ford Truck body.
Ammunition capacity: 120 shells.
Crew: 4.
Used: Light Anti-Aircraft regiments (Royal Canadian Artillery).

Anti-Aircraft Guns

Polsten-Oerlikon Light Anti-Aircraft Gun

Calibre: 20-mm
Ammunition: explosive shells, tracers and incendiaries.
60-round box-magazine.
Practical range: 1/2 mile.
Muzzle velocity: 2 670 ft /sec.
Rate of fire: 460 shells/minute.
Used by: Light Anti-Aircraft Regiments, Royal Canadian Artillery.

Below:
**Centaur AA Mk II.
Twin 20-mm Polsten guns were mounted in a special turret, using the hull of a Centaur IV. Assigned to Anti-aircraft troops of Armoured Regiments, as well as to the Armoured Brigade HQ (two tanks).**

3.7 Inch Anti-Aircraft Gun

Calibre: 94 mm.
Total Weight: 8 3/4 tons
Shell Weight: 27 1/2 lbs
Practical range:
- anti-aircraft: 6 1/4 miles.
- ground role: 11 1/4 miles
Muzzle velocity: 2 574 ft / sec.
Rate of fire:
- manual loading: 10 rounds/min ;

— automatic: 25 rounds / min.
Carriage: four folding trails on two removable axles.
Transport: towed.
Used by: Heavy Anti-Aircraft Regiments, Royal Canadian Artillery (Army reserve formations)

17. Rocket launchers

Conversion of caliber from inches to metric

1 Inch (In.) = 2, 539 cm		3.7 inch	94 mm
.303 inch	7,7 mm	4.2 inch	106 mm
.380 inch	9 mm	4.5 inch	114,3 mm
2 inches	50,8 mm	5.5 inch	139,7 mm
3 inch	76,2 mm	8 inches	203 mm

Land Mattress (Multiple rocket launcher)
(1st Canadian Rocket Battery)

32 launcher tubes mounted on a two-wheel chassis.

Caliber: 7.62 cm.
Weight: 12 1/2 lbs
Range: 2 1/2 - 5 miles depending on the fins at the end of the rockets.
Rockets loaded manually.
Reloading time: 10-12 minutes.
Electrically-fired.
Use and organisation: Battery of twelve rocket launchers operated by gunners of the Royal Canadian Artillery, created 26 October 1944 as the 1st

Canadian Rocket Battery. Its personnel were from the disbanded 112th Battery of the 6th Light anti-Aircraft Regiment. It was committed in November 1944.

Left.
Belgium, 29 October 1944. Loading exercise for this 'Land Mattress' rocket launcher of the 1st Rocket Battery, RCA.
(PAC 138421)

18. Air Observation Post

Mk III Auster Air Observation Post

Maker: British Taylorcraft- Auster.
Engine: De Havilland Gipsy Major 1 rated at 130 bhp.
Length: 21 ft.
Height: 8 ft.
Wingspan: 36 ft 1 1/2 ins.
Weight, empty: 1 098 lbs
Take-off weight:

1 845 lbs
Crew: 2 (pilot: RCAF and observer: RCA)
Use: Light liaison and observation plane used by the Royal Canadian Air Force for spotting targets and adjusting artillery fire.
(PAC photograph)

19. Specialised Artillery Vehicles

Ram II Observation Post (OP) Tank

Maker: Montreal Locomotive Works.
Bridge classification: 30
Engine: aircraft-type air-cooled 9-cylinder radial.
Armour: 1 in to 2 1/2 inches.
Armament: two .30 calibre machine guns.
Crew: 5
Radio: Set No 19. Also a No 18 set, a No 38 set.
Use: fitted with a dummy gun barrel, this tank was used for forward observation by Artillery units.
Note: before the delivery of the

American Sherman tanks in Great Britain, the Canadian-made Rams were used for training AFV crews.

Left and below:
Holland, 1945. Several shots of the Ram Observation Post Tank II in a workshop and in combat
(Public Archives of Canada)

Distribution of artillery pieces among the various Canadian Army formations

Gun	Infantry Divisions	Armoured Divisions	Army Corps	Army
6-Pounder Anti-tank	●	●		
17-Pounder Anti-tank	●	● Tow	● SP Tow	
US M10 Tank Destroyer		●	●	
17-Pounder Archer	●	●		
25-Pounder	● Tow	● SP/Tow		
US M7 Priest 105mm	● (06/44)			●
4.5 inches				●
5.5 inches				●
20 mm Polsten Oerlikon	●	●	●	
40 mm Bofors	●	● SP	● SP Tow	
3.7 in. AA			v	
Land Mattress Projector			● 1	

SP: Self-Propelled. Tow: Towed. 1. As of November 1944

Ford Mfg. Co. 4 x 4 15-cwt Truck

Bridge classification: 4
Engine: Ford V-8 petrol
Rating: 95 bhp.
Max. speed: 50 mph.
Use: Royal Canadian Artillery. Radar equipment for detecting enemy aircraft

within a range of 22 miles. Assigned to Heavy Anti-Aircraft Regiments.

(Tank Museum, Bovington photo)

Formation Sign

This insignia was painted on the front right and rear left on a standard area not exceeding 8 1/2 x 9 1/2 ins.

Unit Serial Numbers (Unit Signs)

Unit Serial Numbers were positioned on the front and the rear right of the vehicle or AFV in the form of digits on a coloured square background. Serial numbers were painted on a 8 1/2 x 9 1/2 inch metal plate attached to the bodywork, or painted directly onto the vehicle.

All units of the same type serving on the same front, used identical serial numbers, whether for the background colours or for the digits.

The unit serial numbers had nothing to do with the actual number of the unit. As a code, they only indicated the arm or the service to which the vehicle or the machine was assigned within the formation (army, army corps, division, brigade...).

In order to identify a unit with the help of the tables on pages 10 to 21, it is important to know beforehand:

1. The number of the division or other formation, determined by observing the Formation Signs on the vehicles and machines, on signposts, or on uniform sleeves.

2. The detailed order of battle of the formation. In the case of divisions, units are always arranged in the same way: within each brigade and from top to bottom, and in the order of precedence for the Infantry Battalions and Armoured Cavalry (see the tables on pp. 10-21).

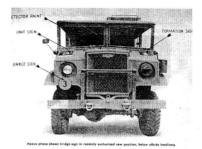

Photograph taken from a period manual:
War Office Publication,
Vehicle Markings 1943.

This photograph is taken from another period manual, *Overseas Routine Order No 1719*.

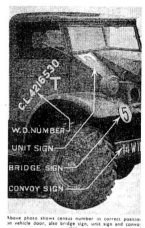

Left. **An actual Unit serial number plate. The vehicle belonged to the 2nd Battalion of a 2nd Brigade of an infantry division. As this item was found in Normandy, it could belong to a vehicle in the Régiment de la Chaudière or the Régiment de Maisonneuve. Only the Formation sign would enable the unit to be identified correctly.**
(Private Collection)

Below: **This table indicates how the colour of geometrical markings identified the regiments in the armoured brigade by order of precedence, and which symbols were given to each squadron within the regiment.**

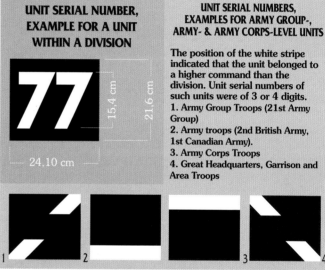

UNIT SERIAL NUMBER, EXAMPLE FOR A UNIT WITHIN A DIVISION

UNIT SERIAL NUMBERS, EXAMPLES FOR ARMY GROUP-, ARMY- & ARMY CORPS-LEVEL UNITS

The position of the white stripe indicated that the unit belonged to a higher command than the division. Unit serial numbers of such units were of 3 or 4 digits.
1. Army Group Troops (21st Army Group)
2. Army troops (2nd British Army, 1st Canadian Army).
3. Army Corps Troops
4. Great Headquarters, Garrison and Area Troops

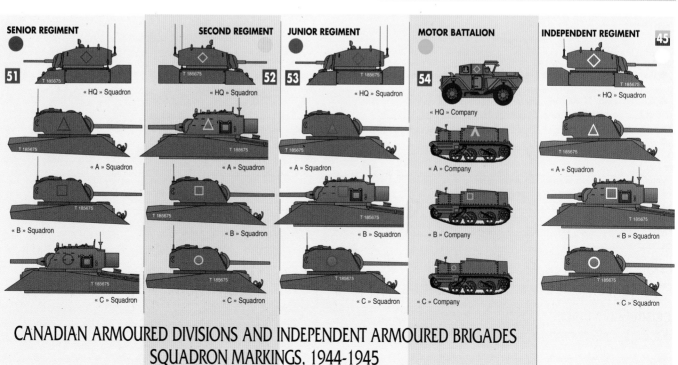

CANADIAN ARMOURED DIVISIONS AND INDEPENDENT ARMOURED BRIGADES SQUADRON MARKINGS, 1944-1945

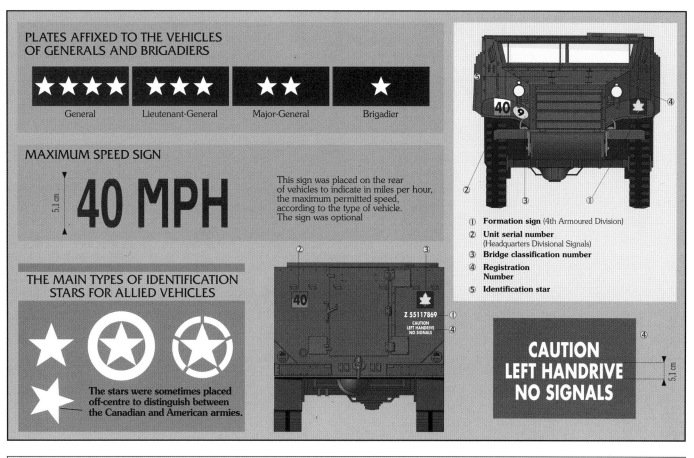

PLATES AFFIXED TO THE VEHICLES OF GENERALS AND BRIGADIERS

★★★★ General
★★★ Lieutenant-General
★★ Major-General
★ Brigadier

MAXIMUM SPEED SIGN

5,1 cm

40 MPH

This sign was placed on the rear of vehicles to indicate in miles per hour, the maximum permitted speed, according to the type of vehicle. The sign was optional

THE MAIN TYPES OF IDENTIFICATION STARS FOR ALLIED VEHICLES

The stars were sometimes placed off-centre to distinguish between the Canadian and American armies.

40

Z 55117869 ①
CAUTION
LEFT HANDRIVE
NO SIGNALS ④

① **Formation sign** (4th Armoured Division)
② **Unit serial number** (Headquarters Divisional Signals)
③ **Bridge classification number**
④ **Registration Number**
⑤ **Identification star**

CAUTION LEFT HANDRIVE NO SIGNALS ④
5,1 cm

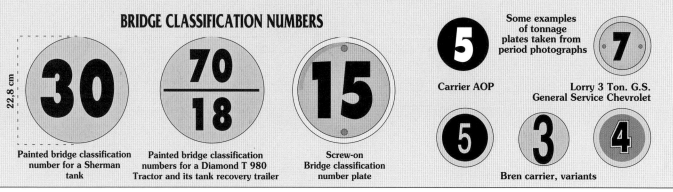

BRIDGE CLASSIFICATION NUMBERS

22,8 cm

30
Painted bridge classification number for a Sherman tank

70/18
Painted bridge classification numbers for a Diamond T 980 Tractor and its tank recovery trailer

15
Screw-on Bridge classification number plate

Some examples of tonnage plates taken from period photographs

5 Carrier AOP
7 Lorry 3 Ton. G.S. General Service Chevrolet

5 **3** **4** Bren carrier, variants

Examples of Unit Serial Numbers (See also Tables Pages 10 to 19)

● 1st Infantry Division, Unit serial number 60 on green background = Princess Patricia Canadian Light Infantry.

● 2nd Infantry Division, unit serial number 67 on a brown background = Fusiliers Mont-Royal

● 4th Armoured Division, unit serial number 54 on red background = Lake Superior Regiment Motor Battalion

● 4th Armoured Division, unit serial number 51 on red background = 21st Army Regiment (Governor-General's Foot Guard.).

Vehicles and AFVs belonging to formations which were above division level (army corps, army, army group) had serial numbers whose background colour remained the same as the divisions but with the addition of a white stripe painted horizontally or diagonally (see box on previous page).

The numbering was also different and comprised 3 or 4 figure numbers in the 100-900 and 1000 to 2700 series.

Registration Number
(War Department number)

This was painted in white figures, 3 1/2 inches high and 2 inches wide on and each side of the vehicle or

heavy vehicle, sometimes on the front, if the shape of the sides did not permit painting.

This figure was always preceded by a category letter, itself preceded by a C for the Canadian Army (Note. the numbers on the plates p. 142 are just examples)

War Department Number prefixes:
A: Ambulance.
C: Motorbike.
E: Heavy Engineering Vehicle.
F: Armoured Car.
H: Tractor or articulated lorry.
L: Lorry over one ton.
M: Light Car, Jeep.
P: Amphibious vehicle.
S: Self-propelled gun.
T: Tank or Bren carrier.
V: Van (RASC).
X: Vehicle towing a trailer.
Z: Small Lorry.

Signpost placed before a bridge across the River Orne near Caen. The bridge was built by the 7th Field Company, Royal Canadian Engineers, 2nd Infantry division. The number 9 indicates the maximum weight allowed across the bridge (9 tons).

Bridge Classification Marking

A yellow 9-inch disk was fixed onto the front right-hand side. It showed a number indicating the category of the weight of the vehicle when fully loaded. This figure had to be equal to or less than, the one indicated on the signposts placed at the entry to bridges and engineering works. The vehicles tow-

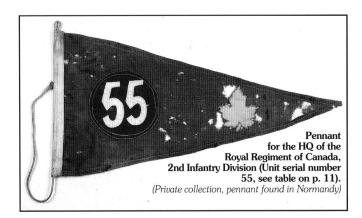

**Pennant
for the HQ of the
Royal Regiment of Canada,
2nd Infantry Division (Unit serial number
55, see table on p. 11).**
(Private collection, pennant found in Normandy)

ing a trailer had two figures separated by a horizontal line on the yellow disk. When the trailer was loaded, only the higher of the two numbers was taken into consideration.

Examples: 2 or 5: Jeep (3/2 with trailer)
4: Daimler 'Dingo'.
5: 15-cwt truck.
7: 3-ton truck.
9: Daimler armoured car.
15: Staghound armoured car.
30:Sherman tank

Armoured Units Markings
(Tactical markings, see page 140, bottom)

These geometrical shapes indicated the position of the armoured squadron within the regiment and the colour, that of the regiment within the brigade (the Troop number was sometimes painted within the shape).

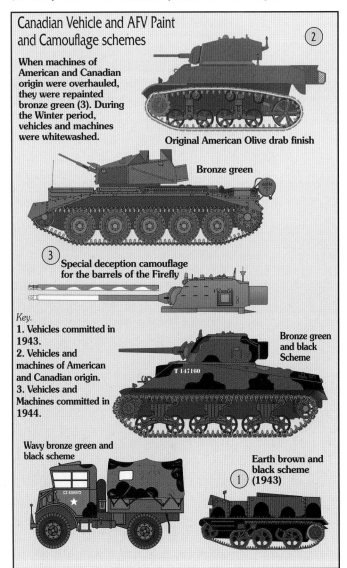

**Canadian Vehicle and AFV Paint
and Camouflage schemes**

② When machines of American and Canadian origin were overhauled, they were repainted bronze green (3). During the Winter period, vehicles and machines were whitewashed.

Original American Olive drab finish

Bronze green

③ Special deception camouflage for the barrels of the Firefly

Key.
1. Vehicles committed in 1943.
2. Vehicles and machines of American and Canadian origin.
3. Vehicles and Machines committed in 1944.

Bronze green and black Scheme

Wavy bronze green and black scheme

Earth brown and black scheme ① (1943)

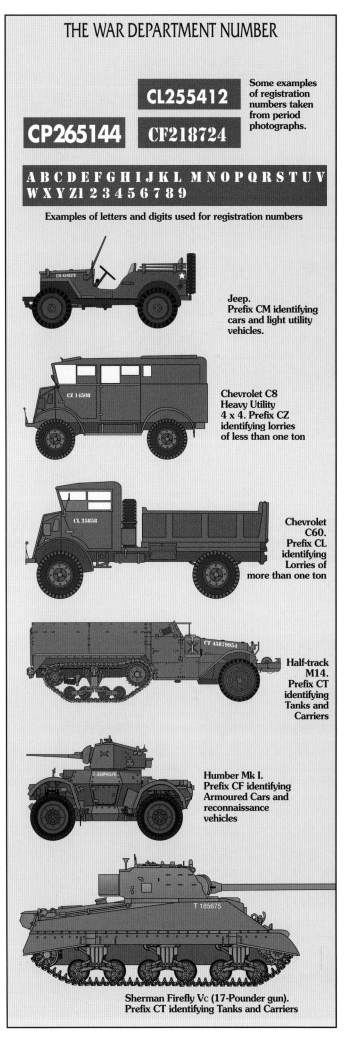

THE WAR DEPARTMENT NUMBER

CL255412

CP265144   **CF218724**

Some examples of registration numbers taken from period photographs.

**A B C D E F G H I J K L M N O P Q R S T U V
W X Y Z1 2 3 4 5 6 7 8 9**

Examples of letters and digits used for registration numbers

**Jeep.
Prefix CM identifying cars and light utility vehicles.**

Chevrolet C8 Heavy Utility 4 x 4. Prefix CZ identifying lorries of less than one ton

Chevrolet C60. Prefix CL identifying Lorries of more than one ton

Half-track M14. Prefix CT identifying Tanks and Carriers

Humber Mk I. Prefix CF identifying Armoured Cars and reconnaissance vehicles

Sherman Firefly Vc (17-Pounder gun). Prefix CT identifying Tanks and Carriers

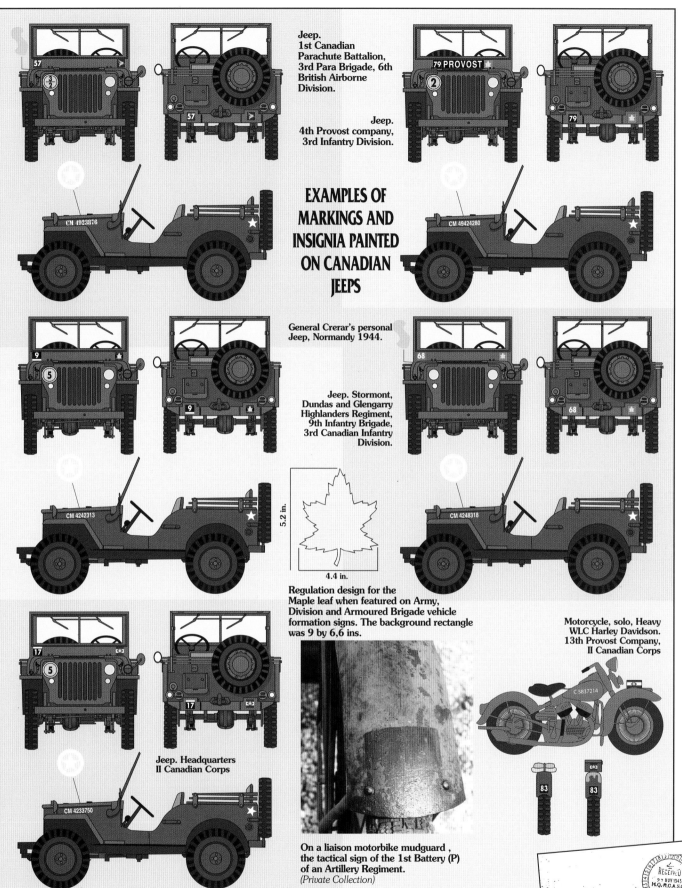

Jeep.
1st Canadian
Parachute Battalion,
3rd Para Brigade, 6th
British Airborne
Division.

Jeep.
4th Provost company,
3rd Infantry Division.

EXAMPLES OF MARKINGS AND INSIGNIA PAINTED ON CANADIAN JEEPS

General Crerar's personal
Jeep, Normandy 1944.

Jeep. Stormont,
Dundas and Glengarry
Highlanders Regiment,
9th Infantry Brigade,
3rd Canadian Infantry
Division.

5.2 in.

4.4 in.

Regulation design for the
Maple leaf when featured on Army,
Division and Armoured Brigade vehicle
formation signs. The background rectangle
was 9 by 6,6 ins.

Motorcycle, solo, Heavy
WLC Harley Davidson.
13th Provost Company,
II Canadian Corps

Jeep. Headquarters
II Canadian Corps

On a liaison motorbike mudguard ,
the tactical sign of the 1st Battery (P)
of an Artillery Regiment.
(Private Collection)

The tactical markings were painted on the turret sides, or on the hull of armoured vehicles (or on the front and rear if the bodywork did not allow otherwise).

surfaces to allow rapid identification from the air, but rarely on tank sides.

Recognition markings

From July 1943 onwards, the white star -in a circle or not - was painted on all Allied vehicles and AFVs. They were of different sizes and placed differently, depending on the unit. They were painted in particular on upper

Heading of a note about Canadian Army vehicle markings, 1943.

EXAMPLES OF MARKINGS ON CANADIAN VEHICLES

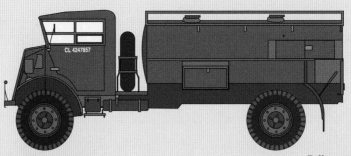

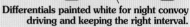

Chevrolet C60 3-Ton 4 x 4
Petrol 800 Gallons.
4th Armoured Division,
RCASC Troop Company.

Differentials painted white for night convoy
driving and keeping the right interval.

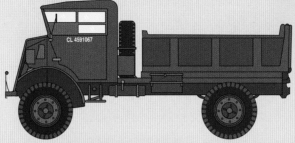

3-ton Chevrolet C60S 4 x 4 Dump Truck, 3rd
Field Park Company, Royal Canadian
Engineers, 3rd Canadian Infantry Division.

Below:
3-ton Ford F60L 4 x 4 Ambulance,
9th Field Ambulance,
1st Canadian Infantry Division.

EXAMPLES OF MARKINGS FOR RCAMC AND RCASC

Examples of Gas detector patches,
painted on any flat surface of the body
with paint which reacted to vesicant
gases.

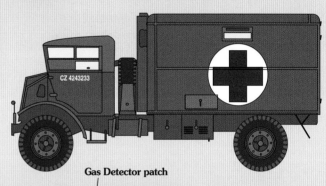

Gas Detector patch

Left:
3-ton Ford 4 x 4 General
Service Lorry, RCASC
Train assigned to 9th
Infantry Brigade, 3rd
Infantry Division.

Below and centre:
Chevrolet C8A 4 x 4
Heavy Utility ambulance,
13th Field Hygiene
Section, RCAMC,
2nd Canadian
Infantry Division.

Differential
painted white.

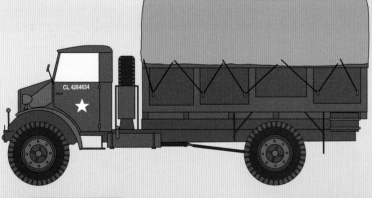

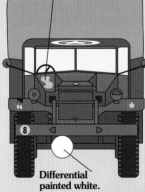

3-ton Chevrolet
CGS 4 x 4 Lorry,
4th Canadian
Armoured
Division.
Divisional
train assigned
to the 4th
Armoured
Brigade.

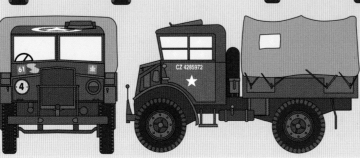

3-ton Chevrolet GS 4 x 4
Lorry, Administrative
Platoon of the Régiment
de la Chaudière,
3rd Canadian Armoured
Infantry Division.

15-cwt Chevrolet or Ford
4 x 4 General Service
Truck, Régiment de la
Chaudière, 8th Infantry
Brigade, 3rd Infantry
Division.

12-ton Model 9814 Diamond T 6 x 4 Prime Mover M 20 Truck of the Royal Canadian Electrical and Mechanical Engineers, 1st Army Troops. (Heavy tank transporter/recovery vehicle).

Right and below:
March 1945, Holland. Painting a 3-ton 4 x 4 Chevrolet of the RCASC attached to a Provost unit (see markings below). The men are wearing the Black Denim Tank Suit with matching beret.

43	8th Provost Company, 4th Armoured Division
84	Troop Coy RCASC
🍁	⑦

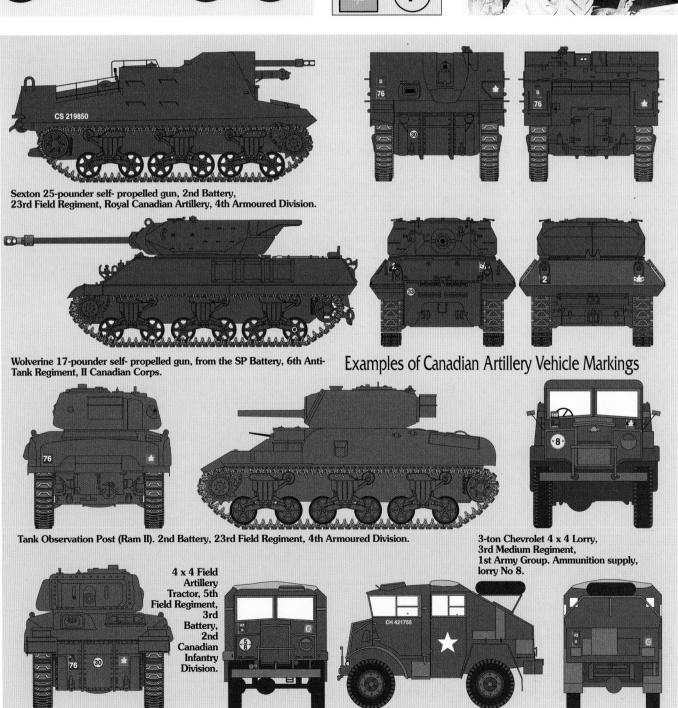

Sexton 25-pounder self-propelled gun, 2nd Battery, 23rd Field Regiment, Royal Canadian Artillery, 4th Armoured Division.

Wolverine 17-pounder self-propelled gun, from the SP Battery, 6th Anti-Tank Regiment, II Canadian Corps.

Examples of Canadian Artillery Vehicle Markings

Tank Observation Post (Ram II). 2nd Battery, 23rd Field Regiment, 4th Armoured Division.

3-ton Chevrolet 4 x 4 Lorry, 3rd Medium Regiment, 1st Army Group. Ammunition supply, lorry No 8.

4 x 4 Field Artillery Tractor, 5th Field Regiment, 3rd Battery, 2nd Canadian Infantry Division.

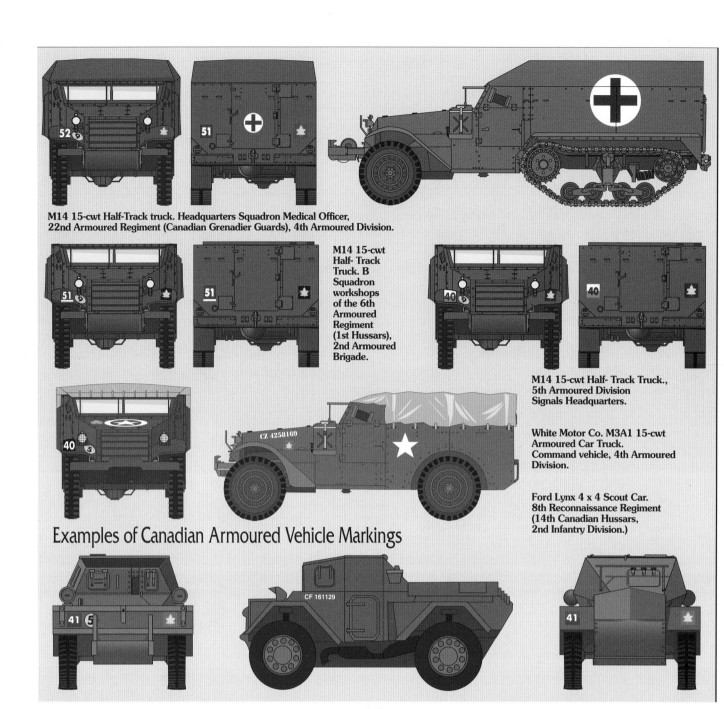

M14 15-cwt Half-Track truck. Headquarters Squadron Medical Officer, 22nd Armoured Regiment (Canadian Grenadier Guards), 4th Armoured Division.

M14 15-cwt Half- Track Truck. B Squadron workshops of the 6th Armoured Regiment (1st Hussars), 2nd Armoured Brigade.

M14 15-cwt Half- Track Truck., 5th Armoured Division Signals Headquarters.

White Motor Co. M3A1 15-cwt Armoured Car Truck. Command vehicle, 4th Armoured Division.

Ford Lynx 4 x 4 Scout Car. 8th Reconnaissance Regiment (14th Canadian Hussars, 2nd Infantry Division.)

Examples of Canadian Armoured Vehicle Markings

Mk II Helmet bearing the Unit Serial Number of a Field Artillery Regiment in an Infantry Division. *(Private collection)*

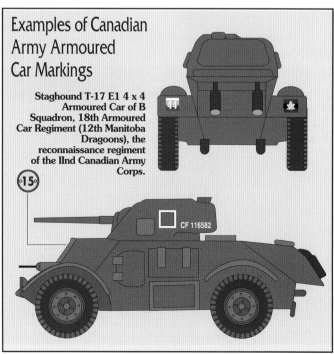

Examples of Canadian Army Armoured Car Markings

Staghound T-17 E1 4 x 4 Armoured Car of B Squadron, 18th Armoured Car Regiment (12th Manitoba Dragoons), the reconnaissance regiment of the IInd Canadian Army Corps.

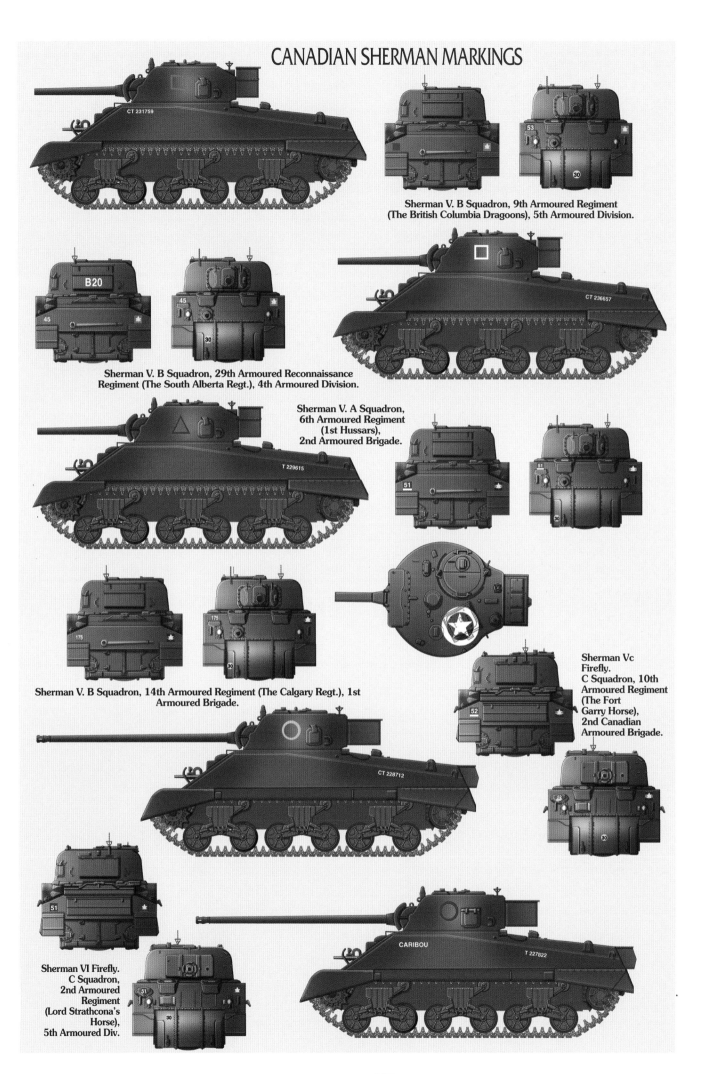

CANADIAN SHERMAN MARKINGS

CT 231759

Sherman V. B Squadron, 9th Armoured Regiment
(The British Columbia Dragoons), 5th Armoured Division.

CT 236657

Sherman V. B Squadron, 29th Armoured Reconnaissance
Regiment (The South Alberta Regt.), 4th Armoured Division.

Sherman V. A Squadron,
6th Armoured Regiment
(1st Hussars),
2nd Armoured Brigade.

T 229615

Sherman V. B Squadron, 14th Armoured Regiment (The Calgary Regt.), 1st
Armoured Brigade.

Sherman Vc
Firefly.
C Squadron, 10th
Armoured Regiment
(The Fort
Garry Horse),
2nd Canadian
Armoured Brigade.

CT 228712

Sherman VI Firefly.
C Squadron,
2nd Armoured
Regiment
(Lord Strathcona's
Horse),
5th Armoured Div.

CARIBOU

T 227822

Holland, 1945. A Sherman 'Firefly' of A Squadron/29th Armoured Reconnaissance Regiment (The South Alberta Rregiment), 4th Armoured Division.
On the rear of the hull one can make out, from left to right the Unit Serial Number 45, the War Department Number and the Tactical Sign. The Formation Sign — a gold Maple Leaf on a green background — is not visible. (PAC)

Normandy, 24 July 1944. General B. Montgomery talking to Lieutenant-General G.G. Simonds, the II Can. Corps Commander. The jeep bears the regulation markings. The Allied star has deliberately been painted off-centre to distinguish a Canadian vehicle.
(PAC 129125)

Official note regulating the presence and the disposition of the various insignia and tactical markings.

Nicknames given to the Shermans of an Armoured Regiment
2nd Armoured Regiment, Lord Strathcona's Horse

Regimental HQ	Armadillo	Brown	Baltic	Caribou
Strathcona	**2nd Troop**	Bader	Bering	**2nd Troop**
Commanding officer	Aspen	Bishop	**4th Troop**	Capri
Screwball	Alder	Barker	Banff	Cork
Second in command	Almond		Barrie	Crete
Scimitar	Apricot	**1st Troop**	Brandon	China
RHQ Troop leader		Beaver	Broadview	
Spartan Troop	**3rd Troop**	Buffalo		**3rd Troop**
Sergeant	Algiers	Broncho	**C SQUADRON**	Chicon
A SQUADRON	Athens	Bear		Chippewa
	Alaska		**HQ Fighting**	Chilliwack
HQ Fighting		**2nd Troop**	Churchill	Chinook
Akbar	**4th Troop**	Balsam	Confucius	
Abdul	Algonquin	Bluebell/Briar	Connoly	**4th Troop**
Attila	Alberta	Buttercup	Conacher	Camrose
Ajax	Aldershot	Birch		Calgary
1st Troop	Argyle		**1st Troop**	Claresholm
Alligator		**3rd Troop**	Cougar	Canmore
Antelope	**B SQUADRON**	Biscay	Condor	
	HQ Fighting	Bengal	Cobra	

Markings and insignia painted on Canadian Stuarts

**Light Tank M3 A3 'Stuart'.
Reconnaissance Troop, 29th Armoured Regiment (South Alberta Regiment), 4th Armoured Division.**

M3 A3 Light Tank, of the Reconnaissance Troop, Headquarters Squadron, 27th Armoured Regiment (The Sherbrooke Fusiliers), 2nd Armoured Brigade.

CHAPTER 11

THE 1st CANADIAN PARACHUTE BATTALION

This unit was formed in July 1942 with volunteers for service parachute duty. The first volunteers were trained at Fort Benning (USA), and at Ringway in Great-Britain for those who had already been transferred overseas. The Canadian school at Camp Shilo (Manitoba) was established in 1943.

The battalion reached Great Britain in July 1943 and was assigned to the British 3rd Parachute Brigade (6th British Airborne Division).

On 6 June 1944, the Canadian paratroopers jumped with the 6th (Br) Airborne Division into Normandy between the Orne and Dives Rivers. In July 1944, they fought in the Forêt de Bavent and advanced towards the Seine Estuary. On 7 September, they returned to Great-Britain. From 20 December 1944 to 18 January 1945, the unit was involved in the Battle of the Bulge. On 23 January, the battalion took part in Operation Varsity (the Rhine Crossing). On 2 May 1945, the Canadians linked with the Russians at Wismar on the Baltic Sea. The Parachute Bn. was the first Canadian unit to be repatriated and landed at Halifax on 21 June 1945 ; it was disbanded on 30 September 1945.

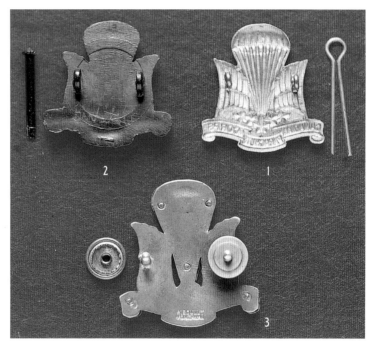

1st Canadian parachute Battalion Cap Badges
1. Beret badge made of brass for issue to all personnel, introduced in 1942.
2. Plastic badge issued from 1944 ; normally replaced the brass badges.
3. Bimetal cap Badge for officers, from 1943.

Below :
1. Shoulder title worn on both sleeves of the Battledress blouse.
2. Canadian paratrooper wings. Obtained after 8 jumps of which the first two from a static balloon (at the Ringway School). The badge was worn above the left hand side BD blouse/Denison smock chest pocket.
3. British Airborne formations generic sign (Pegasus riding Bellerophon). British-made printed on canvas issue insignia, worn on both sleeves of the Battledress blouse.
4. Embroidered variant.
5. British Airborne units strip (printed version), sewn under the 'Bellerophon' insignia.

Paratroopers of the 1st Canadian Parachute Battalion in Belgium on 15 January 1945, after the Battle of the Bulge. The men are wearing British issue kit: Denison Smocks, Airborne Mk I and Mk II steel helmet and Parachutist trousers. *(PA 191136)*

THE PARATROOPERS COMBAT LOAD

● **Rifleman**
— 1 No 4 rifle,
— 1 respirator
— 2 basic pouches with 2 Bren LMG magazines each
— 1 bayonet and frog
— 1 canvas bandoleer with 50 rifle rounds
— 2 grenades in Denison Smock pockets
— 1 Dagger
— 1 Toggle Rope
— 1 Haversack & 1 waterbottle
— 1 Entrenching tool
— 1 General Service shovel or pick

● **Corporal Section Commander**
— 1 Sten Mark V SMG
— 1 respirator
— 1 magazine pouch with seven

magazines for SMG
— 2 grenades
— 1 Dagger
— 1 Toggle Rope
— 1 Haversack and 1 water bottle,
— 1 Entrenching tool
— 1 General Service shovel or pick

● **Bren LMG No1**
— 1 Bren LMG
— 1 Bren gun wallet (p. 120)
— 1 respirator
— 2 basic pouches with 2 Bren LMG magazines each
— 1 Dagger
— 1 Revolver or pistol with cartridge or magazine pocket
— 2 grenades
— 1 Toggle Rope
— 1 Entrenching tool

Contents of Haversack:
— Contents similar to infantry's.
— On airborne operations, two day's food supplies were normally taken in the form of :
— 2 packs of 24-hour rations
— Emergency rations tins were also issued.

NB. The paratroop section followed the same organisation as the regular infantry, shown on pages 25-26.
The items of equipment used by the Canadian Parachute Battalion have been presented in Volume I of the 'Tommy from D-Day to VE-Day'.

Regulation positioning of insignia on the blouse sleeve.
The strip of yellow cloth was worn on both shoulder straps of the blouse and Denison Smock.
It indicated the position of the Canadian Battalion within the British 3 Para. Brigade.
(Reconstruction)

The Rousseau Brothers : Philippe, left and Maurice, right were both Lieutenants in the 1st Canadian Parachute Battalion. They were both killed in action the same year. Philippe, born 1921, died on 6 June 1944 at Gonneville-sur-Mer whereas Maurice was killed on 27 September 1944 at Igney, Alsace.

BATTALION
BATTLE
HONOURS.

(Motto : « Ex Coelis »)
— Normandy landings
— Dives Crossing
— North-West Europe
— Rhine

1st Canadian Parachute Battalion War Strength

(War Establishment, 1942)

	Battalion Headquarters	Headquarters Company						Total HQ Company	3 Rifle Companies (each)			3 Rifle platoons (each)			Total Rifle Company	Total Parachute Bn.
		Company Headquarters	Intelligence Section	Signal Platoon	Mortar Platoon	Defence platoon	Administrative Platoon		Company Headquarters	Mortar Detachment	Anti-tank Section	Rifle Platoon HQ	Rifle Platoon	Total Rifle Platoon		
Lieutenant-colonel	1															1
Major (2nd in Command)	1															1
Majors		1						1	1						1	4
Captains									1						1	3
Adjutant	1								1							1
Lieutenants	1	1		1	1			3				1		1	3	13
Quartermaster							1	1								1
Paymaster (RCAPC)	1															1
Medical Officer (RCAMC)	1															1
Total Officers	6*	2		1	1		1	5	2			1		1	5	26
Warrant Officers Class I	1															1
Warrant Officers Class II		1					2	3	1						1	9
Coy. Quartermaster Sergeants		1						1	1						1	4
Sergeants	4		1	1	4		8	14		1		1	1	4	14	60
Sergeants (RCOC)							2	2								4
Total WOs and Sergeants	5*	2	1	1	4		12	20	2	1		1	1	4	16	73
Corporals	1*	1		1	5	1	4	12	1	1	1		1	3	13	52
Corporal (RCOC)							1	1								1
Privates (39 Lance-Corporals)	18*	6	10	24	27	5	57	129	9	6	6	2	8	26	105	462
Privates (RCOC)							2	2								2
Total	30	11	11	27	37	6	77	169	14	8	7	4	10	34	139	616

Canadian Parachute Battalion Weapons and transport

(War Establishment, 1942)

	Battalion Headquarters	Company Headquarters	Intelligence Section	Signal Platoon	Mortar Platoon	Defence platoon	Administrative Platoon	Total HQ Company	Company Headquarters	Mortar Detachment	Anti-tank Section	Rifle Platoon HQ	Rifle section	Total Rifle Platoon	Total Rifle Company
		Headquarters Company							3 Rifle Companies (each)			3 Rifle Platoons (each)			
Pistols, .45 in. automatic	11	5		8	28	2	2	45	5	7		1	2	7	40
Rifles, .303 in.	17	6	11	10	2	4	75	108	8		6	2	6	20	74
Machine Carbines, 9-mm Sten	2			9	7			16	1	1	1	1	2	7	25
LMGs, .303 in.						2		2					1	3	9
Mortars, 3 in.					4			4		1					2
Mortars, 2 in. (modified)	1														
PIATs (in 1943)						1		1				1		1	3
Grenades, No 68						34		34			17	17		17	68
Grenades, No 36M	48	4	22	56	74	12		168	22	16	14	8	20	68	272
Grenades, No 69												30		30	90
TRANSPORT															
Bicycles, folding	1			8	1			9	1					1	13
Bicycles, non folding							13	13							13
Motorcycles	2														2
Cars, 5-cwt, 4x4, Jeep							5	5							5
Car, 8-cwt, heavy utility							1	1							1
Truck 15-cwt, water							1	1							1
Lorries, 3-ton, 4 wheeled							8	8							8

BATTALION LOSSES

Normandy, 6 June 1944, D-Day Landing
— Killed or died of wounds — 19
— Casualties evacuated — 10
— Missing — 84
Total — 113

Normandy from 6 june to 25 august 1944
— Killed or died of wounds — 65
— Casualties evacuated — 162
— Missing — 101
Total — 328

North-West Europe Campaign 6 June 1944 to 8 May 1945
— Killed or died of wounds — 126
— Casualties evacuated — 291
— Missing — 85
Total — 502

Those missing were mainly Prisoners of War, some of whom managed to escape. The others were liberated in May 1945.

Medals awarded to the Battalion
1 Victoria Cross, **1** Distinguished Service Order, **1** Order of the British Empire (Officer), **1** Order of the British Empire (Member), **3** Military Crosses, **2** Distinguished Conduct Medals, **9** Military Medals, **15** Mentions in Dispatches.

THE CANADIAN PARACHUTISTS' FIGHTING AND JUMP GEAR

On the previous page, a Corporal (Section commander) is carrying his Mk V Sten Gun with the special 7-magazine bandoleer. He is wearing British web equipment. The Camouflaged Denison Smock and helmet are British according to the agreements between British and Canadian Commands stipulating that the British RAOC would provide the Can. para. Battalion with its supplies.

Canadian battledress was kept however, although British Parachutist trousers were worn on 6 June 1944.

Note. Details of British airborne uniforms and equipment have been described in Vol. 1 of the 'Tommy from D-Day to VE-Day'.

The Battalion's Commanding Officers
— Lieutenant-Colonel G.G.P. Bradbrooke from 1942 to 23 august 1944.
— Lieutenant-Colonel J. A. Nicklin (after Major G.F. Eddie's interim command) from 7 September 1944 to 24 March 1945 when he was killed during operation Varsity (Crossing of the Rhine)
— Major, then Lieutenant-Colonel G.F. Eddie from 25 March 1945 to September 1945.

Wearing American Jump Boots in combat was authorised for paratroopers who had won their wings at Fort Benning (Georgia- USA). 989 men were issued with these boots when they qualified - 42 officers and 947 ORs.

THE 1st CANADIAN ARMOUR

The idea for this armoured personnel carrier unit saw the light of day during the preparations for Operation Totalise, planned for on the night of 7-8 august 1944 along the Caen-Falaise axis..

In order to make up for the lack of armoured personnel transport vehicles and on the initiative of General Simonds, CO II Canadian Corps, American M7 self-propelled howitzers issued to 21st Army Group were transformed into personnel carriers .

This transformation entailed removing the 105 mm howitzer and adding armour plates to the hull front, the one-inch space between them being filled with sandbags. The machine was called the 'Kangaroo' and could carry a section of 10 infantrymen. Fifty-five machines of this kind were made ready for the operation.

The new unit's creation

On 28 August 1944, a squadron of four troops was set up and attached to the 25th Armoured Delivery Regiment (the Elgin Regiment). It was commanded by Colonel G.M. Churchill, who remained in command until May 1945.

Its first battle was at Le Havre on 2 September 1944, followed by the fighting at Boulogne and Calais in Northern France. At the end of September, the original Kangaroos were replaced by modified Canadian Rams, produced by Montreal Locomotive Works..

On 24 October 1944, after the Battle of the Scheldt, the 1st Canadian Army created the 1st Canadian Armoured Personnel Carrier Regiment. And on 1 December, the unit was incorporated into the 31st Army Tank Brigade of the British 79th Armoured Division (equipped with all sorts of special AFVs) with which it fought until May 1945.

The regiment lost one officer and 12 men in action and four who died of wounds. The unit was disbanded on 20 June 1945.

Battle honours: Le Havre, Boulogne, Xanten, Lower Meuse River, Roer, Rhineland, Reichwald, Goch-Calcar, Moyland Wood, Rhine Crossing, Groningen.

Below :
Operation Totalise, August 1944. A Kangaroo on an M7 self-propelled howitzer hull. The 105-mm gun port has been closed shut by armour plate.
(Tank Museum, Bovington)

Above :
Holland-Germany, October 1944-May 1945.
Kangaroos based on turretless Ram hulls.
(Tank Museum, Bovington)

'KANGAROO' RAM ARMOURED TROOP CARRIER

Weight: 20 tons.
Length: 18 ft 7 ins.
Width: 9 ft 5 ins
Engine: Continental R975 (aircraft-type) 9-cylinder air-cooled radial petrol engine
Power rating: 400 bhp
Transmission: 5 forwards gears, one reverse.
Armament: one .30 calibre MG in a cupola on the front left-hand side, the driver being on the right. One .50 calibre machine gun (optional)
Armour:
— **Front plate:** 2 ins.
— **Side:** 2 1/2 ins.
Range: 145 miles
Max. speed : 25 mph.
Crew : 1 driver, 1 tank commander, 1 machine gunner (optional).
One Kangaroo would carry one infantry section (ten men).

EXAMPLES OF MARKINGS FOR THE RAMS OF THE CANADIAN ARMOURED PERSONNEL CARRIER REGIMENT

1. Reconnaissance Sign.
2. Tactical sign.
3. Nickname given by the crew.
4. Unit Marking.
5. Formation sign.
6. Number of the machine or the Troop.

MARION 3

(Ram illustrations: All Rights Reserved)

Bibliography

The Canadian Kangaroos in WWII. Kenneth R. Ramsden. Ramsden-Cavan Publishing.

Le 1st Canadian Armoured Personnel Carrier Regiment. Ed Storey, in Militaria Magazine n° 122, September 1995.

Left:
This Trooper of the 1st Canadian Armoured Carrier Regiment is wearing the British-made Tank Suit, Canadian goggles, a British face veil as a neck cloth net and a black Canadian beret.
(Ed. Storey Photo and Collection)

Below:
Insignia of the 1st Armoured Personnel Carrier Regiment
1. Cap Badge (Kangaroo) issued on 28 January 1945. Made in Great Britain by Gaunt Ltd/Birmingham*. Worn on the black beret.
2. Title worn on both sleeves of the Battledress blouse. This was handed out 6 February 1945. The orange letters represented the Royal House of Holland and the Dutchmen serving with the unit. The black stood for the Armoured Corps
3. Formation sign of the British 79th Armoured Division.
4. Formation sign of the 31st Army Tank Brigade (Armoured Brigade after 2 February 1945), worn under No 3.

* Before being issued with this cap badge, the unit wore the Canadian Armoured Corps cap badge (page 60).

PERSONNEL CARRIER REGIMENT

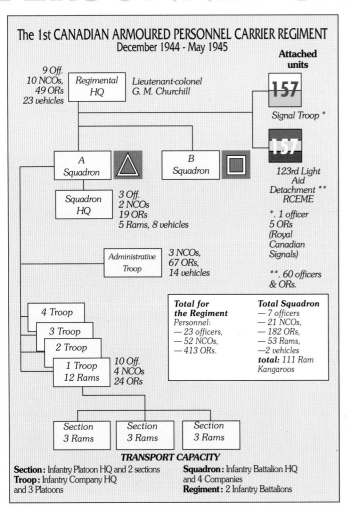

The 1st CANADIAN ARMOURED PERSONNEL CARRIER REGIMENT
December 1944 - May 1945

Attached units

9 Off. 10 NCOs, 49 ORs 23 vehicles — Regimental HQ — Lieutenant-colonel G. M. Churchill

157 Signal Troop *

157 123rd Light Aid Detachment ** RCEME

A Squadron

B Squadron

Squadron HQ — 3 Off. 2 NCOs 19 ORs 5 Rams, 8 vehicles

*. 1 officer 5 ORs (Royal Canadian Signals)

** . 60 officers & ORs.

Administrative Troop — 3 NCOs, 67 ORs 14 vehicles

4 Troop
3 Troop
2 Troop
1 Troop 12 Rams — 10 Off. 4 NCOs 24 ORs

Total for the Regiment
Personnel:
— 23 officers,
— 52 NCOs,
— 413 ORs.

Total Squadron
— 7 officers
— 21 NCOs,
— 182 ORs,
— 53 Rams,
—2 vehicles
total: 111 Ram Kangaroos

Section 3 Rams | Section 3 Rams | Section 3 Rams

TRANSPORT CAPACITY
Section: Infantry Platoon HQ and 2 sections
Troop: Infantry Company HQ and 3 Platoons
Squadron: Infantry Battalion HQ and 4 Companies
Regiment: 2 Infantry Battalions

Appendix 1
OPERATION *JUBILEE*
DIEPPE, 19 AUGUST 1942

After the battle in Hong Kong in December 1941 when two Canadian Battalions — the Winnipeg Grenadiers and the Royal Rifles of Canada — were annihilated, Operation Jubilee was the Canadian Army's first WWII engagement in the European theatre of operations.

Embarkation excercise in Great Britain, July 1942. These two officers belong to the Royal Regiment of Canada (divisional sign combined with the regiment's distinctive green disc). Both have the Mk III Sten gun and a Fairbairn-Sykes commando dagger strapped to the leg.
(Imperial War Museum)

A tricky landing beach

The whole beach was covered with large grey pebbles which were hardly practical for driving tanks and running on. At the top of the beach there was a steep slope culminating in a low wall.

In 1942, the esplanade and the beach were heavily protected by barbed wire and covered by weapons installed in the sea-front houses. A ditch had been dug along the pebble beach. Like most villas, the Casino, all speckled and camouflaged, had been transformed into a formidable strong-point and the cliffs were peppered with machine gun nests. This brief overview serves to show that any landing attempt from the sea was doomed to failure if it had not been preceded by a severe pounding from heavy-calibre naval artillery, and bombed by aircraft.

OPERATION JUBILEE ASSAULT FORCE

SUPREME COMMANDER
Combined Operations, Vice-Admiral Lord Louis Mountbatten
1st Canadian Army: General Mac Naughton.
1st Canadian Corps: Lieutenant General H. D. G Crerar

NAVAL FORCE
Captain John Hughes-Hallett,
Royal Navy [1]

LAND FORCE
Major-General J. H. Roberts [1]
2ND CANADIAN INFANTRY DIVISION

AIR FORCE
Air Vice-Marshall T. Leigh Mallory
Air Commodore Cole [1] (RAF)

Heavy Weapons Support Company. Toronto Scottish

General reserve units
14th Army Tank Regiment (Calgary Regiment)
(Lt.-Col. Johnny Andrews [2])
with B & C Squadrons and one light Command Group

No 3 Commando
(Lt.-Col. Durnford Slater [3], Major Peter Young)
(4 US Rangers)

MISCELLANEOUS SERVICE AND SUPPORT UNITS

4TH CANADIAN INFANTRY BRIGADE
(Brigadier Sherwood Lett)
— **Royal Regiment of Canada**
(Lt.-Col. Catto)
— **Royal Hamilton Light Infantry**
(Lt.-Col. Labatt)
— **Essex Scottish Regiment**
(+ 3 US Rangers)
(Lt.-Col. Jasperson)

No 4 Commando
(Lt.-Col. Lord Lovat, Major D. Mills-Roberts)
(4 US Rangers)

1. Aboard the destroyer Calpe.
2. Killed during the operation.
3. As the landing craft which was carrying him was damaged during the naval engagement, Lt-Col. Durnford-Slater had to hand over command to Major Peter Young.

Below, left:
Embroidered badge of the Canadian Armoured Corps (Tank arm badge) worn on the blouse sleeve of an officer from the 14th Calgary Regiment.

Below, right:
The Calgary Regiment, 14th Army Tank Regiment: Non-regulation (in 1942) Cap Badge and Title, worn at Dieppe.

6th CANADIAN INFANTRY BRIGADE
(Brigadier W. Wallace Southam)
— **Fusiliers Mont-Royal**
(Lt.-Col. Dollard-Menard)
— **Queen's Own Cameron Highlanders of Canada**
(Lt.-Col. Gostling [2])
— **South Saskatchewan Regt**
(Lt.-Col. Merritt)

'A' Royal Marine Commando
(Lt.-Col. J. P. Phillips [2])

5th CANADIAN INFANTRY BRIGADE
— **1 Coy. Black Watch of Canada** (Captain Hicks)
— **2 Rifle sections of the Calgary Highlanders**
The brigade did not take part in the operation, only these units were used as reinforcements for the other two Brigades.

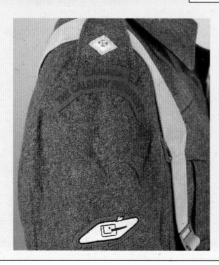

CANADA
THE CALGARY REGIMENT

THE LANDING AT DIEPPE
19 August 1942

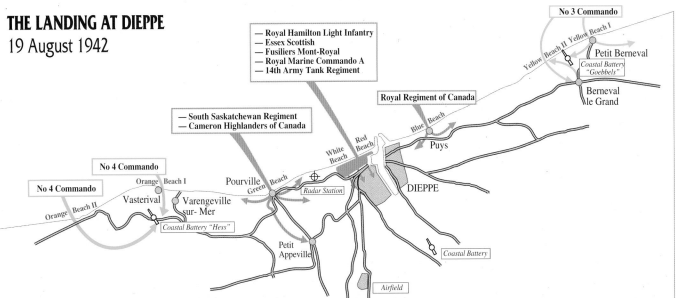

— Royal Hamilton Light Infantry
— Essex Scottish
— Fusiliers Mont-Royal
— Royal Marine Commando A
— 14th Army Tank Regiment

No 3 Commando

Petit Berneval
Coastal Battery "Goebbels"

Yellow Beach II Yellow Beach I

Berneval le Grand

Royal Regiment of Canada

Blue Beach

Puys

— South Saskatchewan Regiment
— Cameron Highlanders of Canada

White Beach

Red Beach

DIEPPE

No 4 Commando

Orange Beach I

Pourville

Green Beach

Radar Station

No 4 Commando

Vasterival

Varengeville sur- Mer

Orange Beach II

Coastal Battery "Hess"

Petit Appeville

Coastal Battery

Airfield

Below.
Magazine published in France under German control, dated 31 August 1942. The photographs were taken by reporters from the Wehrmacht Propaganda Kompanien. On the cover is an 'American civilian Red Cross doctor' who had landed with the assault force giving first aid to Canadian and British casualties.

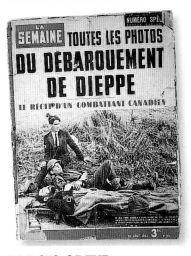

BADGES OF THE CANADIAN 2nd DIVISION AT DIEPPE

1 and 2. 'Cana' shoulder titles.
3. Officer's Divisional insignia.
4. ORs Divisional insignia.
5. The Toronto Scottish (Machine Gun) on a Hodden Grey tartan.

4TH INFANTRY BRIGADE

6. Royal Regiment of Canada.
7. Royal Hamilton Light Infantry.
8. Essex Scottish (McGregor tartan)

5TH INFANTRY BRIGADE

9. Black Watch of Canada. Worn only on the Glengarry. Replaced by a red plume on the Tam O'Shanter.
10. The Régiment de Maisonneuve.
11. Calgary Highlanders (42nd Government Tartan)

6TH INFANTRY BRIGADE

12. The Fusiliers Mont-Royal.
13. Queen's Own Cameron Highlanders (Cameron of Erracht Tartan)
14. South Saskatchewan Regiment.

REGIMENTAL HEADQUARTERS

Name	Number	Type	Tactical Sign
Ringer	T-68881	II	Z2
Regiment	T-31923	II	Z1

DAIMLER SCOUT CARS MK II

Name	Number	Type	Tactical Sign
Horace	F-64318		8
Hector	F-64306		9
Helen			6
Harry			7
Hunter			1
Hare	F-64319		3
Hound	F-64306		2

JEEP

1 landed   CM 4218884

UNIVERSAL CARRIER

1 landed

B SQUADRON

HEADQUARTERS SQUADRON

Name	Number	Type	Tactical Sign
Burns	T-31135	I	F1
Backer	T-68352	II	F2
Bolster	T-31107-R	I	F3

6 TROOP

Name	Number	Type	Tactical Sign
Bob	T-68557	III	6
Bert	T-68560	III	6
Bill	T-68558	III	6

7 TROOP

Name	Number	Type	Tactical Sign
Brenda	T-68760	III	7
Blondie	T-68880	III	7
Betty	T-68176-R	III	7

8 TROOP

Name	Number	Type	Tactical Sign
Beetle	T-68875	I	8
Bull	T-31862	I	8
Boar	T-68176-R	I	8

9 TROOP

Name	Number	Type	Tactical Sign
Butter Cup	T-31655	III	9
Blossom	T-68551R	III	9
Bluebell	T-68759R	III	9

10 TROOP

Name	Number	Type	Tactical Sign
Beefy	T-68177	III	10
Bloody	T-68701R	III	10
Bellicose	T-68175	III	10

C SQUADRON

HEADQUARTERS SQUADRON

Name	Number	Type	Tactical Sign
Calgary		III	F2
Chief		I	F1
Company		I	F3

13 TROOP

Name	Number	Type	Tactical Sign
Cougar		III	13
Cheetah		III	13
Cat		III	13

15 TROOP

Name	Number	Type	Tactical Sign
Caustic		III	15
Canny		III	15
Confident		III	15

This makes a total of 29 Churchill tanks, among which the tank called 'Regiment' of Lt-Col. J.G. Andrews, killed during the operation. Out of 29, two sunk at sea and 27 were destroyed or got bogged down in the pebbles.

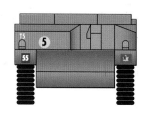

Table realised after 'Dieppe through the lens' - After the Battle Publishers.

Universal Carrier from the Essex Scottish Regiment.

CHURCHILL TANKS AND OTHER VEHICLES LANDED AT DIEPPE.

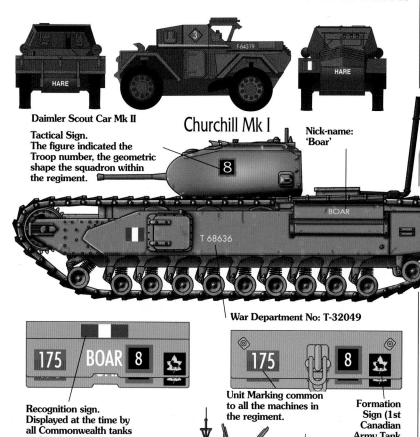

Daimler Scout Car Mk II

Churchill Mk I

Nick-name: 'Boar'

Tactical Sign.
The figure indicated the Troop number, the geometric shape the squadron within the regiment.

War Department No: T-32049

Recognition sign.
Displayed at the time by all Commonwealth tanks and replaced by the standard Allied armies white star.

Unit Marking common to all the machines in the regiment.

Formation Sign (1st Canadian Army Tank Brigade)

Front and back hull markings of 'Cat', a Churchill from 13 Troop.

CHURCHILL INFANTRY TANK

— **Total weight in fighting order:** 40 1/2 tons.
— **Total length:** 24 ft 2 ins.
— **Width:** 11 ft 3 ins.
— **Height:** 7 ft 10 ins.
— **Engine:** Bedford 12-cylinder petrol.
— **Power Rating:** 350 bhp
— **Transmission:** Four forward and one reverse
— **Crew:** 5 of whom 3 in the turret
— **Armour:** 8 ins (front and turret)
— **Max. road speed:** 17 mph.
— **Range:** 94 miles.
— **Armament:**

CHURCHILL MK I

Cast steel turret
One 40-mm gun in the turret
One 7.92-mm machine gun in the turret
One 75-mm howitzer in the hull

CHURCHILL MK II

Cast steel turret
One 40-mm gun in the turret
One 7.92-mm machine gun in the turret
One .7.92-mm machine gun in the hull

CHURCHILL MK III

Welded steel turret
One 57-mm gun in the turret
One 7.92-mm machine gun in the turret
One 7.92-mm machine gun in the hull

In 1943 all Canadian Tank regiments were equipped with American Sherman tanks with which they fought in Northern Italy and North-West Europe.

Left:
Soldier from the Fusiliers Mont-Royal, a French-speaking regiment, wearing combat dress worn at Dieppe.
The life-belt has been slipped under the equipment. He is carrying the No 1 Rifle Mk III* with the Pattern 1907 Bayonet.
(Reconstruction,
Militaria Magazine photo)

Right:
2nd Lieutenant of the 14th Army Tank Regiment (The Calgary regiment) at Dieppe.
(Reconstruction,
Militaria Magazine photo)

Cloth Sleeve Battle flashes of the Canadian 2nd Infantry Division at Dieppe

ORs Formation sign

Officers

Officers (variant)

Divisional Machine Gun Battalion (Toronto Scottish)

4th BRIGADE	5th BRIGADE	6th BRIGADE
Royal Regiment of Canada	Black Watch of Canada [2]	Fusiliers Mont Royal
Royal Hamilton Light Infantry	Régiment de Maisonneuve [3]	Cameron Highlanders of Canada
Essex Scottish	Calgary Highlanders [4]	South Saskatchewan Regt. (officers)

ARMS and SERVICES

RCCS

Royal Canadian Artillery

Royal Canadian Engineers

Royal Canadian Corps of Signals

RCASC

RCOC

CPC

Royal Canadian Army Service Corps

Royal Canadian Army Medical Corps

Royal Canadian Army Ordnance Corps

Canadian Provost Corps

CANADIAN INFANTRY BATTALION, 1942 (theoretical organisation)

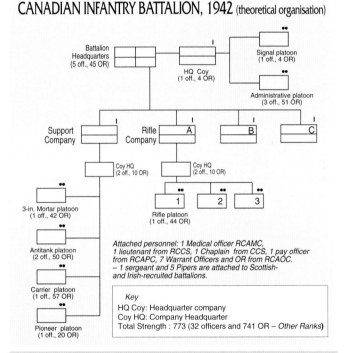

Battalion Headquarters (5 off., 45 OR)

HQ Coy (1 off., 4 OR)

Signal platoon (1 off., 4 OR)

Administrative platoon (3 off., 51 OR)

Support Company

Rifle Company — A — B — C

Coy HQ (2 off., 10 OR)

Coy HQ (2 off., 10 OR) — 1 — 2 — 3

3-in. Mortar platoon (1 off., 42 OR)

Rifle platoon (1 off., 44 OR)

Antitank platoon (2 off., 50 OR)

Carrier platoon (1 off., 57 OR)

Pioneer platoon (1 off., 20 OR)

Attached personnel: 1 Medical officer RCAMC, 1 lieutenant from RCCS, 1 Chaplain from CCS, 1 pay officer from RCAPC, 7 Warrant Officers and OR from RCAOC. – 1 sergeant and 5 Pipers are attached to Scottish- and Irish-recruited battalions.

Key
HQ Coy: Headquarter company
Coy HQ: Company Headquarter
Total Strength : 773 (32 officers and 741 OR – *Other Ranks*)

Select bibliography on the Dieppe Raid

19 août 1942, 4.50 am. Le sacrifice des Canadiens. Philippe Chéron, Thierry Chion, Olivier Richard. 2002. Editions Petit à Petit. BP75-76162 Darnetal Cedex.
Le sacrifice des Canadiens : Dieppe. René Abautret. *Robert Laffont. 1968.*
Opération Jubilee, Dieppe, 19 août 1942. Claude-Paul Couture. France Empire. 1969.
Les Canadiens à Dieppe. Jacques Mordal. **Presses de la Cité. 1982.**
L'aube point sur Dieppe. R. W. Thompson. *Historia Magazine, 1968.*

Commandos and Rangers of WWII. James Ladd. *Mac Donald and Jane's. 1978.*
Militaria Magazine n° 86. Histoire & Collections. September 1992.
39/45 Magazine n° 51. « Massacre à Dieppe ». Editions Heimdal. 1990.
39/45 Magazine n° 73-/74. « Les Canadiens débarquent à Dieppe ». Ronald McNair. Editions Heimdal. 1992.
Dieppe Through the Lens of the German Photographers. Hugh G. Henry Jr et Jean-Paul Pallud. After the Battle 2002.

1. Shoulder titles were adopted at the end of February 1942.
2. A company was committed in support of the 4th Brigade.
3. Unit not committed at Dieppe.
4. Three sections committed in support of the 4th Brigade.

Appendix 2

DIEPPE RAIDS - Canadian Embarkation Strength, Casualties and Rescued.

Units	Embarked Off.	Embarked OR	Killed in action Off.	Killed in action OR	Died from wounds Off.	Died from wounds OR	Died in captivity Off.	Died in captivity OR	Total killed Off.	Total killed OR	Wounded Off.	Wounded OR	POW Wounded Off.	POW Wounded OR	Not wounded Off.	Not wounded OR	Total Off.	Total OR	Total losses[1] Off.	Total losses[1] OR	Return to UK[2] Off.	Return to UK[2] OR
			Dead								*Prisoners of War*											
2nd Division Headquarters Elements	42	48	5						5		7	7	2	5	2	6	11	18	16	18	33	37
Royal Regiment of Canada	26	528	8	199		2	2	16	10	217	2	31	8	95	6	155	16	281	26	498	2	63
Royal Hamilton Light Infantry	31	551	7	172	1	6	2	9	10	187	5	103	7	71	9	88	21	262	31	449	6	211
Essex Scottish Regiment	32	521	5	100		2	1	13	6	115	1	26	3	119	20	240	24	385	30	500	3	49
Fusiliers Mont Royal	32	552	7	98		4	1	9	8	111	2	48	8	103	11	222	21	373	29	484	5	120
Queen's Own Cameron Highlanders of Canada	32	471	5	55	1	7		8	6	70	9	94	3	33	6	125	18	252	24	322	18	250
South Saskatchewan Regiment	25	498	3	75		3		3	3	81	3	159	2	22	7	58	16	239	19	320	13	340
14th Army Tank Regiment (Calgary)	32	385	2	10				1	2	11		4	2	17	13	125	15	146	17	157	15	232
Toronto Scottish Regiment (Machine Gun)	5	120		1						1		8		3		1		12		13	5	115
Black Watch (Royal Highland Regiment) of Canada	4	107	1					3	1	3		6		2	2	59	2	67	3	70	1	43
Calgary Highlanders	1	21																			1	21
Royal Canadian Artillery	14	256	2	11					2	11	1	3	1	7	3	19	5	29	7	40	8	219
Royal Canadian Engineers	7	309	1	22		1	1	2	2	25	3	33	1	36		88	4	157	6	182	4	161
Royal Canadian Corps of Signals	6	72		8				1		9	2	7		3	1	14	3	24	3	33	5	47
Royal Canadian Army Service Corps	1	37		1						1		6		3	1		1	9	1	10		33
Royal Canadian Army Medical Corps	10	116		4						4	0	3		2	1	9	1	14	1	18	9	101
Royal Can. Army Ordnance Corps	1	14		1				1		2		2			2			4		6	1	10
Canadian Provost Corps[3]	2	39	1					1				7				7		11		25	1	21
Canadian Intelligence Corps	2	13		3						3				1		4		5		8	2	5
TOTAL	305	4658	47	760	2	26	7	65	56	851	39	547	37	531	82	1224	158	2302	214	3153	132	2078

Summary totals: Embarked **4963** — Total killed **907** — Wounded **584** — Prisoners of War **1874**[4] — Total losses **3367** — Return to UK **2210**

1. Total losses, all categories.
2. Returned to UK after the operation.
3. Of whom some personnel of the Royal Canadian Mounted Police.
4. Of whom 568 wounded.

Table made up after 'Six years of War' by Colonel Stacey.

Appendix 3

CANADIAN ARMY LOSSES IN NORTHWEST EUROPE 1944-1945

Canadian Army Losses on 6 June 1944 (Land Forces)

Units	Killed	Wounded[1]	Prisoners	Total
Headquarters	1	2		3
Royal Winnipeg Rifles	57	66	5	128
Regina Rifle Regiment	45	63		108
Canadian Scottish Regiment	22	65		87
Queen's Own Rifles of Canada	61	82		143
Régiment de La Chaudière	18	45	42	105
North Shore (New Brunswick) Rgt.	34	91		125
Stormont, Dundas and Glengarry HD	1	13		14
North Nova Scotia HD	4	6		10
Cameron Highlanders of Ottawa	1	3		4
7th Reconnaissance Regiment (17th Duke of York's Royal Can. Hussars)	1	2		3
6th Armoured Regt. (1st Hussars)	22	21		43
10th Arm. Regt. (Fort Garry Horse)	14	11		25
27th Arm. Rgt. (Sherbrooke Fusiliers)		2		2
12th Field Regiment RCA	1	7		8
13th Field Regiment RCA	6	4		10
14th Field Regiment RCA	10	14		24
19th Army Field Regiment RCA	3	18		21
5th Field Company RCE	7	17		24
6th Field Company RCE	11	15		26
16th Field Company RCE	2	10		12
18th Field Company RCE		1		1
Royal Canadian Corps of Signals	4	1		5
Royal Canadian Army Service Corps				
Royal Canadian Army Medical Corps	6	3		9
Royal Canadian Army Ordnance Corps	9	11		20
RCEME		1		1
1st Canadian Parachute Battalion	19	10	84	113
	359	**590**	**131**	**1074**

1. The number includes 25 officers and OR who died of their wounds between 7 and 25 June. (after the 'Campaign for Victory', E. Stacey)

Percentage of casualties according to their causes

Shells, bombs (mortars, aircraft):	60 %	Mines, various traps:	10 %
Small Arms:	25 %	Miscellaneous (incl. accidents):	5 %

Total strength on 4 May 1945 170,000 men[1]

Casualties from 6 to 12 June 1944 (3rd Inf. Div., 2nd Armd Bde and various support units):
Officers: 196 of whom 72 killed.
OR: 2,635 of whom 945 killed.

— From 6 June to 1 October 1944
Killed, evacuated[2], missing:
2nd Infantry Division: 8,211
3rd Infantry Division: 9,263
4th Armoured Division: 3,135
Total: **20,609**

— 6 June 1944 to 22 March 1945
Killed, casualties evacuated, missing: 37,528

— From 6 June 1944 to 4 May 1945 (end of hostilities)
Killed: officers 961; OR 10,375 (Total 11,336)
Wounded: 30,906
Total: **25 889 men**

ITALIAN CAMPAIGN (reminder)

Total strength from 10 July 1943 to February 1945:
92,757 officers and Other ranks
— Killed
Officers: 408; ORs: 4991. Total: 5,399
— Wounded
Officers: 1,218; ORs: 18,268. Total: 19,486
— Prisoners
Officers: 62; ORs: 942. Total: 1,004

1. Out of a total of 237,000 men serving in Northwest Europe.
2. Evacuated casualties: wounded who would never return to active service.

Total PoWs: 2,248 men

MONTHLY EVALUATION OF TROOP CASUALTIES FOR THE WHOLE OF THE 21st ARMY GROUP

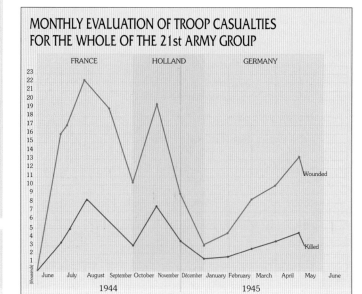

FRANCE — HOLLAND — GERMANY
(June, July, August, September, October, November, December — 1944; January, February, March, April, May, June — 1945). Curves: Wounded, Killed.

1,2,3. Leaflets published in Canada to encourage men to enlist or to underline the n-Nation's huge war effort.
4. Collection of humorous cartoons drawn in 1945 in Holland after the Liberation by Jan Niuewenhys. Surprisingly realistic, these give an accurate rendition of uniforms, insignia and markings of Canadian military vehicles.
5. & 6. Illustrated magazines handed out to Canadian soldiers in canteens and by various charities.

7. The official Canadian Army newspaper in NW Europe. The first continental edition after D-Day was published in Caen, 34, rue Domolombe, on 27 July 1944 (see photo). Later, the editorial team moved to Brussels for the rest of the war in Europe.
8. A selection of official Army manuals used in the making of this book. They were British editions printed in Canada and exact copies of the originals. Several of them were both in French and in English.

TECHNICAL BOOKS

— **Sexton Jr., D. J.** . *Guide to Canadian Shoulder Titles, 1939-45.* Pass in Review Publications, 1987.
— **Chartrand, René.** *Canadian Forces in WWII.* Osprey, 2001.
— **Tripp, F. R.** *Canadian Army in WWII. Badges and histories.* Unitrade Press, 1983.
— **Mazéas, Daniel.** *Insignes canadiens, Revised edition.* Military Historical Ste, 1985.
— **Grimshaw, Major L. E.** *Ex Coelis, the badges and Insignia of the Canadian Airborne forces.* (available from L. Grimshaw, 612 Fay Street, Kingston, ON K7L 4V1. Canada).
— **Army Historical Section.** *The Regiments and Corps of the Canadian Army.* Queen's Printers, Ottawa, 1964.
— **Beldam, Barry.** *Canadian Vehicle Markings.* Barry Beldam, 1996.
— **Canadian Military Historical Society.** *Canada's Fighting Vehicles, 1943-45.* W. A. Gregg, 1980.
— **Wise, Terence.** *Military Vehicle Markings, WWII.* Ryton Publications, 1994.
— **Edwards, C. A.** *Formation signs of the Canadian Army.* Pass in Reviews Publication, 1985.
— **Dorosh, M. A.** *Dressed to Kill.* Military Artifact, 2001 (Military Artifact/Service publications. PO Box 33071, Ottawa, Ontario K2C 3Y9 Canada).

HISTORICAL WORKS IN ENGLISH

— **Hartigan, Dan.** *A rising of Courage, 1st Canadian Parachute Battalion.* Drop Zone Publishers, Calgary, Canada, 2000.
— **Munro, Ross.** *Gauntlet to Overlord.* MacMillan

Co., Canada, 1946.
— **McAndrew, Bill; Graves, Donald E.; Whitby Michael.** *Normandy 1944, The Canadian Summer.* Art Global Inc., Montréal Québec, 1994.
— **Granatstein, J. L.; Morton, D.** *Bloody Victory.* Lester & Orpen Dennys Ltd, Toronto Canada, 1984.
— **Williams, Jeffery.** *The Long Left Flank.* Leo Cooper Ltd., London, 1988.
— **Graves, Donald, E.** *South Albertas. A Canadian Regiment at War.* Robin Brass Studio (10 Blantyre Avenue, Toronto, Ontario, M1N 2 R4, Canada), 1988. An outstanding book and source on the Canadian Armoured Regiment.
— **Harclerode, Peter.** *Go to It. History of the 6th Airborne Division.* Bloomsbury Publishing, second printing, 1990.
— **Wiles, John A.** *Out of the Clouds. The history of the 1st Canadian Parachute Battalion.*
— **Horn B.; Wyczynski M.** *Tip of the Spear.* Dundurn Press (8 Market Street, Suite 200, Toronto, Ontario M5E 1M6. Canada). Another recommended book, more than 300 unpublished photos of Canadian paratroopers.

HISTORICAL WORKS IN FRENCH

— **Militaria Magazine n° 59/60.** July 1990. Special British and Canadian Paratroopers in Normandy issue.
— **Henri, Jacques.** *La Normandie en flammes.* Corlet, 1984.
— **Vasseur, A. G.** *Boulogne 1944.* Presses de la Cité, 1969.
— **Chrétien, Guy.** *Les Canadiens dans la bataille.* Lafond-Caen, 1990-2002.
— **Bernage, Georges.** *Les Canadiens face à la*

Hitlerjugend. Heimdal, 1991.
— **Bernage, Georges.** *Mourir pour l'Abbaye d'Ardenne.* Heimdal, 1991.
— **Desquesne, Rémy.** *Les Canadiens au secours de l'Europe.* Mémorial de Caen, 1994.
— **Roy, Reginald H.** *Débarquement et offensive des Canadiens en Normandie.* Ed. Trecare, Québec, 1986.
— **Marchand, Gérard.** *Le régiment de Maisonneuve vers la victoire.* Les Presses libres, Montréal, 1980.
— **Barbe, Dominique.** *Charnwood.* Corlet, 1994.
— **Cormier, Ronald.** *J'ai vécu la guerre.* Editions d'Acadie, Canada, 1988.
— **Florentin, Eddy.** *Stalingrad en Normandie.* Perrin, 2002 (new edition).
— **Florentin, Eddy.** *Le Havre à feu et à sang, 1944.* Presses de la Cité, 1985.
— **Florentin, Eddy.** *Opération Paddle (la poursuite).* Presses de la Cité, 1994.
— **Florentin, Eddy.** *Montgomery franchit la Seine.* Presses de la Cité, 1994.
— **Copp, Terry.** *Guide canadien des champs de bataille de Normandie.* Distributed by Heimdal, 1994.
— **Stacey, colonel C. P.** *La Campagne de la Victoire.* Ministère de la Défense Nationale, Ottawa, 1960.

INTERNET SITES.

http://www.bcregiment.com/ber.rcac.htm
http://www3.sympatico.ca/chrjohnson/tacsign

See also the bibliography on pages 140-141 of the Tommy from D-Day to VE-Day, Vol II for other books in connection with the Canadian Army in NW Europe.

After the end of hostilities, announced officially on 8 May 1945, a Canadian Military Mission headed for Berlin. The first meeting with the Russians occurred on the Elbe. This gunner from the Royal Canadian Artillery poses with two of his comrades-in-arms. Going home was now only a question of time.
(Public Archives of Canada Photograph)

ACKNOWLEDGEMENTS

I should like to extend my thanks to my Canadian friends without whose help this book would not have seen the light of day. While not belittling the contribution of others, I would first like to mention *Jocelyn Garnier* who, with infinite patience, answered my unending questions.

But also *Richard Martin*, Curator of the Régiment de la Chaudière Museum, as well as Major *Michel Litalien* of the Public Archives of Canada, who supplied me with unpublished documents which were the foundation of this book.

I would also like to thank, still in Canada: *Louis Grimshaw*, *Michel Perrier*, Miss *Carmen Harry* of the Royal Canadian Mounted Police Museum, Lieutenant *Deschênes*, *Ed Storey*, *Clive M. Law*, Lt-Col. *J.W. Ostiguy* of the Régiment de Maisonneuve and *René Chartrand*.

In France I would like to thank all the team at *Histoire & Collections* (the publishers of this book) very warmly. In particular, I must mention my friend *Philippe Charbonnier*, the Editor of *'Militaria Magazine'* whom I harassed endlessly with e-mail to send and requests for translations and who turned out to be an outstanding photographer. As well as getting through his daily tasks, Philippe put himself entirely at my disposal to re-read, correct, and annotate a good number of the pages of this book. My other friend, *Jean-Marie Mongin*, Managing Director at *Histoire & Collections* who is the real artisan of this book, must not be left out either. For weeks on end, he had to put up with my demands, corrections, additions and various delays, all without batting an eyelid.

I should also like to thank the following: *Bernard Petitjean*, *Robert Le Chantoux*, Lieutenant-Colonel T. *Darly*, *Patrick Lengrand*, *Philippe Laurent*, *Marc Landry*, *Ludovic Fortin*, *Xavier Sieur*, *Laurent Rougier*, *J.-M. Boniface*, *François* and *Patrice Bouchery*, *Nancy Bouchery-Waille*, *Alain Brogniez* and *Frédéric Finel*, as well as *Eric Limosin*.

My thanks also go to the two Norman collectors (who wish to remain anonymous) who opened their doors and shared some of their treasures with me.

Several major militaria dealers and shops were also instrumental: *Military Antiques* Fay Street in Kingston, Ontario, Canada ; *Michel Perrier Militaria Toutes Nations* in Union Boulevard, Saint-Lambert, Quebec; and the *Overlord* (rue de la Folie Méricourt, Paris 11e) and *Le Poilu* (rue Emile Duclaux, Paris 15e) shops in Paris, France.

Drawings, design and lay-out by Jean-Marie MONGIN and André JOUINEAU (drawings of Canadian Soldiers in pages 5, 26 and 36), Antoine POGGIOLI and Yann-Erwin ROBERT

ISBN: 2-913903-51-7

Publisher's number: 2-913903

A book published by
HISTOIRE & COLLECTIONS
SA au capital de 182 938, 82 €

5, avenue de la République
F-75541 Paris Cédex 11
Telephone (33-1) 40 21 18 20
Fax   (33-1) 47 00 51 11

This book has been designed, typed, laid-out and processed by *The Studio A&C*, fully on integrated computer equipment.

Printed by *Zure*, Spain,
European Union
July 2003